Modeling the Past

Modeling the Past

Archaeology, History, and Dynamic Networks

John Terrell, Mark Golitko,
Helen Dawson, and Marc Kissel

berghahn
NEW YORK · OXFORD
www.berghahnbooks.com

First published in 2023 by
Berghahn Books
www.berghahnbooks.com

© 2023 John Terrell, Mark Golitko, Helen Dawson, and Marc Kissel

All rights reserved. Except for the quotation of short passages for the purposes of criticism and review, no part of this book may be reproduced in any form or by any means, electronic or mechanical, including photocopying, recording, or any information storage and retrieval system now known or to be invented, without written permission of the publisher.

Library of Congress Cataloging-in-Publication Data

A C.I.P. cataloging record is available from the Library of Congress
Library of Congress Cataloging in Publication Control Number: 2023004645

British Library Cataloguing in Publication Data

A catalogue record for this book is available from the British Library

ISBN 978-1-80073-869-0 hardback
ISBN 978-1-80073-870-6 ebook

https://doi.org/10.3167/9781800738690

I agree that the view of Nature which I have maintained in these lectures is not a simple one. Nature appears as a complex system whose factors are dimly discerned by us. But, as I ask you, Is not this the very truth? Should we not distrust the jaunty assurance with which every age prides itself that it at last has hit upon the ultimate concepts in which all that happens can be formulated? The aim of science is to seek the simplest explanations of complex facts. We are apt to fall into the error of thinking that the facts are simple because simplicity is the goal of our quest. The guiding motto in the life of every natural philosopher should be, Seek simplicity and distrust it.

—Alfred North Whitehead,
The Concept of Nature, Trinity College (November 1919)

Unlike the scientific hypothesis, a model is not verifiable directly by experiment. For all models are both true and false. Almost any plausible proposed relation among aspects of nature is likely to be true in the sense that it occurs (although rarely and slightly). Yet all models leave out a lot and are in that sense false, incomplete, inadequate. The validation of a model is not that it is "true" but that it generates good testable hypotheses relevant to important problems.

—Richard Levins,
"The Strategy of Model Building in Population Biology" (1966)

Contents

List of Illustrations — viii
Acknowledgments — xi

Introduction. History Matters — 1

1. Dynamic Relational Analysis — 10
2. Start with a Question — 33
3. Theories of History — 59
4. Modeling Theories — 83
5. Developing Hypotheses — 109
6. Gathering Information — 129
7. Analyzing Data — 148

Conclusion. So What? — 178

Glossary — 195
References — 199
Index — 225

Illustrations

Figures

1.1.	An elementary social network.	16
1.2.	Relational contingencies in the category "network models."	29
1.3.	Mississippi Valley watershed.	31
2.1.	Islands in the southwest Pacific.	41
2.2.	Network model of social connections in the New Guinea region given a maximal distance of 220 km.	46
2.3.	Network model of social connections in the New Guinea region given a maximal distance of 360 km.	47
2.4.	Obsidian at sites in the New Guinea region dating before 3,500 years ago.	52
2.5.	Obsidian at sites in the New Guinea region dating between 3,500–2,000 years ago.	53
3.1.	Facts matter, but what is a fact?	61
3.2.	Theories are assumptions about why things are the way they are (or appear to be).	63
3.3.	Theories of history differ in how far we are responsible for what happened.	65
3.4.	What would a Bronze Age world system look like?	75
3.5.	Matrix of contacts between regions in the Mediterranean around 1500–1200 BC.	77
3.6.	A Mediterranean Bronze Age "small world" network.	78
3.7.	Two models of history.	79

4.1.	The word "model" can have different meanings.	86
4.2.	Biblical and modern accounts of human origins.	90
4.3.	Darwin's model of what he called "the great Tree of Life."	91
4.4.	Graphic of the Iroquois type of kinship terminology system.	92
4.5.	The trellis model of recent human evolution.	96
4.6.	Two models of why people in the Pacific are diverse.	99
4.7.	Map of the Pacific showing places included in the study.	100
4.8.	Network mapping of the localities included in the genome scan.	102
4.9.	Nearest-neighbor structuring of interaction among the localities represented.	103
4.10.	Network mapping of only the Pacific Island populations in the genome scan.	104
4.11.	The contingencies of the three models discussed.	106
4.12.	A simple template for comparing two or more contingency models.	108
5.1.	Using Bayes' Theorem and the probability that someone sixty years of age or older in Wisconsin died.	114
5.2.	Bayes' Theorem modeled as a 2×2 contingency table.	116
5.3.	Recording how much confidence you have in a contingency in the past.	120
5.4.	A subjective baseline analysis using Bayes' Theorem.	121
5.5.	A three-dimensional ternary graph.	125
6.1.	Categorical thinking, relational thinking, and model building compared.	131
6.2.	"The Blind Men and the Elephant."	133
6.3.	Dates of the earliest Neolithic sites in the Mediterranean.	138
7.1.	A ceramic typology.	153
7.2.	Age of Miss America and murders by steam, vapors, and hot objects.	156

7.3.	Settlements in Mesoamerica dated to between ~900–600 BC.	160
7.4.	Two ways of explaining language diversity in New Guinea.	163
7.5.	Apportionment of variation.	166
7.6.	A selection of New Guinean bone daggers.	167
7.7.	A social network model of 1,720 communities.	170
7.8.	Results of Partial Mantel tests.	173
7.9.	A mapping of some of the possible contingencies.	175
8.1.	Why history matters.	181
8.2.	How experience and facts matter.	192

Tables

0.1.	Categorical vs. Relational Thinking.	7
3.1.	Structural Theories of History.	66
3.2.	Functional Theories of History.	68
3.3.	Ecological Theories of History.	69
3.4.	Participant Theories of History.	70
3.5.	Control Theories of History.	72

Acknowledgments

We want to thank those who helped us while we were writing this book: Stephen Acabado, Dean Anthony Arcega, Cyrus Banikazemi, Michael Armand Canilao, Ronald "Sonny" Faulseit, Adam Johnson, William Kelley, Antti Lahelma, Robin Meyer-Lorey, Angus Mol, Vivian Scheinsohn, and Peter Sheppard. We also want to thank our friends on social media who have commented on our posts about this book for their encouraging words and suggestions.

INTRODUCTION
History Matters

Network science has true potential to integrate the knowledge acquired in diverse fields of science. Given the ubiquity of networks in our world, the results of the theoretical and practical study of networks might help solve some of the major challenges confronting society.
—Katy Börner, Soma Sanyal, and Alessandro Vespignani,
"Network Science" (2007)

At its most basic, network analysis examines how entities connect to other entities. These entities, commonly called nodes, can represent any number of objects: cells in a body, people, species, households, and even cities have all been the subjects of network analysis.
—Stefani Crabtree and Lewis Borck,
"Social Networks for Archaeological Research" (2019)

Despite all disclaimers, it is only when science asks why, instead of simply describing how, that it becomes more than technology. When it asks why, it discovers Relativity. When it only shows how, it invents the atomic bomb, and then puts its hands over its eyes and says, *My God what have I done?*
—Ursula K. Le Guin,
The Language of the Night (1979)

- Relational Analysis
- Relational vs. Categorical Thinking
- Research Models and Hypotheses
- Modeling the Past
- Key Points

The philosopher George Santayana famously wrote that "Those who cannot remember the past are condemned to repeat it." Or, as the anarchist poet Peter Lamborn Wilson wrote, "Those who understand history are condemned to watch other idiots repeat it." Joking aside, it is clear that what we experience today reflects a host of past events that still impact our lives in the present—and not necessarily in beneficial ways, as anyone encountering racial discrimination can readily attest to.

Another famous saying goes, "Rome wasn't built in a day." Nor did it fall in a day, even if historians can point to a moment in time and a particular event marking the formal end of the Western Roman Empire. Why this hesitation? It is far from certain what the Roman Empire was like on 4 September 476 when the "barbarian" general Odoacer removed the child emperor Romulus Augustus from the throne and declared himself king. Nor is it known whether life was all that different on the fifth of September that same year for the average person living then anywhere in Italy. Historians point to a multitude of economic, social, and possibly even climatic contingencies that cumulatively resulted in what had once been one of the dominant political forces on earth ceasing to exist in a functional sense, even if many of its institutions, ideas, and practices remain with us to this day.

It is also clear that many people care about what happened in the past, even about events as remote as the end of the Western Roman Empire, and for a variety of different reasons. For instance, some are now drawing clear links between migration and border security two millennia ago to justify their arguments for closing borders to keep modern "barbarians" outside the proverbial gates (Argote-Freyre and Bellitto 2012).

So yes, history matters. Yet let's not be naïve when making this claim. As every good politician, cruise line operator, or museum director knows, history also sells—as anyone who has visited the Tower of London has experienced firsthand. Furthermore, if packaged well as a marketable commodity, history can be profitable (Hofmann et al. 2021).

This is not a book, however, about history or the commercialization of archaeology. This is a book about how we can learn from history in ways that may make a difference in how each of us lives our life during our time on earth from birth to death, from the cradle to the grave. Hence in the final chapter we discuss what we consider to be the main lessons and implications of history, and how we should strive towards decolonizing its study.

The kind of history we have in mind is not timeless, but the amount of time that needs to be taken into account to learn history's lessons is not something that can be easily framed in days, years, or centuries. We will be suggesting instead that how much time is required to see history's patterns largely depends on what is the specific question about the past you are asking history to answer either for your own enlightenment or for the world's general benefit. Are the patterns we are looking for likely to have taken just a short while to develop or many centuries?

We are also going to be arguing that how history is patterned is often something that cannot be learned if all you have to work with is what people have recorded in one way or another for one reason or another. Why is this so? Often simply because nobody had realized "back then" they needed to "write this down for posterity." But another reason is perhaps less obvious. Because no one realized then what was happening or why (Holland-Lulewicz and Roberts Thompson 2021).

Hence the answers to many of the questions about history we want to ask must be pieced together from what was back then little more than "this and that." Here is why, therefore, this book is also about archaeology and the analytical sciences that are so much a part of what scholars are using nowadays to marshal evidence for or against "this or that" opinion, belief, or logical claim about how the world works and why.

More to the point, in the last half century or so, interest in using network modeling and relational analysis to study history has also grown steadily. Nowadays it is even said there has been a major new science in the making—network science—capable of radically changing our fundamental understandings of the world and how it works (Börner, Sanyal, and Vespignani 2007; Crabtree and Borck 2019; Kolaczyk 2009). How can such modeling and analysis, therefore, be used to explore the history of our relationships with one another and the impact that our species has had on the world around us?

Relational Analysis

Thanks to cell phones, computers, and online social media services, the words *network* and *networking* are familiar to many today. So, too, at least in the academic world, is the phrase *social network analysis* (SNA).

In recent years, a small and widely dispersed academic community of archaeologists and historians has been encouraged by the growing popularity of network analysis in the sciences to work together toward the ambitious goal of reconstructing history and human relationships in the past (Brughmans and Peeples 2018; Crabtree, Dunne, and Wood 2021). Although these efforts have been promising, it remains uncertain how successful such undertakings can be (Mills 2017; Pálsson 2021; Peeples 2019). Social relationships rarely leave unambiguous material traces. Connecting archaeological observations with social realities has never been simple. Nor are the research tactics of SNA easy to use when those whom you are studying and writing about are not around to watch, listen to, and survey (Carrington, Scott, and Wasserman 2005).

> ❖ **network** [ˈnet-ˌwərk] *noun*: a group or system of interconnected people or things. There are differing specific definitions of the word network as a noun depending on the kind of network being discussed (Kolaczyk 2009: 3–10). For instance: graph neural networks (Zhou et al. 2020), computer networks (Chowdhury, Kabir, and Boutaba 2010), and social networks (Sekara, Stopczynski, and Lehmann 2016).

This book, therefore, is an introduction to an alternative strategy for using relational analysis in archaeology and other historical sciences. Instead of reconstructing social ties as the principal goal, we will show you how relational thinking can be used to develop testable hypotheses about covariation and causal patterning in the past. While the hypotheses considered can, of course, be about how particular types of social relationships may have been instrumental in the past, they need not be. Using a modeling strategy that we call *dynamic relational analysis* (DYRA), they can also be about relationships—*causal contingencies*—of many forms among people, places, and things.

Since both SNA and DYRA have strengths as well as weaknesses, we start off Chapter 1 in this book by comparing how these two alternative ways of modeling the world differ in their basic assumptions about how the world works. However, we want to emphasize that both of these research strategies share something vitally important in common. They are alike in how they try to cultivate the unconventional way of thinking about things called *relational thinking*.

Relational vs. Categorical Thinking

We have written this book for three reasons. First, we show how to use DYRA to explore, model, and try to understand the complex global history of our species. Reduced to bare bones, relational analysis is a way of understanding the world around us—a way called *relational thinking*—that is liberating but challenging (de Nooy 2003; Kosiba 2019; Sanger 2021: 743–46). Why? Because relational thinking is largely counterintuitive to how the human brain evolved over millions of years to become our primary way of navigating how we experience things and events in the world we live in.

Although a full explanation would be a lengthy one, briefly stated here is the reasoning behind why we see relational thinking as basically counter to how we all normally deal with things and events. Evolution has given each of us a brain that is remarkably large and flexible in how it handles life's demands (Terrell and Terrell 2020). Thus equipped, each of us is not only able to meet—more or less successfully—what life throws at us. We are also clever enough—and socially skilled enough—to be able to dumb down the world we live in. Why? To make what we must deal with as predictable and generally as benevolent as humanly possible. However, none of us is omnipotent or truly omniscient. The old chestnut "my brain is full" may be a comic expression, but there are metabolic and practical limits to what a human brain can do (Simon 1978). Therefore, in the interests of efficiency and speed, it is not surprising that our brains as biologically constructed survival tools favor *categorical thinking* (Lupyan and Bergen 2016: 411–12; Michel and Peters 2021; Monod 1971: 154; Tse 2013).

> ❖ **categorical** [ˌkadəˈgôrək(ə)l] *adjective*: unambiguously explicit and direct.
>
> **category** [ˈkatəg(ə)ri] *noun*: a class or division of people or things regarded as having particular shared characteristics.

> **relational** [rɪˈleɪʃ(ə)n(ə)l] *adjective*: concerning the way in which two or more people or things are connected.

What is this conventional way of thinking about the world and our place in it? As magnificent as it is, the human brain is predisposed to accept without too much bother that if something looks like a duck, swims like a duck, and quacks like a duck, then it probably is a duck (Allport 1954; Chattoraj et al. 2021; Michel and Peters 2021; Schurgin 2018).

Saying this somewhat more formally, if something comes across to us as seemingly the same as something we have already experienced, we are predisposed to believe "this is just that again" despite the fact that in reality it may not be "just another one of those." Often such pragmatic thinking is good enough—especially when we have deliberately dumbed down the world to make things we come across in life more *alike*, more *the same* than they might otherwise be. Yet such thinking can also make it easy for us to make mistakes, to miss the fact that something really is not the same kind of thing or event (Allport 1954: 170–74).

There is no denying that categorical thinking can be an efficient and practical way of dealing with the world and everyday events. However, as we will be emphasizing repeatedly in this book, we live in a world that is *relational*, not categorical. Despite what common sense may tell us, things do not really exist first and foremost all on their own, and only later may become connected with, linked to, tied to, dependent on, etc. other similarly "disconnected" things. More often than not, things are the way they are because they are connected with, linked to, etc., other things.

Research Models and Hypotheses

The second reason we decided to write this book is more conventional. We do not believe the currently available networks toolkit adds up to an entirely new science in its own right. But we agree with others that there is now a suite of well-developed methods and procedures for doing relational analysis that can be used productively to study the past.

In the chapters that follow, we will be arguing, however, that these tools are best used to turn our ideas and propositions about the past into useful models (see Chapter 4) and research hypotheses (Chapter 5). Why do we say this? Because modeling the past in this way can help you see more clearly not only what you believe you already know, but

Table 0.1. Categorical vs. Relational Thinking.

Categorical Words kind, type, size, density, family, group, community, village, tribe, city, state, nation, empire...	**Relational Words** relational, contingent, situational, circumstantial, consequential, adaptive, intentional, purposeful...
Categorical Concepts individual, population, region, isolation, network structure, migration, admixture...	**Relational Concepts** contingency, link, tie, relationship, event, agency, learning, mobility, collaboration, competition, adaptation, cost, benefit, risk, innovation...

also what you do not as yet know—and therefore, what you still need to find out about the human past and the role that our species has played in shaping the world we live in.

> ❖ **model** ['mädl] *verb*: devise a representation, especially a mathematical one (of a phenomenon or system).

For this reason, we think it is unfortunate that network modeling today is commonly seen as a specialized type of data analysis. Initially we thought of calling what we offer you in this book "dynamic relational modeling." However, upon reflection, we elected instead to continue using the usual term "analysis." We want to acknowledge in this way that while developing the ideas and methods described in this book, we have drawn on many of the same analytical precedents that are now also part of modern network modeling in general, and SNA in particular (see Chapter 1).

Modeling the Past

Third, as we discuss in some detail in Chapter 1, contemporary SNA has adopted an intentionally narrow outlook on what is worth studying using the methods and statistical tools of modern relational analysis. In the words of Stanley Wasserman and Katherine Faust, two of the foremost authors in this field: "the methods of social network analysis provide formal statements about social properties and processes" (Wasserman and Faust 1994: 11). We have found this research focus on social relationships to be not only limiting but often also unhelpful. As human beings, we may like to believe we are the masters of our fate, but one of the reasons for studying history is to unravel why things happen that are, in fact, not under our control, and why our intentions can backfire and take us down paths that we should have avoided.

We also believe the study of history is not just about documenting what happened in the past, but also about figuring out why things happened the way they evidently did. Yet we have worked as archaeologists and anthropologists long enough to know all too well, for instance, that the biologist and Nobel Laureate François Jacob was being more than just metaphysical or mysterious when he titled his popular book about science and evolution *The Possible and The Actual* (1982). If the word "actual" is another way of saying "true" or "existing in fact," then the best that any of us can hope to do regardless of our training is to pin down as well as we can what may be the most likely, the most plausible, explanations for what we are finding. But rarely, if ever, what is certifiably the true and actual explanation.

When you read Jacob's short and delightful book, you soon learn that the word "possible" in his title refers to how the human mind tries to decide what can or cannot be possibly true in the real world. "Whether in a social group or in an individual, human life always involves a continuous dialogue between the possible and the actual. A subtle mixture of belief, knowledge, and imagination builds before us an ever changing picture of the possible" (1982: vii–viii).

Without claiming to be as eloquent as François Jacob, we have written this book as a guide to using the logic and strategies of relational thinking to craft and then evaluate possible answers—or as we like to call them, *plausible models*—to fundamental questions of How? and Why? in the study of history.

Key Points

1. This is a book on how to use dynamic relational analysis (DYRA) to explore, model, and understand the complex global history of our species.

2. We live in a world that is relational, not categorical. Things do not simply exist all on their own, and only later become connected with, linked to, tied to, dependent on, etc. other similarly disconnected things. More often than not, things are the way they are because they are connected with, linked to, etc. other things.
3. The methods and procedures of dynamic relational analysis can be used to turn our ideas, assumptions, and working historical models into testable research hypotheses.

CHAPTER 1

Dynamic Relational Analysis

Recte enim Veritas Temporis filia dicitur, non Authoritatis
(For rightly is truth called the daughter of time, not of authority).
—Francis Bacon, *The New Organon* (1620)

A corollary of the highest importance may be deduced from the foregoing remarks, namely, that the structure of every organic being is related, in the most essential yet often hidden manner, to that of all other organic beings, with which it comes into competition for food or residence, or from which it has to escape, or on which it preys.
—Charles Darwin, *On the Origin of Species* (1859)

- Consequential Relationships
- What Is Relational Analysis?
- Social Network Analysis
- Dynamic Relational Analysis
- Working Assumptions
- Modeling Complexity
- Defining Relational Contingencies
- Types of Network Models
- Chapter Summary
- Key Points

Scholars today who are using relational thinking in their research do not need to be told by anyone that network science is still "under development," as the familiar although cryptic saying goes (e.g.,

Broekaert, Köstner, and Rollenger 2020; Cegielski 2020; Collar et al. 2015; Corneli, Latouche, and Rossi 2018; Holland-Lulewicz 2021; Holland-Lulewicz and Roberts Thompson 2021). In this chapter, we sketch what we see as some of the major differences between traditional social network analysis (SNA) as long practiced by scholars around the world and what in this book we will be calling dynamic relational analysis (DYRA).

Consequential Relationships

The quotation above from Charles Darwin's *On the Origin of Species* (1859) captures the reason, as well as the major theme of this book on archaeology, history, and dynamic relational analysis. *Things and people exist as such because they are connected and interdependent*—sometimes competitively, as Darwin says, but not always, and not always intentionally. Moreover, and more to the point of this chapter, how and why we are all connected and interdependent is rarely haphazard and totally unpredictable. Being thus linked contingently together—that is, *networked*—often leads to the patterning of things and events over time and space. And when change happens, it is often more predictable than some of us would like to acknowledge.

This book is about how to look for such patterning in the history of how the world works. Why is this worth doing? We will discuss this question in the conclusion of this book. Briefly considered here at the start, however, the challenge of global climate today can be used to highlight why we think studying history this way is worthwhile.

Albert Einstein taught us that time is relative. So, too, is change and history. You have to know what used to be to decide whether something is now different from what it once was. Is the Earth's climate changing, and not in a direction that will be good for us? Are we somehow responsible for what is happening, if this is true? Can we do anything? Or are we at the mercy of the weather and our own past foolishness, like it or not?

We do not intend to debate climate change in this book. We merely want to note that according to the theoretical physicist Carlo Rovelli, reality is a complex network of contingencies that we arbitrarily divide up into sequences of past, present, and future (Rovelli 2017: 70–73). Furthermore, we are also given to thinking about things as "things." But what is a thing? As Rovelli has eloquently observed:

> [A] war is not a thing, it's a sequence of events. A storm is not a thing, it's a collection of occurrences. A cloud above a mountain is not a thing, it is the condensation of humidity in the air that the wind blows over the mountain. A wave is not a thing, it is a movement of water, and the water that forms it is always different. A family is not a thing, it is a collection of relations, occurrences, feelings. And a human being? Of course it's not a thing; like the cloud above the mountain, it's a complex process, where food, information, light, words, and so on enter and exit. . . . A knot of knots in a network of social relations, in a network of chemical processes, in a network of emotions exchanged with its own kind. (Rovelli 2018: 99–100)

Although talked about nowadays as if climate change is an identifiable "something," like wars, storms, clouds, waves, and human beings, this isn't true. Whatever you take climate change to be, what these two words paired together mean is obviously something that is complex and arguably changing because of how things—yes, there often seems no easy way to avoid using this word—down here on earth are now and always have been linked, tied, contingent, and interdependent. In a word, it is the very nature of things not to be "standalone" but rather contingent and thus "networked."

Therefore, deciding *whether*, *how*, and *why* the Earth's atmosphere may now be dynamically changing depends not only on knowing how things are now, but also on knowing how they used to be. Hence history is not just about things that are over and done with. Consequently, it would be decidedly naïve to believe that the past is merely something that is "behind us."

What Is Relational Analysis?

Simply described, network science is "the *study of the collection, management, analysis, interpretation, and presentation of relational data*" (Brandes et al. 2013: 2, italics in original). However, if this description strikes you as less than helpful, you are not alone. Practitioners of this newly self-proclaimed science often appear to be writing about a new way to organize research data and perform sophisticated statistical analyses—about methodology, not about science. For instance, according to one well-known expert in this field: "social network analysis is an orientation towards the social world that inheres in a particular set of *methods*. It is not a body of formal or substantive social theory" (Scott 2000: 37).

❖ Social Network Analysis

Social network analysis provides a precise way to define important social concepts, a theoretical alternative to the assumption of independent social actors, and a framework for testing theories about structured social relationships. (Wasserman and Faust 1994: 17)

Central to the theoretical and methodological agenda of network analysis is identifying, measuring, and testing hypotheses about the structural forms and substantive contents of relations among actors. (Knoke and Yang 2008: 4)

A class of networks with one of the longest histories of systematic study, dating back to at least the 1930s, is that of social networks (i.e., networks representing the interactions among a collection of social entities or "actors"). (Kolaczyk 2009: 5)

Network analysis is about structure and position. (Borgatti, Everett, and Johnson 2018: 10)

❖ Dynamic Relational Analysis

Studying the changing relational contingencies among people, places, and events over time and space of differing character, cause, and probability.

In light of such an uninspiring portrayal of modern relational analysis, we need to say at the start not only what relational analysis is, but also why we decided to write this book about a way of doing network science we call *dynamic relational analysis* (DYRA), which differs in several important ways from what is now called *social network analysis* (SNA).

Since both SNA and DYRA have strengths as well as weaknesses, we begin by comparing how these two alternative ways of doing relational analysis differ in their basic assumptions about how the world works.

Social Network Analysis

In SNA, how all of us live, work, and are in other ways engaged with others of our kind between the cradle and the grave is formally called "links," "ties," "connections," or "edges" (the latter is a term taken directly from the formal mathematics of graph theory; Harary, Norman, and Cartwright 1965). As described by Stanley Wasserman and Katherine Faust, for instance, "social network analysis is concerned with understanding the linkages among social entities and the implications of these linkages. Actors are discrete individual, corporate, or collective social units" (Wasserman and Faust 1994: 17). Furthermore: "Actors are linked to one another by social *ties*. . . . the range and type of ties can be quite extensive. The defining feature of a tie is that it establishes a linkage between a pair of actors" (1994: 18).

A few examples in keeping with their usage of the word "tie" would be these: how one person evaluates someone (e.g., as a friend); how material resources are transferred (e.g., gifts, lending or borrowing things); our biological relationships (e.g., kinship); our physical connections (e.g., roads, rivers, and bridges); and our behavioral ties (e.g., sending emails or talking together).

Fundamental also in SNA is the assumption that relationships "among actors can be of many different kinds, and each type gives rise to a corresponding network [type]" (Borgatti et al. 2018: 4). Furthermore, it is assumed that the relationships involved are "continuously persistent"—such as being someone's brother or friend—with the qualification, however, that calling social ties "persistent" does not mean they never end. All that is implied is that while a given tie exists, it is functioning continuously within its particular network type (Borgatti et al. 2018: 1–4).

Therefore, what is fundamental to this way of understanding how people deal with one another and the world around them are these two key assumptions in SNA generally taken to be self-evidently true, both of which are questionable when seen from the perspective of DYRA:

1. **Networks are structured and observable *systems of relationships* that *persist* as such, apart from those participating in them.** "Network models conceptualize structure (social, economic, political, and so forth) as lasting patterns of relations among actors" (Wasserman and Faust 1994: 4). "Relations are not the properties of agents, but of systems of agents" (Scott 2000: 3). "Relational ties among actors are primary and attributes of actors are secondary" (Wasserman and Faust 1994: 8). Or as the authors of one recent survey of network analysis in sociology have written: "People differ not only with respect to the social networks they come to inhabit but also in their ability to capitalize on their networks in order to get ahead" (Smith et al. 2020: 165).

2. **Networks are formed and structured by the *type of relationship* creating them.** To repeat what we quoted earlier: "Relations among actors can be of many different kinds, and each type gives rise to a corresponding network" (Borgatti et al. 2018: 4). The contacts, ties, and connections relating one agent to another "cannot be reduced to the properties of the individual agents themselves" (Scott 2000: 3). Said more colloquially, a network is more than the sum of its parts, and it can be analyzed as a unity exhibiting its own typifying characteristics.

From the perspective of SNA, networks are also often described and analyzed in ways asking us to treat the relationships involved as static rather than dynamic, and the networks being analyzed as things or entities.

3. **Social networks as entities** (Figure 1.1a). A basic premise of modern SNA has long been the idea that there are recognizable (more or less) bounded groups, collections, classes, or systems of actors who interact with one another in the real world, and "who for conceptual, theoretical, or empirical reasons are treated as a finite set of individuals on which network measurements are made" (Wasserman and Faust 1994: 19).

Furthermore, as Barbara Mills, a prominent advocate for the use of SNA methods and associated ideas in archaeology, has written: "The overarching network theory linking current archaeological approaches is that connections define probabilities for interaction in the past, the structure of those interactions, and how position in the network creates both opportunities and constraints for actors" (Mills 2017: 383).

But do social networks exist? After all, as the applied mathematician and computer scientist Vedran Sekara and his colleagues have remarked: "Social systems are in a constant state of flux, with dynamics spanning from minute-by-minute changes to patterns present on the timescale of years" (Sekara et al. 2016: 9977; also Knoke and Yang 2008: 6). Furthermore, as David Knoke and Song Yang (2008: 15) ask rhetorically in their widely used handbook *Social Network Analysis*: "Where does a researcher set the limits when collecting data on social relations that, in reality, may have no obvious limits?"

A key issue, therefore, is how does one draw a line around a social network—a far from trivial concern. Moreover, as Mills has further ob-

16 • Modeling the Past

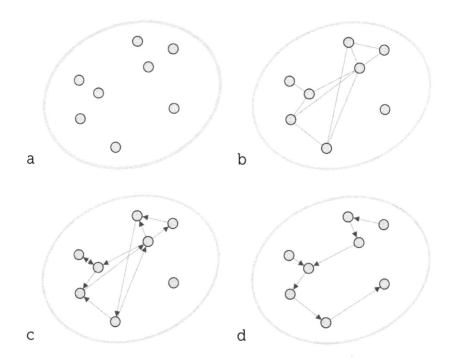

Figure 1.1. An elementary social network drawn as (a) a bounded composite group, entity, or unit of analysis (b) with internally structured relationships among the enclosed social actors (c) having causal relationships, (d) and performing in an integrated way as a purposeful system or goal-oriented process. © John Edward Terrell.

served, the word *network*—as in the expressions *whole network, complete network,* or *entire network* (Knoke and Yang 2008: 14; Wasserman and Faust 1994: 22)—is something of a misnomer at least in archaeology "because the boundaries or samples, as in any other archaeological analysis, are defined by the archaeological problem" (Mills 2017: 383; also Wasserman and Faust 1994: 19–20).

4. **Social networks as structures** (Figure 1.1b). According to Stephen Borgatti at the University of Kentucky and his colleagues, a "fundamental axiom of social network analysis is the concept that structure matters" (Borgatti et al. 2009: 893). Why? Because, for instance, "teams with the same composition of member skills can perform very differently depending on the patterns of relationships among the members."

Given this focus on the structuring, or patterning, of social relationships within classes, or categories, of things, or sets of things, called networks, it is understandable why SNA is often seen as a way of doing a particular kind of social research called *structural analysis*. For instance, in their monumental textbook *Social Network Analysis: Methods and Applications* (1994)—seen by many in the social sciences as the bible of structural analysis—Stanley Wasserman and Katherine Faust are careful to define what they mean by the phrase *network structure*: "the presence of regular patterns in relationship." By regular, they mean "lasting patterns of relations among actors" (1994: 3–4).

As we will be noting frequently in the following chapters, however, one of the obvious limitations of using conventional SNA methods and theories in archaeology is that it is not self-evident when, if ever, history is patterned in repetitive, predictable, and lasting ways. Perhaps on the brief timescale of most structural analyses in sociology it may be reasonable to say, as Wasserman and Faust have, that "regularities or patterns in interactions give rise to structures" (1994: 6–7). But how likely is it that when measured over longer runs of time, human history is patterned in lasting and meaningful ways (Lorenz 2011)? Far from being a self-evident prior assumption, exploring the patterning of history instead needs to be one of the primary goals of historical research.

Furthermore, in SNA the evident bias in favor of documenting what might be called "structural causation" is commonly also said to favor—as we noted previously—the prior assumption that "relational ties among actors are primary and attributes of actors are secondary" (Wasserman and Faust 1994: 8)—a claim that historians would surely be reluctant to accept without serious debate and qualification (Butterfield 1955).

5. **Social networks as causes** (Figure 1.1c). In keeping with what we just noted about structure, it is commonly assumed in SNA that the focus of research should be on "the connections or ties that connect entities—known as nodes, vertices, or actors—rather than the entities themselves" (Mills 2017: 380; also Borgatti et al. 2018: 2; Knoke and Yang 2008: 4–5; Newman 2010: 36). However, as Schortman (2014: 168) among others has emphasized, the word "network" can be a verb as well as a noun. Rather than seeing networks as bounded and structurally configured relational entities, the evident patterning over time and space of human relationships can be viewed instead as open-ended social, political, and economic formations constituted by, and inseparable from, human aims and actions. Furthermore, Schortman (2014: 171) has also

emphasized that analyzing social relationships using the seemingly precise mathematical measures of SNA easily tempts us into transforming the dynamic interplay of social life into seemingly rigid constraints and obligations.

Therefore, many researchers in recent years have opted to reverse what Schortman has called "the causal arrow implicit in structural analyses" (2014: 171) to focus instead on *networking* as something that people do rather than on *networks* as more or less fixed social arrangements within which people live and try to go about their daily lives. Or as Mills has stated, even if the structuring of ties among actors or nodes is consequential, it is wise "to look at how actors structure networks and networks structure interactions among actors" (Mills 2017: 380).

> ❖ **system** ['sistəm] *noun, pl* systems: a set of things working together as parts of a mechanism or an interconnecting network.

6. **Social networks as systems** (Figure 1.1d). As Wasserman and Faust (1994: 19) have noted, another supposition commonly accepted in SNA is that to "a large extent, the power of network analysis lies in the ability to model the relationships among systems of actors." If so, then how is a *system* different from a structure? Or should we take these two words to mean basically the same thing? (Kolaczyk 2009; Newman 2010: 1–3)

Not necessarily. It is often stated in the literature on SNA that the structural relationships which are the primary interest of such network studies should be viewed as dynamic processes (Knoke and Yang 2008: 6; Scott 2000: 30; Wasserman and Faust 1994: 8–9). For instance, this would seem to be what Wasserman and Faust had in mind when they wrote:

> Social network theories require specification in terms of patterns of relations, characterizing a group or social system as a whole. Given appropriate network measurements, these theories may be stated as propositions about group relational structure. Network analysis then provides a collection of descriptive procedures to determine how the system behaves, and statistical methods to test the appropriateness of the propositions. (1994: 22)

Being a stickler for definitional clarity may not be a charming scholarly trait, but in our opinion the seeming willingness on the part of those doing SNA to use words such as "structure," "system," and "process" as if they all mean basically the same thing strikes us as confusing and unhelpful.

Dynamic Relational Analysis

History shows repeatedly that our reliance as a species on the pragmatic (and often self-serving) strategy of mentally putting things, people, and experiences into separate and seemingly distinct mind boxes—into different groups, kinds, types, or categories—can make it hard to see and pay sufficient attention to how things, people, places, and experiences are almost always linked and interrelated rather than separate and distinct. Hence, perhaps the most fundamental premise of both SNA and DYRA is that—unlike categorical thinking that takes it for granted things exist apart from one another (and may only subsequently become linked, tied, or connected with one another)—the thinking so fundamental to all styles of relational analysis assumes instead that things exist as such *because* they are interrelated (Rovelli 2017).

> ❖ **dynamic** [dī'namik] *adjective*: characterized by constant change, activity, or progress.
>
> **dynamic relational analysis**: studying changing *relational contingencies* among people, places, and events over time and space of differing character, cause, and probability.

When stated as we just did, thinking relationally may sound more like an advertising slogan than a working proposition. An example, therefore, may help illustrate more concretely what makes relational thinking so central to network modeling and relational analysis.

Example

Humans as a rule are not only ready, willing, and able to forge and maintain relationships with others of their kind, we are also remarkably skilled at coming up with playful excuses to do so. Moreover, it is obvious that spectator sports such as tennis or baseball involve more than just simple dyadic relationships between two individual players. The social complexity of sporting events is even more apparent for games like soccer and football that call for the coordination of players both within and between the two opposing teams on the field. Indeed, the complexity of human relationships is perhaps even more apparent among the fans watching the sporting events being played out right before their eyes. For some sports, it might even be argued that most of the real relational action is in the bleachers, not down on the field.

What can be said about this simple example? Regardless of how well or how poorly those on the field are playing by the rules of a game, it is obvious, for instance, that football and soccer are team sports. They are human engagements that "exist" only as such when played relationally. True, sports fans may want to idolize individual players whom they single out as "winners." Yet even so, as every coach knows, the key to winning a game is how well everybody on the team does what needs to be done.

Working Assumptions

Given this example, how does DYRA differ from conventional SNA? It is customary, after all, in SNA to say that human relationships are dynamic processes, not just static structures (Borgatti et al. 2018: 8–10). Furthermore, although the focus may be on networks as structures, it is also generally acknowledged in SNA that people can apply "their knowledge about networks to leverage advantages" and "transform the relational structures within which they are embedded, both intentionally and unintentionally" (Knoke and Yang 2008: 6; Scott 2000: 14). Therefore, in what ways do the working assumptions of SNA and DYRA differ?

1. **Whole networks, or working models?** The strategy in SNA of using graph theory (Harary et al. 1965; Kolaczyk 2009) to model human relationships mathematically as sets of points—some or all of which have connecting lines (Figure 1b)—commits SNA not only to the goal of describing the patterning formed by the lines but also to the premise that such linking patterns shape and may also explain the behavior of the individuals (points) included (Scott 2000: 19). What may be less obvious is that this mathematical approach can also be an analytical and interpretative Catch-22. It can give you something but not necessarily what you want or need.

To analyze patterns of points and lines constructed using graph theory, you must assume that the structures being characterized are "whole networks" (as noted above). Furthermore, to do something meaningful with relational information about network structuring, you must also assume that there is an "underlying system of interest" that can be analyzed statistically to reveal the inherent impact and importance of these bounded structural relationships (Kolaczyk 2009: 51).

As already stated, however, one of the basic suppositions of SNA as a social science is that human relations "are in a dynamic flux, with the final balanced outcome—if it is achieved—resulting from the actions and compromises of all the participants involved" (Scott 2000: 14). Consequently, as Wasserman and Faust observed years ago, the methods used in SNA "must be applied to a specific set of data which assumes not only finite actor set size(s), but also enumerable set(s) of actors. Somehow, in order to study the network, we must enumerate a finite set of actors to study" (1994: 32).

These analytical requirements are generally acknowledged in SNA. As John Scott has written: "the question of the *selection* of data is one that does pose considerable problems for social network analysis. These selection problems concern the boundedness of social relations and the possibility of drawing relational data from samples" (Scott 2000: 53; also Knoke and Yang 2008: 15–20; Wasserman and Faust 1994: 31–33; see Chapter 6, this volume).

A number of strategies have been used in SNA to work around the confounding issues of boundary definition and data sampling. In DYRA, however, the issues of what to study and how to sample are approached differently. Somewhat ironically—to borrow what John Scott (2000: 54) wrote about SNA—from the perspective of DYRA, researchers "are involved in a process of conceptual elaboration and model building, not a simple process of collecting pre-formed data."

In keeping with Scott's observation, the primary goal of DYRA is *not* to collect relational information and then analyze these data to reveal the structural patterning latent within them. *Instead, the basic goal is to model and then investigate the* **relational contingencies** *that may have led to what evidently happened in the past.*

❖ The focus of historical research using DYRA is on modeling and then investigating the relational contingencies—popularly called "the causes"—that may explain what happened in the past.

2. **Describing networks, or exploring research questions?** The minimal unit of social life defined in SNA is called a *dyad*—the "contact, connection, or tie between a pair of actors" (Knoke and

Yang 2008: 7). It is not a foregone conclusion, however, that when a dyadic pair of actors is further linked with other actors (and pairs of actors), the composite set of relationships (lines, links, contacts, connections, ties, etc.) thus formed gives rise to an instrumental "whole set" or "working network." Common sense suggests that what happens within any given dyadic pair *could* influence, affect, alter, change, and so forth what then happens within others who are also relationally engaged with those in that dyadic pair. At issue however, are the basic questions *how? why?* and *so what?*

This is one reason that the *basic unit* in DYRA—if for some reason there is a need to talk about one—is not the structural dyad, but instead *the probability that an observed outcome, result, or consequence* (X_{t+1}) *can be attributed to a previous set of conditions* (X_t) *and what has happened* (Y) *that may have led to this outcome* (see Proposition 1.2). A playful example of a rolling and ultimately consequential series of such contingencies which may be familiar to many would be the Mother Goose Rhyme about a horseshoe nail.

❖ For Want of a Nail
For want of a nail the shoe was lost.
For want of a shoe the horse was lost.
For want of a horse the rider was lost.
For want of a rider the message was lost.
For want of a message the battle was lost.
For want of a battle the kingdom was lost.
And all for the want of a horseshoe nail.

3. **Categorical ties or relational probabilities?** Earlier we noted that one of the common working assumptions in SNA—somewhat ironically—is the categorical premise that networks are formed and structured by the particular types of relationship creating them. Not only does this supposition imply that social ties are inherently causal but also that they are enduring (or at least repetitive) and generally are all of one discernible type or another.

Even if it is appropriate to say, for example, that someone who is a *friend* is "a person whom one knows and with whom one has a bond of mutual affection, typically exclusive of sexual or family relations," and it is common parlance to talk about "friendship networks," why we have friendships with other people is a widely varying dimension of human social life. Although the expression *friendship network* can be a convenient shorthand way of talking about social relationships, it would be naïve to assume that what is being talked about can be so easily categorized. Put simply, the grounds for friendship can be many, diverse, and variable in their importance, timing, and impact. Therefore, to offer a specific example, another way of talking about how SNA and DYRA differ in their working assumptions is to contrast what in SNA is called *homophily* with the concept of *relational probability* as used in DYRA and in the modeling of dynamic Bayesian networks (DBNs; Meyer-Delius et al. 2008).

However difficult it may be to pin down and define, there is little doubt that the degree to which people are actively engaged with one another varies greatly in character and probability. Decades ago, however, Mark Granovetter argued—and others since have also—that "the stronger the tie connecting two individuals, the more similar they are, in various ways" (Granovetter 1973: 1362). This categorical premise is now commonly referred to in SNA as *homophily*, "the tendency for people to like people who are similar to themselves on socially significant attributes" (Borgatti et al. 2018: 6). This tendency, insofar as it is an analytically (and psychologically) useful claim, may be plausible, but this explanation for why people may be involved with one another offers a very narrow view for why people do become involved, however momentarily or enduring the relationship.

In DYRA, therefore, the concept of homophily is rarely used. Instead, the focus is on determining the relational probability that there will be ties, links, or associations between individuals, places, and things that are *contingent* and hence *inherently variable* in their character, frequency, duration, and predictability.

Consequently, it is unnecessary in DYRA to assume that the ties, links, etc. will be (or need to be) of one kind or another. *Until observed to be otherwise, the default assumption in DYRA instead is that the relationships involved will be variable in their kind, duration, and consequences.* The defining question is not whether there is a tie, link, or association between the people, places, or things under consideration, but rather how probable and diverse those connections may be.

4. **Analyzing networks, or building models?** It would be the height of academic conceit to claim that anyone can easily resolve the motives, modalities, and rewards of someone's dealings with another human being into regular, predictable, and lasting relational patterns. To call upon a familiar platitude, how well does anyone

even know their own spouse or children? Surely, therefore, to propose that one can usefully fathom the latent patterning of ties, connections, linkages, and the like among a seemingly interrelated multitude of people who may or may not belong to a bounded and easily defined group would be seemingly outrageous. Hence the focus of historical research using DYRA is not on analyzing abstract social networks, but on *modeling the varied and changing contingencies that may have led to the relationships and events in the past being studied.*

Modeling Complexity

The undeniable complexity of our relationships is not just a social phenomenon. Over half a century ago, the biologist Richard Levins wrote insightfully about the challenges of dealing simultaneously with the genetic, physiological, and age heterogeneity of species that are changing and evolving under the fluctuating influences of other species in heterogeneous environments. The problem, he wrote, is how to deal with such complex realities:

> The naive, brute force approach would be to set up a mathematical model which is a faithful, one-to-one reflection of this complexity. This would require using perhaps 100 simultaneous partial differential equations with time lags; measuring hundreds of parameters, solving the equations to get numerical predictions, and then measuring these predictions against nature. However:
>
> (a). There are too many parameters to measure; some are still only vaguely defined; many would require a lifetime each for their measurement.
>
> (b). The equations are insoluble analytically and exceed the capacity of even good computers.
>
> (c). Even if soluble, the result expressed in the form of quotients of sums of products of parameters would have no meaning for us. (Levins 1966: 421)

As he then went on to say, what is needed are ways to tackle complexity that preserve the essential features of the problem being studied without becoming entirely swamped. Perhaps following the advice of the great French mathematician, physicist, and philosopher Henri Poincaré (1905: 152–55), Levins favored using simple mathematical models that are flexible and often graphical instead of trying to write formal and elaborate mathematical equations (Orzack and Sober 1993).

However, Levins acknowledged that there is a price paid for such generality and flexibility. "There is always room for doubt as to whether a result depends on the essentials of a model or on the details of the simplifying assumptions." (Levins 1966: 423). Given this inherent uncertainty, here is what Levins advised biologists to do:

> [T]reat the same problem with several alternative models each with different simplifications but with a common biological assumption. Then, if these models, despite their different assumptions, lead to similar results we have what we can call a robust theorem which is relatively free of the details of the model. Hence our truth is the intersection of independent lies. (1966: 423)

In this book, we advocate following the same advice in the study of history.

Defining Relational Contingencies

It would be rare to find a scientist who would disagree with Richard Levins about the inherent complexity of the real world. In archaeology, much has been written in recent years about the entanglement of human beings with things and places around them, and the difficulties of pinning down good answers even for the most basic questions of *why? how?* and *so what?* (Hodder and Mol 2016). Anthropologists, too, have devoted similar attention to the many interdependencies linking the social, biological, and physical worlds (Ingold 2015, 2017).

> ❖ **cause** [kôz/ /kɔz] *noun*: a person or thing that gives rise to an action, phenomenon, or condition.
>
> **contingency** [kənˈtinjənsē, kənˈtɪndʒənsi] *noun*: a future event or circumstance which is possible but cannot be predicted with certainty.
>
> **contingent** [kənˈtinjənt] *adjective*: occurring or existing only if (certain circumstances) are the case; dependent on.
>
> **variable** [verēəb(ə)l, vɛriəb(ə)l] *noun*: (*mathematics*) a quantity which during a calculation is assumed to vary or be capable of varying in value.

From this perspective, the contingencies involved in any relationship are likely to be many and variable in their form, frequency of occurrence, and consequences. DYRA can be seen, therefore, as a way of adopting Levins's modeling strategy to cut through the Gordian Knot of the boundless tangle of things and events in the real world that the anthropologist Tim Ingold has called life's "meshwork" (Ingold 2015, 2017).

How can untangling this meshwork, this Gordian Knot, of things and events be accomplished? A common strategy is to try to reduce—model—life's complexity mathematically. There are many at least in the world of science who would insist that until you have done so, you cannot legitimately claim you understand what you are dealing with. As we will say repeatedly in this book, however, we do not agree that the "gold standard" of scholarship is the mathematical equation. From the perspective of DYRA, mathematics is a modeling strategy, not the only road to go down, and certainly not the only high road to take.

One reason we have for insisting on modeling complexity in more ways than mathematical is that the word "variable" is generally taken in mathematics to mean something (a "factor" or "function") that can vary "within itself," and hence the degree to which it does so determines ("causes") the computed outcome with some degree of probability. *For example*: If we assume $(x + 3)(x + 1) = x^2 + 4x + 3$, and we know that $x = 3$, then the answer is 24. But if $x = 4$, then the answer is 35. This way of thinking about what is a *variable* holds even in the case of differential equations that assume the phenomenon of interest is a function of something that is continuously changing. For example:

N is the size of a population at a moment in time **t**

r is the rate of change (growth) in **N** over a moment in time

dN/dt = rN is the exponential rate of change in the size of a population over a moment in time

Please do not get us wrong. Although we do not believe writing mathematical equations is the only strategy of choice when modeling the past, there is no denying that mathematics can be a useful *modeling strategy*, and that differential equations can be a particularly useful way to model change in a measurable variable (such as population size) over time.

However, from the perspective of DYRA, we are not just interested in modeling how a variable changes "within itself" over time—even when an equation such as that just given for exponential population growth is modified to capture the reality that population growth is contingent not only on the size of a population at any given moment in time but also on how its observed rate of growth may also change (i.e., is variable) depending on the resources available for the survival of that population. To be truly useful as a research tool, therefore, the exponential equation **dN/dt = rN** needs to be modified to take into account another variable, **K,** defined as the "carrying capacity"—the maximum size of a population—that is sustainable with a specific type of "environment": **dN/dt = rN(1-N/K)**.

Adding a variable such as **K** to a mathematical equation for exponential growth is obviously a logical way to admit what common sense tells us: populations (whatever we take this word to mean) cannot continue to grow and grow over time until they become infinite in size. But what does **K** represent in the real world? What is an environment? How do you measure the carrying capacity of such a place, or thing, or whatever an environment may be?

Nobody doubts the concept of carrying capacity can be used to good purpose, for instance, in ecology, agriculture, and fisheries research (Wu and Hu 2020). Here, however, we champion another strategy. Instead of assuming that the world's complexity can be reduced to one, two, or even a handful of "variables," we suggest it is more useful to think of history as a changing set of *contingencies* which may vary not only "within themselves" but also in their impact on what may come about as a result, or *consequence*.

Hence, we think "contingency" is a good word to use, but not because a dictionary would define it as meaning a "future event or set of conditions that cannot be predicted with certainty" (see definition section). Instead, we favor defining this word when used in DYRA as "what may need to be taken into account when you are trying to explain what may collectively lead to change over time and space in what is being studied." For those who are mathematically inclined, we offer worked statistical examples of what we have in mind in Chapter 5.

❖ Types of Relational Contingencies

> **circumstantial** [ˈsərkəmˌstans] *adjective*: a fact or condition connected with or relevant to an event or action; an event or fact that causes or helps to cause something to happen.
>
> **consequential** [ˌkänsəˈkwen(t)SHəl] *adjective*: following as a result or effect.

situational [ˌsɪtʃəˈweɪʃ(ə)n(ə)l] *adjective*: relating to or dependent on a set of circumstances or state of affairs.

Granting that studying complexity calls for both simplification and careful problem-driven selection of what is to be included in the models constructed, we have found it also useful to distinguish (Figure 1.2) between *situational contingencies* X_t that are seen as pre-existing ("prior," i.e., previously established, conditions), and *circumstantial contingencies* Y that are newly arising or are considered to be changing during the time interval being modeled. In both cases, only those contingencies are included in any given model that are arguably the most likely ones contributing to ("causing") what we are trying to model dynamically—outcomes we refer to as the *consequential contingencies* X_{t+1} of the time interval being studied.

Stated more formally, *causal statements* (Mumford and Anjum 2013) can be framed as propositions (Gerring 2008) about the likely temporal pathways leading from a *prior situation* X_t to an *observed outcome* X_{t+1} through a sequences of possible intermediate *circumstantial changes* or *events* Y:

$$X_t + Y \longrightarrow X_{t+1} \qquad \text{Proposition 1.1}$$

We want to emphasize, however, that we consider DYRA to be a way to model and evaluate associations—popularly called correlations and explanations—among selected contingencies. Like SNA, what we are calling DYRA is not a formal body of theory or a specific set of hypotheses. Therefore, propositions such as Proposition 1.1 must be *hypothesized* as part of model building (see Chapters 4 and 5). Only after doing so does it make sense to try to confirm—to seek support for—the relational patterning in the implied temporal pathway (Proposition 1.2) where P is the probability that the intermediate set of hypothesized contingencies Y has contributed to outcome X_{t+1}.

$$P(X_t + Y) \longrightarrow X_{t+1} \qquad \text{Proposition 1.2}$$

Types of Network Models

Figure 1.2 recognizes five basic types, or classes, of relational models differing in their primary characteristics. We emphasize that all of the five real-world examples also included in the right-hand column are

	situational X_1	circumstantial Y	consequential X_2	adaptive	intentional	purposeful	EXAMPLES
STRUCTURAL	✓	✓	✓				Mississippi River watershed
FUNCTIONAL	✓	✓	✓				your body's circulatory system
ECOLOGICAL	✓	✓	✓	✓			natural ecosystems
PARTICIPANT	✓	✓	✓	✓	✓		Facebook users' group
CONTROL	✓	✓	✓	✓	✓	✓	Flint, Michigan water system

Figure 1.2. Relational contingencies in the category "network models." © John Edward Terrell.

in themselves relational models, i.e., generalized representations. Consider, for example, the Mississippi River watershed modeled as a structural network:

> The situational X_t, or prior condition, of any given watershed varies depending on a wide range of contingencies such as the local hydraulic gradient, underlying geological variability, riverbed conductance, riverbed thickness, width of the riverbed length, gradient of the riverbed, and the like (Ghysels et al. 2019). Similarly, the subsequent (that is, the changing, or "dynamic") performance of a watershed—for instance, whether and when flooding occurs X_{t+1}—is contingent on a range of circumstances Y_n such as groundwater conditions, the amount of rainfall within a given period of time, and general atmospheric conditions (e.g., air temperature).

❖ Types of Relational Contingencies

> **adapt** [əˈdapt] *verb*: make (something) suitable for a new use or purpose; modify.
>
> **evolve** [ēˈvälv] *verb*: develop gradually, especially from a simple to a more complex form.
>
> **intent on/upon** [inˈtent] *adjective*: resolved or determined to do (something).
>
> **purpose** [ˈpərpəs] *noun*: the reason for which something is done or created or for which something exists.

Now it would be questionable indeed to suggest that the evolving network of channels in a watershed over time—the Mississippi River being one example—is more than an unintended byproduct of our planet's global atmospheric system at work. On the other hand, the human circulatory system has clearly evolved biologically as a dynamic functional network (Proposition 1.3) that needs to be modeled and analyzed as a *feedback cycle* regulating vital bodily functions:

$$X_1 + Y_1 \longrightarrow X_2 + Y_2 \longrightarrow X_1 \qquad \text{Proposition 1.3}$$

Unlike functional networks, ecosystems are evolving networks (Proposition 1.4) within which change among the contingencies, although neither intentional nor purposeful, leads to historical changes that are adaptive rather than cyclical along what might be called developing *temporal pathways*:

$$X_t + Y_1 \longrightarrow X_{t+1} + Y_2 \longrightarrow X_{t+2} \qquad \text{Proposition 1.4}$$

Finally, the bottom two types of networks given in Figure 1.2 add the contingencies of *human agency* and *intentionality* (for which, Proposition 1.1 applies when **Y** is interpreted as choice, deliberate selection, etc.) and *purposeful behavior* (for which, propositions 1.3 and 1.4 apply). Although perhaps obvious, including the contingencies of intentionality and choice can significantly alter the likelihood of modeled outcomes (see Figure 5.5) because—being goal-driven—those engaged in deliberative acts are likely, in the words of one philosopher of history, to look for alternative causal pathways leading to their targeted goals (Tucker 2010: 69; also Terrell 1986). Although we will not enter into such a discussion here, there is substantial evidence that the neural underpinnings of intentionality and choice are comparable to those leading to historical outcomes at the individual and social levels of human agency (Tse 2013).

Chapter Summary

In the sciences, a good model is one that offers us a reasonably plausible explanation for how and why something happens. Similarly, in the study of history, a good model is one that does the same for how and why something may have plausibly happened—that is, with some degree of likelihood—in the past.

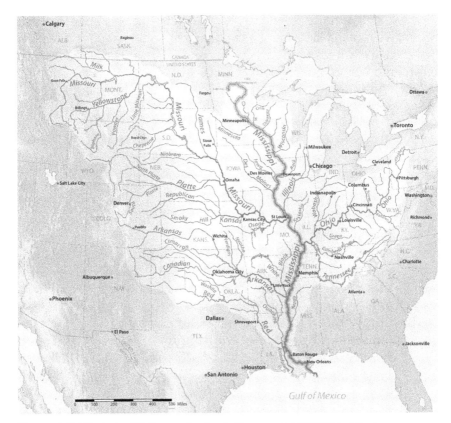

Figure 1.3. Mississippi Valley watershed. Shannon1, CC BY-SA 4.0, via Wikimedia Commons.

As we have now described them, conventional SNA models are structural models. As such, they are basically deterministic models. While in practice, such models are often modified by researchers to make them more dynamic and responsive as portrayals of changing circumstances, they are essentially timeless categorical depictions having the simple logical form $X_t \rightarrow X_{t+1}$ (which might be summarized as "what you had is what you get"). Furthermore, although SNA models are about the patterning of social relationships rather than about rainfall and watersheds, it might even be said that SNA models formally have much in common with structural watershed network models (Figure 1.3).

In contrast, dynamic relational analysis challenges us to do what Richard Levins suggested we do when faced with the inherent complexity of the world and causation. Treat the same problem with several alternative models each with different simplifications but with a common working premise. Then, despite their differing assumptions, these several ways of thinking about a problem may lead to a robust theorem that is relatively free of the faults of any one of them. "Hence our truth is the intersection of independent lies." (Levins 1966: 423)

Key Points

1. The focus of historical research using DYRA is not on analyzing social networks, but is instead on modeling and then investigating the *relational contingencies* that may explain what happened in the past.
2. One of the limitations of using conventional SNA methods and theories in archaeology is that it is not self-evident that what happened in history was patterned in repetitive and enduring ways.
3. Studying complexity calls for both simplification and problem-driven selection of the contingencies to be included in the models constructed.

CHAPTER 2
Start with a Question

One of the first things one notes about scientists is the fact that a large part of their time is spent in thinking about things in a question-answering way. They want to find out something, and all of their activities are designed to bring them answers to questions. (Of course, a good part of the trick to being a first-rate scientist is in asking the right questions, or asking them in ways that make it possible to find answers.)

—Anne Roe, *The Making of a Scientist* (1953)

Turing thinks carefully about how humans perform computations. He realizes that any computation can be broken down to a sequence of simple steps. Then he constructs theoretical machines capable of performing each of these steps. These machines, which we now call Turing machines, are capable of doing any computation. After this, he shows that you don't need a different machine for each different algorithm, you can design one machine that can compute any algorithm.

—Chris Bernhardt,
Turing's Vision: The Birth of Computer Science (2016)

- Asking Questions
- What Is a Good Question?
- Picturing the Possible
- The Logic of Research
- Planning a Research Project
- Example: Ancient Voyaging in the Pacific
- Chapter Summary
- Key Points

Many of the questions asked of history are about guilt and innocence, blame and restitution. For instance, who was Jack the Ripper? Was the virus causing Covid-19 artificially created at the Wuhan Institute of Virology in China? Alternatively, the questions asked are often about cause and consequences. Why did the supposedly unsinkable luxury passenger liner RMS Titanic sink during its maiden voyage on 15 April 1912, after hitting an iceberg in the North Atlantic? Why wasn't President Donald Trump re-elected on Tuesday, 3 November 2020?

Of the many questions that can be asked of the past, the ones we find most helpful and revealing are those not only about how and why things happen but also about how likely is it that such things may yet happen again in the future. Questions about the patterning of history strike us as not only great questions to ask, but also challenging questions to answer.

Wanting to understand how the world works does not guarantee you may be able to control what happens and why. Nor does wanting to understand what happened in history mean you can change the past. Yet it would be foolish to believe you could attempt the former without knowing about the latter. This is why this book is not about interpreting the past. This book is about trying to understand and explain what happened in the past to be better prepared for what could happen in the future.

In *The Nature of Historical Explanation*, the British philosopher Patrick Gardiner (1922–1997) argued against the grandiose assumption that philosophers of history ought to be able to "answer questions about the meaning or purpose of the historical process, the nature of human destiny, the course of human history, and the future of mankind" ([1952] 1961: ix). At the same time, however, he was careful to point out that someone interested in philosophy might legitimately "be very interested in the kind of evidence an historian might bring forward" to substantiate their claims, and "in the criteria he uses for deciding whether or not a connection existed" say, between the Protestant Reformation in the sixteenth and seventeenth centuries and the rise of capitalist economies ([1952] 1961: x).

Similarly, someone in computer science interested in mathematics and real-world applications might not be historically inclined, but nonetheless may want to know how and why Alan Turing (when he was only twenty-four years old) came to write his now legendary paper in 1936 on the theory of computation—an intellectual contribution widely heralded as leading to the development of modern digital computers. The easy answer, of course, would be that Turing was able to do what he did because he was a genius (Bernhardt 2016). This answer, however, tells us nothing. Such an explanation is equivalent to saying that people sleep because they are sleepy or do idiotic things because they are stupid. Explanations such as these merely turn good questions about how and why into poor answers that are not only meaningless but are also effectively useless—unless, of course, the aim is not to answer the questions *how* and *why* but simply to get off the hook of having to come up with adequate explanations.

Asking Questions

Some would argue that archaeologists spend too little time confronting the challenges of writing history (Terrell 2013b). Often it seems (at least to us) that many archaeologists take it more or less for granted that their research findings contribute somehow directly to historical understanding, with scant attention to the British historian E. H. Carr's famous question: *What is History?* (Carr 1961; see Chapter 3, this volume).

Journalists have long followed the helpful advice that any news story worth putting into print (or these days, online) should answer six fundamental questions: *What? Where? When? Who? How? Why?* We have the impression, however, that for many historians and archaeologists, the minimally acceptable set of questions need only be the first four of these to the neglect of *how?* and *why?* As one of Terrell's dissertation advisors many years ago said to him: "Just stick to the facts and leave the interpretation to others." (This individual was later removed from Terrell's doctoral committee by the other members.)

We have never been convinced that merely answering the first four questions is all that anyone must be able to do to claim they are writing about history and not just gathering facts and figures about the past (Clark and Terrell 1978). Furthermore, we are convinced that there is a seventh question that must not be neglected. *So what?*

We include this seventh question not only because granting agencies and foundations nowadays insist on asking applicants to explain in a convincing fashion why they should be given financial support to be able to do what they say they want to do. The real reason we have for invoking this seventh question, nonetheless, is similarly straightforward.

Phrased briefly, *not all questions that can be asked are worth the time, effort, and money required to answer them.* And not just because, as the old cliché goes, curiosity may kill the cat. But, also because even with the best will in the world, *there may be no feasible way to answer some questions however worthy they may be.* Equally important to note for those of us who are archaeologists, anthropologists, and historians is that some questions may be ones that in all honesty we simply cannot help resolve.

What Is a Good Question?

A more picturesque way of underscoring the importance of thinking long and hard about what research questions to ask and try to answer is to invoke what we like to call the "Goldilocks Rule." What do we mean by this? Some questions are too big to try to answer, some are too trivial. The art of doing research is finding the happy medium between these two extremes. As the renowned evolutionary biologist Robert H. MacArthur wrote years ago: "The only rules of scientific method are honest observations and accurate logic. To be great science it must also be guided by a judgment, almost an instinct, for what is worth studying" (1972: 1). Change his focus from science to history, and we believe the same can be said about studying the past.

If so, then what makes a question a good one for anyone interested in history to ask and try to answer? Obviously, there is no easy way to make this kind of assessment, but nonetheless, we think there are three questions that can be used to guide such judgments, to borrow MacArthur's word.

1. What makes the question you want to ask worthwhile?
2. Given what can currently be achieved, how likely is it that this question is answerable?
3. If so, how can you help answer it?

If these three questions strike you as self-evident, please note in particular how the last one has been phrased. As we will be arguing repeatedly in this book, given the complexity of things—and, therefore, the complexity of the past—asking how someone can *help answer* a good question is a far more realistic challenge than asking how they can answer worthy historical questions all on their own.

Picturing the Possible

We are convinced that dynamic relational analysis (DYRA) can be used to turn ideas and propositions about what happened in the past into testable research hypotheses. Toward this end, we have endorsed the view favored in the last century by the biologist François Jacob that science is a continuous dialogue between the possible and the actual: "A subtle mixture of belief, knowledge, and imagination builds before us an ever-changing picture of the possible" (1982; see Introduction, this volume).

In Chapter 1, we introduced the modeling strategy promoted by another biologist, Richard Levins (1966, 1968, 2006). As the philosopher of science Michael Weisberg wrote retrospectively a number of years ago, Levins's contributions to the philosophy of biology a half century ago "are notable for their attention to the complex issues facing practicing theoreticians" when they are analyzing "complexity and the theoretical strategies necessary to deal with it" (Weisberg 2006: 603).

Levins favored using qualitative methods of mathematical analysis and model building to study highly complex phenomena. Furthermore, when dealing with such challenges, he said, a healthy approach is one that makes use of "a cluster of abstractions" drawn from different perspectives, different temporal and horizontal scales, and assuming different givens (Levins 2006: 741).

In 2006, looking back over what he had written previously, Levins offered a number of basic observations about the nature of complexity. Several of these are germane not only to the study of biological complexity but also the study of history:

- Things are more richly connected than is obvious.
- Things are the way they are because they got that way.
- The dichotomies into which we split the world—biological/social, physiological/psychological, genetic/environmental, random/deterministic, intelligible/chaotic—are misleading and eventually obfuscating. (Levins 2006: 742)

Being an evolutionist, the second of these observations was Levins's rather quaint way of acknowledging that understanding biological complexity calls for understanding history, too, not just biology.

Back in the 1960s, Levins was one of a half-dozen or so mathematically inclined population biologists, all then in their early to mid-thirties, who were self-consciously working together to advance the idea that the best way to tackle complexity is to be willing to simplify and accept that "a satisfactory theory is usually a cluster of models" rather than an unmanageable but seemingly all-encompassing single model. Although he was writing specifically about mathematical modeling, what Levins concluded has much broader applicability:

> A mathematical model is neither an hypothesis nor a theory. Unlike the scientific hypothesis, a model is not verifiable directly by experiment. For all models are both true and false. Almost any plausible proposed relation among aspects of nature is likely to be true in the sense that it occurs (although rarely and slightly). Yet all models leave out a lot and are in that sense false, incomplete, inadequate. The validation of a model is not that it is "true" but that it generates good testable hypotheses relevant to important problems. A model may be discarded in favor of a more powerful one, but it usually is simply outgrown when the live issues are not any longer those for which it was designed. (Levins 1966: 430)

Levins challenged all of us to consider questions that at first may sound almost painfully simple, but are actually profound. "Why are things the way they are instead of a little bit different? Why are things the way they are instead of very different? The first is the question of self-regulation and homeostasis. The second is the question of evolution, development and history" (2006: 742).

With both of these questions in mind, we now offer you what we have found to be a useful sequence of steps to follow that can turn good research questions about the history of people, places, and things into useful models, reasonable hypotheses, and effective research strategies for tackling what Levins highlighted as evolution, development, and history.

The Logic of Research

There are no fixed rules about how to do research and write up your findings. However, there is some scholarly agreement on what the characteristics of a good research report are:

1. Clearly stated research question and hypothesis,
2. Relevant review of current knowledge,
3. Well-designed experimental approach [that is clearly reported],
4. Clearly explained and illustrated results, and
5. Conclusions that are supported by the results. (Yore, Hand, and Florence 2004: 356)

We want to emphasize again that the first item on this list of desirable characteristics is not only important, but also that having clearly stated questions or hypotheses is not all that is critical to successful research. It is essential to be transparent about the importance of knowing not only why and how answering the question you have elected to ask makes sense, but also may make a real difference in how the world is understood and dealt with by all of us, not just by those doing the research involved. The *so what?* question is one that should never be overlooked.

Planning a Research Project

Although there may be no fixed way to get from start to finish when doing a research project, we have found that not only is having a well-conceived plan of action important when crafting a funding proposal, but also that this is the only reliably way to ensure that you will not be wasting your time and talents on a project likely to fail. With this practical aim in mind, therefore, here are the formal research steps we have found helpful. Alternative guidelines, of course, are available elsewhere in print and on the Internet, too.

- **Problem statement**
    1. What is the question being asked?
    2. Why is this question important?
- **Current theories**
    3. Background information
    4. What are some of the possible explanations?
- **Working model**
    5. Which explanations may be the most plausible ones?
    6. How may these particular explanations be modeled so that they can be evaluated?
- **Working hypothesis**
    7. What are your working hypotheses derived from these models, and what do you expect your data will show you given these propositions?
- **Evidence and analysis**
    8. A step-by-step description of the evidence available and the analyses done.
- **Evaluation and discussion**
    9. How does this new evidence support or refute your working hypotheses?
    10. How would additional research narrow the field of likely solutions?

Keeping these ten steps in mind, here is one example drawn from our own research on the history of the Pacific Islands illustrating how we have used this approach to study the deep past in this vast region of the world.

Example: Ancient Voyaging in the Pacific

It has become increasingly uncertain in recent years just when it was that our species began to leave our African homeland (Rito et al. 2019). Even so, the archaeological evidence now available seems sufficient to suggest a few things. Those who did so were successful tens of thousands of years ago in traveling as far to the east as Australia and New Guinea—and ultimately the Americas, too. At least some people then must have also had the technology and the voyaging skills needed to leave the Asian mainland and travel from island to island throughout Southeast Asia and the New Guinea region (Roberts et al. 2020; Veth et al. 2019).

Problem Statement

1. What is the question being asked?

It is known archaeologically that the initial human colonization of Australia and the islands in the New Guinea region of the southwest Pacific took place at least ~50,000–65,000 years ago; in contrast, the first settlement of islands to the east in the Pacific beyond the Solomons Archipelago (Figure 2.1) apparently did not happen until ~3300–2800 BP (Bedford et al. 2019). Why was there such a long pause before anyone voyaged eastward out of sight of land away from the Solomons to colonize islands in the more remote parts of the Pacific?

2. Why is this question important?

Background information: Evolution has made us a markedly social species. Nowadays cell phones, the World Wide Web, and the like are making it easy for many of us to stay in touch with others anywhere on earth at any time of day or night. However, at least since the Enlightenment in the seventeenth and eighteenth centuries, it has been generally assumed that (a) intimacy—both social and geographic—is a decisive characteristic of our social networks, and (b) as a consequence,

Start with a Question • 41

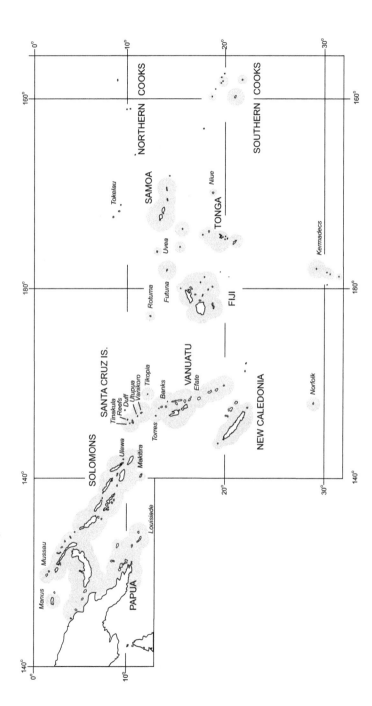

Figure 2.1. Islands in the southwest Pacific. Shaded areas indicate the maximum distances from which high land can be seen from sea level given optimal conditions (Irwin 2008: fig. 5). © Geoffrey Irwin and the University of Hawai'i Press, reproduced with permission.

the social formations popularly known as "families" and "tribes" are the primary and most important building blocks of our social lives.

These twin assumptions have led to the popular idea that as our forerunners traveled away from Africa, they necessarily changed in fundamental ways. Why? Supposedly because for most of human history, we lived in small, isolated, and often hostile social groups ("tribes"), each out of contact with others (Pinker 2002; Wilson 2012)—a view of our history as a species that the anthropologist Alexander Lesser (1961) called "the myth of the primitive isolate"—a way of modeling our past (and in the eyes of some, also social life in seemingly far off and allegedly "primitive" places today) as a mosaic of separate and distinct societies and ethnic traditions (Barth 1969). Although we have come across few who would agree with us, this myth is alive and well in the working assumption that our species (and other species, too) is subdivided into "populations," and it is somehow meaningful to study how "admixed" these supposed isolates have become (Pritchard, Stephens, and Donnelly 2000) since 1492 when Columbus and his three ships left Spain searching for a western sea passage to the East Indies.

There is no doubt, of course, that our species is diverse both in its ways and in its physical appearance. The standard explanation for our obvious diversity is one rooted for many of us (Stocking 1987) in the traditional biblical story of humankind's exodus from the Tower of Babel (Genesis 11:1–8). It has long been assumed that our human differences must be showing us that for most of the history of our species, the reach of our social networks has been extremely limited. For most of human history, life for all of us must have been a time of social isolation and hostility towards anyone perceived as strange, odd, and untrustworthy.

Further information: It is perhaps not surprising, therefore, that the spatial patterning of human diversity in the Pacific has long inspired historical narratives about ancient migrations from the Asian mainland out into this island world by radically (and racially) different ethnic groups, peoples, or populations (Terrell 2006; Terrell, Hunt, and Gosden 1997). Although the number of these presumed migrations has varied over the centuries since Europeans themselves arrived for the first time in the Pacific, nowadays it is commonly said that these supposedly decisive historical human migrations were at least two in number. With rare exceptions (e.g., Allen and O'Connell 2008), the demographic scale and social organization of these two presumed major human relocations have never been adequately specified, and their historical existence has simply been taken for granted.

The first of these two migrations—one that took place evidently soon after *Homo sapiens* first left Africa—is said to have led to the discovery and colonization of the habitable islands in the Pacific near the Asian mainland ~50,000–65,000 years ago. By all accounts, today's Australians and New Guineans are to be seen as the lineal descendants of these adventurous early pioneers, whoever they were.

The second presumptive migration out into the Pacific from Asia and nearby Taiwan began according to most writers today after the last global Ice Age, starting from Taiwan sometime around 6,000 years ago. Those involved have usually been described as an ethnically (and racially) distinctive people, a population unlike anyone who was then already living on New Guinea or elsewhere on the islands immediately east of New Guinea. It is also commonly said that these new arrivals spoke a language that historical linguists say can be assigned to the historic Austronesian family of languages (which are spoken today throughout much of the Pacific and even as far to the west as the island of Madagascar off the African coast; Pawley 2007; Terrell and Welsch 1997).

Consequently, the story of how our species came to inhabit the islands of the Pacific Ocean is more than just a question about process and history; it touches both on how we think about our diversity as a species, and perhaps also how we think about the motivations and capabilities of those who are indigenous to these islands.

Initial working assumptions: Given the timing of this posited second major colonization event, one currently popular historical assumption is that those traveling in the more recent migration had already mastered the skills and navigational know-how that would later prove to be essential for voyaging successfully beyond the Solomons. However, it is far from self-evident why these hypothesized newcomers would have had such skills and know-how since the distances to be navigated among the islands in Southeast Asia are similar to those in the New Guinea regions as far east as the Solomons. If it is true that necessity is the mother of invention, the need and motivation to develop such expertise would presumably have been lacking.

Current Theories

3. Background information

For something like 227,000 of the last 250,000 years, sea levels around the world were ≥10 meters below their current stand. Back then what is now called New Guinea—the second largest island in the world with a land area of ~808,000 km sq—was merely a thickset projection of land on the northern flank of the continent now called Australia. Until the Holocene sea-level rise had slowed down ca. 7,000 years ago, and coastal sedimentary environments had begun to stabilize around the world, much of what is now New Guinea's northern coastline was probably steep and uninviting (as much of it still is), except where favorable local circumstances may have trapped eroding sediment in sandbars, coastal lagoons, and small river deltas (Terrell 2002).

Therefore, given what is presently known or may be surmised about the geomorphological history of New Guinea, it is likely that this island has played a significant role in shaping the history of the Pacific Islands: first as a lengthy land barrier to travel between the islands of Southeast Asia and the rest of the Pacific to the east during the last Ice Age, and then later as a bridge (or perhaps, more accurately, as a socially integrated voyaging corridor) rather than a deterrent to travel between Asia and the Pacific after ~6,000–7,000 years ago.

4. What are some of the possible explanations?

What then are a few of the likely explanations for the delay in settling the Pacific east of the Solomons? Several elementary explanations might account for the long delay in colonizing the islands east of the Solomons:

- Until a few thousand years ago, perhaps nobody in this part of the world thought there would be any islands to colonize east of the Solomons since those farther out in the Pacific are geographically too far away to be seen from there, and it can take weeks on the open sea to reach some of them (Figure 2.1).
- There may have been no compelling reason for anyone to risk voyaging over such uncertain and immense distances of open sea until a few thousand years ago.
- Until then, nobody in the Solomons or elsewhere in the New Guinea area knew how to build ocean-going vessels and risk the dangers of lengthy open sea journeys.

Of these three explanations, which might be the most probable one? The first two are basically what might be called "why explanations." They are about human motivations. As such it may be difficult to examine these explanations archaeologically. The third, however, raises a substantive "how question."

If it is assumed that this last possibility is indeed the most likely one, is there archaeological evidence suggesting that what it takes to voyage successfully far from land was only a recent addition to the skills and knowledge base of those living in the region of New Guinea and the Solomon Islands?

Working Model

5. Which of these explanations may be the most plausible one?

Archaeologists and others have long favored the explanation that our species stalled at the Solomon Islands for so many thousands of years before moving eastward out into the Pacific because people there did not have the right voyaging skills and ocean-going boats (Irwin and Flay 2015; Montenegro, Callaghan, and Fitzpatrick 2016). Furthermore, the archaeologist Geoffrey Irwin at the University of Auckland has suggested what the design characteristics of the type of boat introduced from Island Southeast Asia by Austronesian-speaking foreigners around 3,500 years ago may have been: "a single-outrigger canoe with a hull made from dugout log, and its freeboard raised with lashed-on strakes. The sail was a simple two-spar rig of a kind usually described as an 'oceanic spritsail,' and the canoe may have changed direction relative to the wind by some mode of tacking rather than shunting" (Irwin 2008: 15).

6. How may this explanation be modeled so that it can be further evaluated?

There is currently no direct archaeological evidence attesting to what the hypothesized new type of canoe would have been like. Linguistic reconstructions of words for canoe parts (Pawley and Pawley 1994) as well as engineering studies of the performance characteristics of likely types of hulls and sails (Irwin and Flay 2015) when taken together suggest that these ocean-going vessels were indeed single-outrigger canoes with sails (cf. Anderson 2018; Cochrane 2018: 540). Nonetheless, although direct archaeological evidence is lacking, it is still possible to construct simple yet plausible relational models of what may have been the impact of such a new type of canoe on local social networks in the New Guinea region 3,000–4,000 years ago (Golitko and Terrell 2021).

To do so, it is necessary to take certain real-world constraints into account, such as where people are likely to have been living in this region of the Pacific back then, and how far they may have customarily traveled from place to place by sea. We should also take to heart a basic principle of formal modeling. Begin with a simple model having few moving parts, so to speak. See how well this basic model fits

46 • Modeling the Past

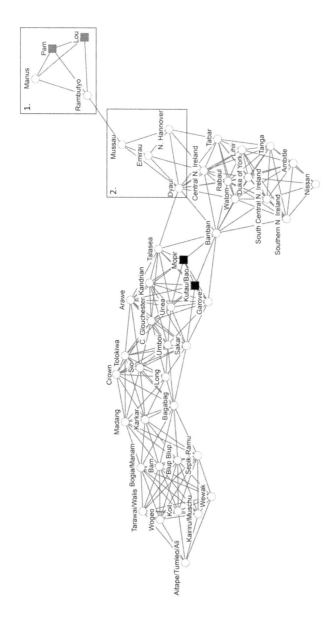

Figure 2.2. A simple network model of plausible social connections between places around the Bismarck Sea in the New Guinea region of the Pacific given a maximal possible voyaging distance of 220 km. The black and gray squares are the obsidian sources. Assuming straightforward "down-the-line" movement of obsidian from these sources, locations in Area 1 are expected to have received a predominance of Admiralty Island (Lou and Pam) obsidian; in Area 2, roughly similar percentages of both Admiralty and New Britain (Kutau/Bao and Mopir) obsidian, and in the rest of the area, predominantly New Britain obsidian. © Mark L. Golitko.

Start with a Question • 47

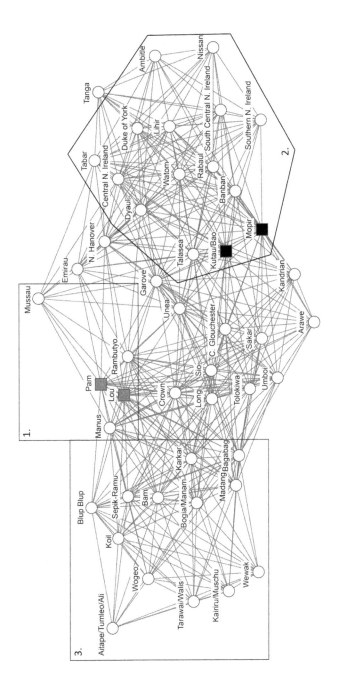

Figure 2.3. A simple network model of plausible social connections between places around the Bismarck Sea given a maximal possible voyaging distance of 360 km. The black and gray squares are the obsidian sources. Assuming straightforward "down-the-line" movement of obsidian from source regions, places in Area 1 are expected to receive a predominance of Admiralty Island (Lou and Pam) obsidians; places in Area 2, obsidian primarily from New Britain sources; and those in Area 3 almost exclusively obsidian from Admiralty sources. Sites not included in these three areas should receive roughly equal amounts of material from the two source areas. © Mark L. Golitko.

what is known about the problem under consideration. Then gradually add more contingencies—more complexity—to see whether doing so improves the "performance quality" of the model being constructed (Levins 1966).

An elementary model of routine voyaging from place to place around the fringes of the Bismarck Sea off the north coast of New Guinea, for instance, can be constructed as follows (Figures 2.2 and 2.3). First, identify places (in SNA they would be labeled as "nodes") known archaeologically or suspected for other reasons to have been the locations of human settlements in the past. Second, draw connections among these places using their geodesic distance apart from one another as the solely determining criterion (i.e., linkage contingency).

In Figures 2.2 and 2.3, as just stated, we have placed the nodes shown at locations where it seems likely there may have been human settlements in the past—localities such as major islands, the mouths of rivers, coastal lagoons, and so forth. These are the sorts of places where people today are most likely to live along the shores of the Bismarck Sea off the northern coastline of New Guinea (Terrell 2006).

In Figure 2.2, we have linked together all of these identified locations at a distance of 220 km or less from one another. This maximal distance was chosen as this is the longest archaeologically documented distance traveled in this part of the Pacific over the sea prior to ~3,500 years ago—specifically, this is the sea distance between the Admiralty Islands and New Guinea. It is known archaeologically that people had crossed this water gap by 12,000 years ago at the latest based on evidence of their presence found at Pamwak rock shelter in the Admiralty Islands (Irwin 1992: 20–21).

In Figure 2.3, we have again linked these locations, but this time at a maximal sea distance of 360 km—the distance of open sea that had to be sailed between the islands at the southeastern end of the Solomons Archipelago and those in the Reef/Santa Cruz Islands farther to the east, the first landfalls beyond the Solomons known to have been colonized sometime around 3,200–3,000 years ago (Irwin 1992: 20–21).[1]

Working Hypothesis

7. What are your working hypotheses derived from this model, and what do you expect your data will show given these propositions?

Current archaeological evidence from the north coast of New Guinea suggests that between the first human settlement of the Pacific region and the stabilization of the world's sea levels ~6,000–7,000 years ago, few people were living anywhere along this coastline. By the time sea levels had risen near present stands, however, many coastal areas in Island Southeast Asia and the New Guinea region had probably begun to develop into rich floodplains, river deltas, and lagoons (Terrell 2006). Consequently, by the mid-Holocene, New Guinea serving as a land barrier between Asia and the Pacific may have finally given way to new commerce and intercourse as coastal people began to travel and socialize with far greater reach (Terrell 2002).

Furthermore, by the mid-Holocene, coastlines throughout the western Pacific may have become productive enough to support sizable human populations. If so, then it seems plausible that sooner or later advances in canoe-building and navigation that had already been developed in Island Southeast Asia were being adopted by at least some of the coastal communities that had sprung up along the northern coast of New Guinea and elsewhere as far to the east as the northern Solomons Archipelago (Figure 2.1).

Evidence and Analysis

A step-by-step description of the evidence available and the analyses done.

One type of indirect evidence of intercommunity travel in this part in the past is the archaeological distribution of obsidian, or volcanic glass. Excavated obsidian pieces are nowadays often used by archaeologists working in the Pacific to trace the scale of social interactions across space and time (Summerhayes 2009).

It is known that obsidian was once widely exchanged among local communities in the Pacific (as it has been elsewhere in the world, too) for this is one of the few materials that preserve well in the tropical archaeological record. It can also be fairly easily traced by chemical or other means back to its specific geological source since natural volcanic glass is found only at a small handful of places in the Pacific region: of relevance to the analysis we present here are sources on a few offshore islands in the Admiralty Islands off the northeast coast of New Guinea, and around the Willaumez Peninsula on the island of New Britain just east of New Guinea.[2]

There are many contingencies that could be included in modeling how historical changes in voyaging technology might have shaped the distribution of obsidian as a locally valued raw material, including the patterning of wind and ocean currents, the probabilities of reaching different places alive and in good health, and social factors including the social uses of obsidian and whether people were willing to transport obsidian from place to place.

To evaluate the hypothesis that major changes in the distribution of obsidian might be accounted for by the introduction of new sailing technology and the resulting ability to make longer voyages than previously undertaken, we assumed first that (a) mined obsidian as a raw material was probably moved from its natural source to other locations in the New Guinea region via what archaeologists have called "down-the-line" exchange (Renfrew 1977) either being passed from village to village between people who knew one another personally, or by being distributed by middlemen traders. If so, then (b) the distance through such networks from the source would probably have affected the amount of obsidian that reached any given locality.

For instance, places nearer to the geological sources on New Britain (in terms of how many intermediary communities must be traversed) should have a higher frequency of New Britain obsidian than that of obsidian from the more distant Admiralty Island sources—assuming that someone in each community along the way took some of the obsidian given to them, and then passed the remainder (or allowed it to be passed) further down the line to people in other places.

To test this simple model here, we have collected information on all chemically sourced obsidian from archaeological assemblages in the Pacific, divided into three broad time periods (6000–3000 BP, 3000–2000 BP, and post-2000 BP, although we will not consider this later period in this book). At present, the archaeological record of the Pacific is not robust enough to parse out the chronology to a finer degree than this.

When obsidian was first sourced archaeologically in the Pacific, it was obtained largely from excavated contexts dating to either the last 2,000 years, or from sites associated with Lapita ceramics (a style of pottery in the Pacific dating ~3,000 years ago thought to have been made originally by incoming Austronesian-speaking migrants). Recent findings, however, suggest that by around 6000 BP, large-stemmed obsidian objects were being widely traded in the Bismarck Archipelago (where several of the obsidian sources are located), along the north coast of mainland New Guinea, out to the island of Buka in the northern Solomons, and even into the rugged central highlands of New Guinea (Shaw et al. 2020; Torrence and Swadling 2008). The sources currently known for these stemmed objects closely match the expectations of our 220 km voyaging model, although we have not modeled inland transport into the interior of New Guinea.

In Figure 2.4, the distributional occurrence of New Britain and Admiralty Islands obsidian at sites suspected of predating ~3,500 years ago is shown against a map of the places we included in our simple network models. The Pacific archaeological record, particularly for mainland New Guinea, is less robust than in other regions of the world (and less so than those of us working there would like!), but to a first approximation, the 220 km voyaging distance model seems capable of generating the kinds of relative source frequencies observed in the archaeological record.

We are on firmer footing in evaluating the distribution of obsidian after about 3,500 years ago when pottery appears in the archaeological record, and sites are now easier to locate archaeologically. As predicted, near to the obsidian sources themselves, obsidian from the nearest source is generally the most abundant, while away from sources, we do see that most archaeological sites contain obsidian from both New Britain and the Admiralty Islands in variable proportions (Figure 2.5). For instance, New Britain obsidian is present in the St. Matthias group, but is less frequent than the closer Admiralty sources, while Admiralty obsidian is present on New Ireland and northern New Britain, but generally at lower frequencies than the closer New Britain sources. There are some slight deviations from our model, as might be expected. We do not, for instance, take into account the frequency with which a particular network link was traversed, which might change some of the model predictions (and could certainly be incorporated into a later version of this model).

Evaluation and Discussion

9. How does this new evidence support or refute the hypothesis being evaluated?

What does this model tell us about the past? We have not tried to evaluate all possible explanations for changes in obsidian distribution around the Bismarck Sea during the period between 6,000–2,000 years ago. Nor have we directly addressed the question of what languages people may have spoken (or who was steering the canoes). We have, however, shown that assuming improvements in voyaging capabilities through the introduction of new technology and knowledge is a sufficient explanation for some changes observed in the archaeological record during this period in the human settlement of the Pacific.

52 • Modeling the Past

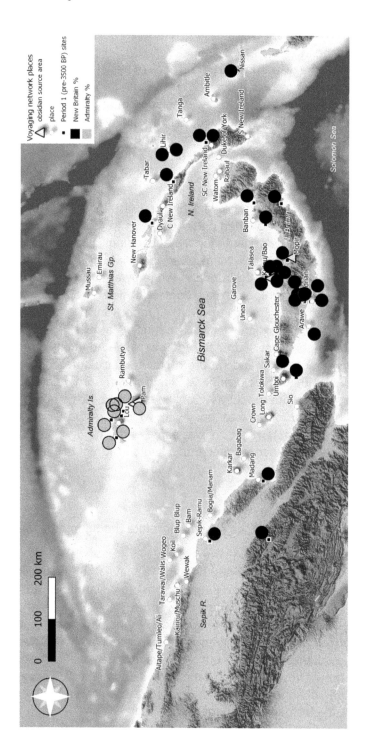

Figure 2.4. Obsidian frequencies at archaeological sites (black and gray segments of pie charts) dated to or suspected of dating to before 3,500 years ago. Sites included in our voyaging models and obsidian sources are also shown (white) as are volcanic obsidian source areas (gray triangles). © Mark L. Golitko.

Start with a Question • 53

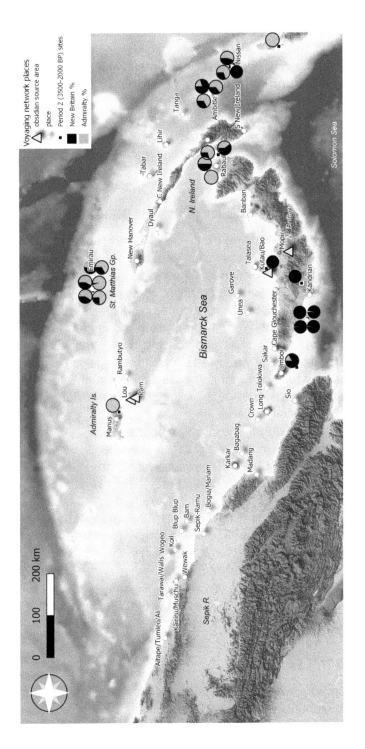

Figure 2.5. Obsidian frequencies (pie charts) at archaeological sites dated to or suspected of dating between 3,500–2,000 years ago. Sites included in our voyaging models and obsidian sources are also shown (white) as are volcanic obsidian source areas (gray triangles). © Mark L. Golitko.

Perhaps more to the point of broader theoretical questions, it seems likely that the introduction of new voyaging skills and technology, whether by Austronesian-speakers or not, merely broadened the range over which pre-existing social ties could reach, rather than transforming a world of largely isolated hostile communities into one of regular social contact. However, in this analysis, we have included no assumptions about what might have been the motivations people had to voyage from place to place, only about their ability to do so given the distances involved.

10. How would additional research narrow the field of likely solutions?

One major advantage of being explicit about how model expectations are generated is that shortcomings are then obvious when compared to existing knowledge. As mentioned, there are a number of ways that we could make these models more complex, for instance by adding wind and current information, by weighting links by distance, changing how many people we assume were living at each locality (and how much obsidian they kept as a result), and so forth. These models, however, also show where potentially relevant information is lacking, and provide expectations for what we might find if we did have such information.

For example, it is known archaeologically that obsidian from the sources in the Admiralty Islands and New Britain did reach the north coast of New Guinea during the last two thousand years. However, with the exception of the stemmed obsidian tools mentioned previously that have been dated to ~6,000–3,500 years ago, no one currently knows how much and what sorts of obsidian may have been reaching locations on New Guinea for the following 1,500 years (Golitko, Schauer, and Terrell 2013; Golitko and Terrell 2021). Additionally, finding and excavating sites younger than ~3500 BP might tell us both whether our models correctly predict obsidian distribution in areas that have not yet been studied archaeologically, and also whether people were actually living in all the places we have included in our models. If what is found does not fit these models, we at least know that we need to go back to the drawing board, and update or replace them.

Summary of This Example

Taken on its own, archaeologically documented change over time in the spatial distribution of obsidian from different natural sources tells us nothing directly about how or why this may have happened. Needless to say, the same can be said about most of the nondocumentary evidence used to make inferences about history—for example, genetics evidence (Posth et al. 2018).

Linking material evidence with the most plausible explanations for it is a relational exercise that is far more challenging than popularly believed. Years ago, Paul MacKendrick (1914–1998), a Classics professor at the University of Wisconsin, gave his popular book on the ancient monuments and archaeological history of Italy the fanciful title *The Mute Stones Speak* (MacKendrick 1960). Would that they only could.

One of the mysteries of human history is how and why *Homo sapiens* left Africa and was able to move eastward for over eight thousand miles to reach Australia and New Guinea ~50,000–65,000 years ago. Equally mysterious, why did those who got that far simply stop—or so it seems—at the Solomon Islands in the southwestern Pacific until ~3,500 years ago? Given what had already been accomplished in moving across the globe, intuition suggests that people surely must have tried to move farther eastward. Yet they did not succeed for tens of thousands of years.

For all we know, the obvious reason may be the right one. Perhaps people in the Pacific simply did not have the navigational skills and sailing technology required to conquer the open seas east of the Solomons. If so, then what happened around 3,500 years ago that apparently changed the odds, and made what had been previously impossible not only feasible, but also successful?

Chapter Summary

Before moving on to the next chapter where we will be talking about how to use relational thinking to compare and analyze theories about history, we want to end this one by summarizing what we have been discussing using the notation we introduced in Chapter 1.

$$|\text{--Step 1--}|\text{--Step 2--}|$$
$$X_1 + Y_1 \rightarrow X_2 + Y_2 \rightarrow X_3 \rightarrow \qquad \text{Proposition 2.1}$$

Step 1. During the Last Glacial Maximum (Veth, Ward, and Ditchfield 2017) and well into the Holocene, what is now New Guinea and Australia must have been mostly a land barrier X_1 between Southeast Asia and islands farther out in the Pacific. Why? Because the northern coastline of what is now New Guinea is not just ~1,800 miles long, but back then was also mostly uninhabitable until the stabilization Y_1 of world sea levels ~6,000–7,000 years ago (Terrell 2006). By then, however, with the gradual development of lagoons, river deltas, and the like starting in the early Holocene, human settlement along this coastline would have become more feasible, and it seems probable that social ties X_2 would have started developing among these newly established local communities (Welsch and Terrell 1998).

Step 2. Using archaeologically recovered pieces of volcanic glass (obsidian) as an material proxy for the movement of people in the past from place to place through their social ties, we have assumed—in keeping with conventional thinking today—that sometime around the middle of the second millennium BC, the skills and technologies needed for travel by sea over long distances and out of sight of land were introduced to people locally in the New Guinea region by foreigners coming over for one reason or another from Island Southeast Asia.

Using the linear (geodesic) distances between known or likely settlement locations as the only specified contingency Y_2, we have shown how two alternative graph models can be drawn, picturing how improvements in canoe-making and voyaging prowess may have led to changes X_3 around three thousand years ago in the geographic distributional patterning of obsidian transport and usage.

What we have sketched as an elementary temporal pathway (Terrell 1986), or sequence, of defined steps (Proposition 2.1) leading from a prior condition, or situation X_1, to a subsequent one X_3 is an attempt to pin down and model the past in a formal step-by-step manner. However, every model is a simplification of reality, and hence every model is figuratively speaking a lie. This is why, as Levins wrote, "our truth is the intersection of independent lies."

With this thought in mind, we want to emphasize that hypothetical temporal pathways from X_n to X_{n+1} should be seen only as historical claims of a greater or lesser probability having the elementary form previously discussed in Chapter 1:

$P(X_t + Y) \longrightarrow X_{t+1}$ Proposition 1.2

One final thought: we want to emphasize that on their own, the network diagrams we have drawn showing how variation in the distribution of obsidian in the archaeological record may be patterned chronologically neither prove nor disprove that a new type of voyaging canoe was introduced to the New Guinea region around the middle of the second millennium BC. These mappings tell us something about the past, but it would be misleading to take what they seem to be saying too confidently. Furthermore, these relational mappings suggest *how* it may have finally become possible to voyage successfully beyond the Solomons. Yet on their own, they tell us nothing about *why* anyone three or four thousand years ago decided to try their luck on the open sea by doing so.

Key Points

1. We should take to heart a basic principle of formal modeling. Begin with a simple model having few moving parts, so to speak.
2. Some questions are too encompassing to try to answer, some are too trivial. The art of doing historical research is finding the happy medium between these two extremes.
3. As the biologist François Jacob remarked, science is a continuous dialogue between the possible and the actual: "A subtle mixture of belief, knowledge, and imagination builds before us an ever-changing picture of the possible" (1982: vii–viii).
4. There is general agreement on what are the characteristics of a good research report:
    a. Clearly stated research questions and hypotheses
    b. Careful review of current knowledge
    c. Well-designed research strategy
    d. Clearly described and illustrated research results
    e. Conclusions that are supported by these results.
5. The advantage of being open and explicit about how a research problem is being modeled is that it can be easier to see what is known and what must still be discovered about the real world and the past.

Notes

1. Not all of these routes were necessarily traveled regularly. As is still the case today, it is likely that shorter distances were much more regularly traveled

than longer distances. In the Pacific, for example, there is often a particular season of the year for traveling on longer voyages when weather and current patterns are most favorable; some links may have been used as little as once a generation or so. Our only assumption is that beyond the maximal distance allowed in any given model, voyages were either impossible, or so unlikely to succeed given existing capabilities that they almost never occurred. Consequently, they would have had little or no impact on the social world of people living around the Bismarck Sea.
2. Obsidian from Fergusson Island in the Massim area of southeastern New Guinea has not been found in any excavated archaeological assemblages on the north coast of the New Guinea mainland dating prior to ~1000 BP.

CHAPTER 3

Theories of History

The future is dark, the present burdensome; only the past, dead and finished, bears contemplation. Those who look upon it have survived it: they are its product and its victors. No wonder, therefore, that men concern themselves with history. The desire to know what went before, the desire to understand the passage down time, these are common human attributes.

—G. R. Elton, *The Practice of History* (1967)

Yet the history of ancient Rome has changed dramatically over the past fifty years.... That is partly because of the new ways of looking at the old evidence, and the different questions we choose to put to it. It is a dangerous myth that we are better historians than our predecessors. We are not. But we come to Roman history with different priorities—from gender identity to food supply—that make the ancient past speak to us in a new idiom.

—Mary Beard, *S.P.Q.R.: A History of Ancient Rome* (2016)

- Writing History
- Theories vs. Models
- The Role of Human Agency
- Five Types of Theories
- Example: Maritime Interaction in the Bronze Age Mediterranean
- Why So Many Theories?
- Chapter Summary
- Key Points

History matters, but what is history? The influential British historian Edward Hallett Carr (1892–1982) did not shy away from asking this question and then turning it into a book appropriately titled *What is History?* (1961). While he was not reluctant about offering us his own answer to this deceptively simple question, he was also willing to admit that it has been answered by others in many differing ways. He was even willing to accept that the best answer might simply be that history is whatever historians write.

Perhaps, but if relational thinking is to be used productively to study history, the resolve that anything goes is not a helpful piece of advice. Like it or not, it is necessary to know in some detail what it is we are writing about, and why we might hope others would be grateful that we are.

Writing History

In Chapter 1, we said that according to convention, there are six questions journalists try to answer when they are writing a news story: *who, what, where, when, why,* and *how*. Archaeologists are trained how to find evidence about *what, where,* and *when*—and sometimes perhaps even *who*. Writing history, however, calls for trying to answer also *why* and *how* (Figure 3.1), as well as the important but often neglected question, *so what?*

This last question is about relevance. As we said at the end of Chapter 1, knowing not just what happened in history but also how and why can shape how we see ourselves, how we understand others, and what we think it means to be human. But writing about history is not just worthwhile. Writing history is also challenging. How do you draw the line between credible theories about history and fanciful or even intentionally misleading ones?

We do not think we need to argue that, as the popular saying goes, facts matter when it comes to evaluating the credibility of ideas, explanations, and the like. Our experience has been, however, that it is not always seen how facts are not like potatoes, onions, or turnips that are ready for harvest and just need to be dug up. Facts alone are never enough to make sense of the world.

As depicted in Figure 3.1, there is an added challenge. The "what" composition of something solid and down to earth—for example, how to classify various types of soil (left in this figure)—is fairly straightforward and indisputable. On the other hand, in archaeology, skillfully

Theories of History • 61

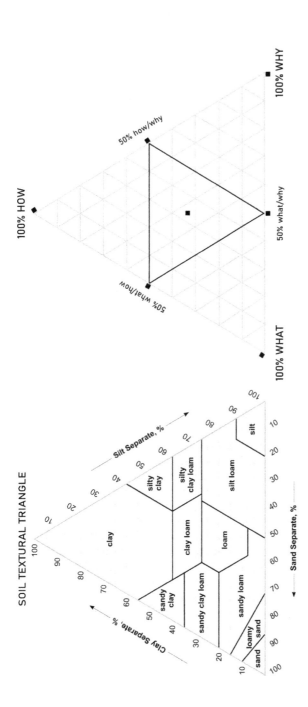

Figure 3.1. It is popularly said that "facts matter." This sounds right, but what is a fact? Moreover, not all facts are easy to pin down and gather for research purposes. Ironically, it is easier for archaeologists to establish the types of soils they are digging into than discover the significance of what they are finding underground. *Left*: Soil textural triangle (source: Flickr, [CC BY 2.0], public domain https://www.flickr.com/photos/natureserve/16890073330). *Right*: In the study of history, a good theory is one that leads you to discover not just *what* happened, but also *how* and *why*. Evidence bearing on these two other questions can be elusive, or totally lacking. Good historical explanations are those that can be said to fall somewhere within the inverted triangle at the center of this graph where there is a balance of evidence bearing on all three questions. © John Edward Terrell.

done excavations and laboratory work may be able to document some of what is needed to understand what happened in the past, but it is far from easy to dig up facts about "how" and "why." Yet, of what use is an explanation without evidence about both of these critically important questions?

Without belaboring the issue, this is why facts alone are never enough, and why there is always the need for good theories to tie together the available facts.

Theories vs. Models

The words "just a theory" usually come across as judgmental and dismissive. So, too, the words "I have a theory" often carry with them the hint that what is about to follow is likely to be some half-baked idea more suitable for derision than serious consideration. Yet all on its own, perhaps due in part to the scientific reputation of Albert Einstein, this word sounds grand—the perfect label for ideas and insights that are brilliant and probably hard to understand, yet awesome, perhaps even revolutionary.

The four of us would never claim we truly understand Einstein's theory of special (or general) relativity, or why replacing, say, the "particles" at the heart of theoretical particle physics with the one-dimensional "strings" of string theory leads to a viable theory of quantum gravity—and according to some, even a distinctly promising "theory of everything." However, there is something we think we do know, and that is where to draw the line between what is a "theory" and what is a "model."

> ❖ **theory** ['THirē] *noun, pl* theories: a supposition or a system of ideas intended to explain something, especially one based on general principles independent of the thing to be explained.
>
> **assumption** [əˈsəm(p)SH(ə)n, əˈsəm(p)ʃ(ə)n] *noun*: a thing that is accepted as true or as certain to happen, without proof.

The definition of theory that we have relied on while writing this book (see definition section) strikes us as overly generous. The word *supposition* seems right, but saying a theory is a "system of ideas in-

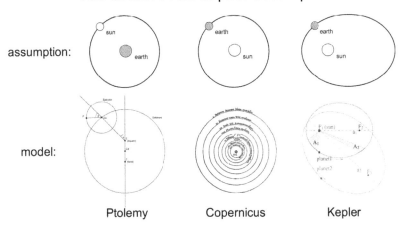

Figure 3.2. Theories (*top*) are assumptions about *why* things are the way they are (or appear to be); models (*bottom*) are assumptions about *how* things are able to be the way they are (or appear to be). An example from the social sciences would be the assumptions that we live in social networks, social fields, or social playing fields (Martin 2003; Welsch and Terrell 1998). Images, *top row:* © John Edward Terrell. *Bottom row*: Wikimedia Commons, public domain. https://commons.wikimedia.org/wiki/File:Copernicus percent27s_image_of_planetary_system_(1543).tif; https://upload.wikimedia.org/wikipedia/commons/6/6d/Ptolemaic_system.png; https://upload.wikimedia.org/wikipedia/commons/thumb/a/ab/EquantPtolemee.svg/2256px-EquantPtolemee.svg.png; https://upload.wikimedia.org/wikipedia/commons/thumb/9/98/Kepler_laws_diagram.svg/1910px-Kepler_laws_diagram.svg.png.

tended to explain something" sounds more like a suitable definition of what a "model" is, not what a theory is.

Although "supposition" would not be an inappropriate word to use, when writing about theories, we prefer the word *assumption* even though this same dictionary makes it sound like assumptions are merely claims, ideas, beliefs, and so on that are accepted as true or certain without proof. We would argue to the contrary that what is both characteristic and sometimes deceptive about assumptions is that they are claims, ideas, etc. that we are often not even aware of accepting as somehow true or certain, that is, *prior assumptions* that are unquestioned and simply *taken for granted*.

What then do we see as the basic difference between the theories we will be discussing in this chapter and the models we will be writing about in the next one? *Theories are assumptions about WHY things are the way they are (or appear to be); models are assumptions about HOW things are able to be the way they are (or appear to be).*

❖ What Kind of Theory Is It?

We have previously divided relational models (Figure 1.2) into five basic types: structural, functional, ecological, participant, and control. These categories can be used to classify many of the theories of history, proposed by scholars and others, which differ in how much credit for what happened in the past should be given to:

> **structural theories** (Table 3.1)—pre-existing (prior) situational contingencies (examples: theories of geographical, racial, and cultural determinism; see Table 3.1).
>
> **functional theories** (Table 3.2)—homeostatic relations returning a changing situation back to its prior (situational) contingencies (examples: theories of genetic immunity, conservative politics, and religion).
>
> **ecological theories** (Table 3.3)—changing physical and biological contingencies among species (examples: theories of climate change, adaptation, and domestication).
>
> **participant theories** (Table 3.4)—the motivations of those involved (examples: theories of revitalization, conspiracy, and scientific revolutions).
>
> **control theories** (Table 3.5)—the need to socially regulate major contingencies involved (examples: theories of social control, supply networks, and warfare).

The Role of Human Agency

One of the major issues that historians deal with is the role of human agency in shaping and perhaps even dictating what happened. Who

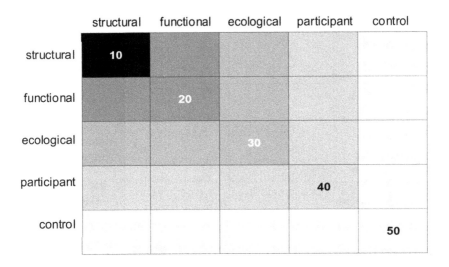

Figure 3.3. Theories of history differ in how far we are said to have been responsible for what happened in the past. Although the numerical values shown here are arbitrary, this table illustrates how the degree of human control over what can happen in the five types of networks identified in Chapter 1 is likely to vary from a little (10) to a lot (50). © John Edward Terrell.

was responsible? Did they know what was happening? If so, what did they do? What were their intentions? How did they respond and did it make any difference? As a broad generalization, the five types of relational models we have labeled as such differ in how prominently human agency and intentionality have played a decisive role in determining what has happened in the past (Figure 3.3). These five categories, therefore, can be used to sort out some of the countless theories that have been advanced to account for what is known—or thought to be known—about human history.

Five Types of Theories

Structural Theories of History

As noted in the earlier chapters, conventional descriptions of networks in SNA may give the impression they are deterministic configurations that shape, but are not easily shaped by, those caught up in them. Few experts would say, however, that this impression is correct. Even

Table 3.1. Structural Theories of History.

	X_t *Situational contingencies*	Y *Circumstantial contingencies*	X_{t+1} *Consequential contingencies*
Geographic determinism	Natural resources are not evenly distributed geographically.	Only recently did humans begin to interact with people outside their own geographic home region.	Historically some people have been naturally better equipped to succeed in the enduring Darwinian struggle for existence.
Example	\multicolumn{3}{}{Jared M. Diamond, *Guns, Germs, and Steel: The Fates of Human Societies* (1997)}		
Racial determinism	Humans are naturally divided into different racial types, and the European "Nordic race" is inherently superior to all others.	Since Colonial times, Nordic Americans have been "outbreeding" with immigrants and inferior lower-class individuals.	If this miscegenation (genetic admixture) continues, the superior Nordic race in the United States will cease to exist.
Example	Madison Grant, *The Passing of the Great Race* (1916)		
Cultural determinism	"The history of all hitherto existing society is the history of class struggle." —*The Communist Manifesto*	Those who control the means of production reap its rewards, and the those in the working class are forced to sell their labor	Class struggle and ultimately, revolt by the working masses leading to the establishment of socialist societies.
Example	Karl Marx, *A Critique of Political Economy* (1867, 1904)		

in SNA, networks are usually seen as dynamic rather than fixed and unchangeable.

Nonetheless, descriptions of social networks often make them sound as if how they are relationally structured not only frames but may also determine what happens over time within them. For example, according to the popular writer Jared M. Diamond (1997), the comparative historical success of people around the world since the last Ice Age was largely predetermined by the uneven geographically structured availability of certain key natural resources that can be exploited for human purposes, both physical (materials for the production of weapons, for instance) and biological (plants and animals suitable for cultivation and domestication by humans).

Stated more generally, the commonsense idea that there may only be so much that any of us can do to alter the situations in which we find ourselves has long been an important and controversial theme in the study of history.

Functional Theories of History

In Chapter 1, we cited the body's circulatory system as an example of what are called homeostatic networks—often referred to in such cases as "systems" or "feedback systems"—that are able to handle change in ways that more or less effectively return contingent relationships to their prior or "original" state of equilibrium, X_1.

$$X_1 + Y_1 \rightarrow X_2 + Y_2 \rightarrow X_1 \qquad \text{proposition 1.3}$$

There are many theories of history taking as one of their central propositions the claim that people are inherently conservative; that what anthropologists have long favored calling "cultures" are basically systems of learned norms, values, beliefs, and the like "designed" either knowingly or not to maintain something often called "law and order"; and that those who are already better "preadapted" in one way or another to a changing situation are more likely to survive and even prosper.

Ecological Theories of History

Saying history matters does not mean, however, that the dynamism inherent in all five of the network types is the same. In addition to the contingencies influencing what can happen over time and space in

Table 3.2. Functional Theories of History.

	X_t *Situational contingencies*	Y *Circumstantial contingencies*	X_{t+1} *Consequential contingencies*
Genetic immunity	Geographic isolation until recently led to local "herd immunity" to disease morbidity and mortality.	European colonization of the New World after 1492 led to the introduction of foreign diseases.	Range expansion led to the transmission of diseases into areas where people were not immune to them.
Example	Ann F. Ramenofsky, Alicia K. Wilbur, and Anne C. Stone, "Native American Disease History" (2003)			
Conservative politics	Socially isolated individuals who want to escape the apparent senselessness of human existence.	Totalitarian propaganda caters to their incapacity to handle the messy contingencies of the real world.	By willfully flouting commonsense evidence and arguments, the totalitarian leader wins a mass following.
Example	Hannah Arendt, *The Origins of Totalitarianism* (1951).		
Religion	Ecclesiastical understandings of what it means to be "saintly" maintained by the Papacy in Rome.	Locally popular ideas about what it takes to be a virtuous and genuinely "saintly" individual.	Continuing struggle to maintain the parameters of religious orthodoxy and centralized authority.
Example	André Vauchez, *Sainthood in the Later Middle Ages* (1997)		

Theories of History • 69

Table 3.3. Ecological Theories of History.

	X_t Situational contingencies	Y Circumstantial contingencies	X_{t+1} Consequential contingencies
Climate change	Until ~6,000–7,000 BP New Guinea and Australia formed a single landmass.	World sea levels only stabilized near their present stand ~6,000 years ago.	Before then, New Guinea was basically a barrier between people and places to the east and west.
Example	John Terrell, "The 'Sleeping Giant' Hypothesis and New Guinea's Place in the Prehistory of Greater near Oceania" (2004)		
Environmental adaptation	*Zea mays* was grown for centuries before settled village agricultural systems developed locally.	Maize was grown locally long enough for selection to lead to the development of Northern Flint maize.	There is no evidence showing rapid transitions to settled village life following the adoption of maize.
Example	John P. Hart and William A. Lovis, "Reevaluating What We Know about the Histories of Maize in Northeastern North America: A Review of Current Evidence" (2013).		
Domestication	Landscapes differ in the species and their abundance found there.	How people exploit other species varies depending on the species and on how they are harvested.	Any species may be called "domesticated" when another species knows how to exploit it.
Example	John Terrell et al., "Domesticated Landscapes: The Subsistence Ecology of Plant and Animal Domestication" (2003)		

Table 3.4. Participant Theories of History.

	X_t *Situational contingencies*	Y *Circumstantial contingencies*	X_{t+1} *Consequential contingencies*
Revitalization	A socially pervasive feeling that life is becoming more difficult and established ways are no longer working.	A deliberate, socially organized effort to construct a more satisfying way of life.	A new way of dealing with life mostly administered by political rather than religious leaders.
Example	Anthony F. C. Wallace, "Revitalization Movements" (1956)		
Conspiracy	Misinformation is being deliberately spread online, particularly on social media platforms.	"Fake news" may lead to political polarization and undermine democracy.	Data, however, show news consumption is mostly dominated by online mainstream and many television news sources.
Example	Jennifer Allen et al., "Evaluating the Fake News Problem at the Scale of the Information Ecosystem" (2020)		
Scientific revolutions	Scientific research usually relies on well-established ideas and practices.	Sometimes, however, normal explanations fail to account for key observations.	Old ideas and practices may then be replaced with "revolutionary" new ones.
Example	Thomas S. Kuhn, *The Structure of Scientific Revolutions* (1970)		

the two network types already discussed—*structural* and *functional*—the dynamism of ecological networks, as Charles Darwin long ago observed, is the product of contingencies that are adaptive (Williams [1966] 2018). Note, however, that Darwin and most evolutionary biologists today would agree that the dynamism of ecological networks is "blind" (Dawkins 1996); although there are theories about history that are based on arguments to the contrary (Chardin 1959; Ruse 2013). Said simply, intentionality is not considered to be a contingency of ecological networks—at least not until we humans become involved.

Participant Theories of History

In an eloquent address given to the Historical Association at its annual general meeting at Cambridge, England, on 31 December 1953, the renowned and controversial historian Herbert Butterfield (1900–1979) argued that history can be seen as "an intricate network formed by all the things that happen to individuals and all the things that individuals do" (Butterfield 1955: 2). From this theoretical perspective:

> the influences and ingredients which an age or an environment supply are churned over afresh inside any human personality, each man assimilating them, combining them and reacting to them in his peculiar way. The result is that nobody is to be explained as the *mere* product of his age; but every personality is a fountain of action . . . capable of producing new things. (Butterfield 1955: 4)

In participant theories of history, the contingencies of human control and decision-making are seen as far more deterministic of what has happened than is likely in the previously mentioned theories.

Control Theories of History

As the evolutionist Edward O. Wilson documented in his controversial book *Sociobiology* in 1975, most species on earth are social in the minimal sense that they are able to deal with others of their own sort at least long enough to help reproduce their kind. However, a society is not just a random collection of organisms that happen to find themselves in more or less the same place at the same time for a particular reason. To be called a society, those involved need to be involved with one another socially (Wilson 1975: 7).

Table 3.5. Control Theories of History.

	X_t Situational contingencies	Y Circumstantial contingencies	X_{t+1} Consequential contingencies
Social	Under favorable circumstances, human numbers are likely to increase.	New subsistence strategies are developed to meet to their growing size.	Hierarchies arise to cope with the developing human needs.
Example	Robert L. Carneiro, "On the Relationship between Size of Population and Complexity of Social Organization" (1967)		
Supply	Water is a critical natural resource.	Dependable access to water may require substantial irrigation, human labor, and social management.	Centralized and despotic control of the labor force required to manage irrigation.
Example	Karl A. Wittfogel, *Oriental Despotism* (1957)		
Migration	Established ownership norms and communal strategies maintaining egalitarian social forms.	Emergent inequality intrinsic to the Neolithic (farming) lifestyle.	Rapid fissioning by early farming communities in the Mediterranean.
Example	Thomas P. Leppard, "Process and Dynamics of Mediterranean Neolithization (7000–5500 BC)" (2022)		

This simple wisdom, however, can be easily misconstrued in two basic ways. Being engaged with others socially does not necessarily mean (a) collectively all of those involved comprise a single and enduring functional entity of some kind, or (b) collectively they form something that can be called a bounded and discrete society.

The premise that our species is structured naturally into separate geographically recognizable and functioning social groupings of differing scale and historical significance has been an accepted idea about ourselves and our past possibly for as long as our kind of being could put our thoughts into words (Furholt 2021; see also Chapter 2, this volume). As the anthropologist Fredrik Barth observed decades ago, practically all social science reasoning has long been grounded on the commonsense idea that we humans live in more or less discrete social, political, and economic collective entities with well-defined boundaries—clusters of individuals variously called "tribes," "ethnic groups," "populations," "races," "societies," or "cultures" (Barth 1969). More recently, the sociologist Rogers Brubaker similarly commented that "few social science concepts would seem as basic, even indispensable, as that of group" (Brubaker 2004: 7).

As we discussed in Chapter 1, for instance, it has long been recognized in SNA that most of the available statistical methods used for structural analysis presuppose that what is being analyzed is a bounded social unit of some sort. In other words, regardless of how mathematically sophisticated SNA methods may be, it is ironically often necessary to assume that groups, communities, societies, populations, and the like are real rather than analytically defined "units of analysis"—in a word, convenient (and, yes, often useful) fictions.

Furthermore, while evolution has made us an impressively social species in many ways, we are not able to read each other's minds and inner thoughts. The best any of us can do to get along and live with one another successfully is to watch and listen to what others are doing and saying. It is not surprising, therefore, that paleontologists, biological anthropologists, archaeologists, and others have spent considerable time and effort trying to understand not only when in the past our primate ancestors started to behave socially with each other in more or less human-like ways, but also how and why human societies (however you elect to define them) began to grow as large and evidently complex as they seem to be nowadays.

Prior to World War II, writing about the origins of both human sociality and organizational complexity was commonly framed as a story about the evolution of Civilization with a capital "C" (e.g., Childe 1942;

Toynbee [1934] 1961). Due perhaps to the obvious barbarism of the last world war, however, theories about what had previously been described as the "March to Civilization" were largely recast as theories about the "evolution of complex societies" and the emergence of ancient city-states here, there, and elsewhere after the end of the last Ice Age (e.g., Service 1975).

Among the contingencies invoked to account for the rise of prehistoric city-states and growth of politically complex societies are: (a) population growth following the domestication of plants and animals after the Pleistocene, (b) the subsequent need for irrigation systems for water management, (c) the increasing frequency and violence of warfare due to population growth and intercommunity competition, and so on (Feinman 2012; Johnson and Earle 2000). Furthermore, how to define complexity as a phenomenon, and how to account for variation in the apparent amount, or levels, of social complexity found both historically and ethnographically in different locations around the world have been and still are major issues of considerable uncertainty and academic debate (Daem 2021), as the following example will illustrate.

Example: Maritime Interaction in the Bronze Age Mediterranean

Problem Statement

Long-distance maritime contacts between the eastern and western shores of the Mediterranean Sea (some 700 km as the crow flies between Greece and Sicily) were first established in the early part of the Bronze Age (from about 2000 BC) (Dawson 2021a). What led people to sail such distances? What were the consequences for the communities involved? Did they change the course of history in the Mediterranean in ways that earlier would have been unlikely and even unachievable?

Current Theories

One widely accepted explanation is that merchant ships traveled east-west from what is now modern Greece to Italy in search of raw materials to satisfy the needs of the "palace economies" of the Near Eastern and Aegean regions. They were after metals, particularly tin and copper (the main ingredients of bronze alloys), mineral resources such as amber, sulfur, and alum, as well as organic products. Extensive copper

Theories of History • 75

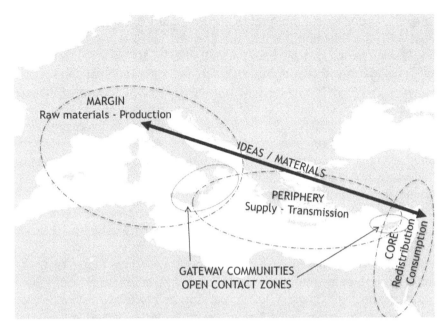

Figure 3.4. What would a Bronze Age world system look like? (adapted from Dawson and Nikolakopoulou 2020: fig. 1). © Helen Dawson.

sources are located in Italy in Sardinia, coastal Tuscany, and the Alpine region, as well as Iberia and Cyprus; while tin is found in Sardinia and Cornwall (Iacono et al. 2021). As these resources are widely scattered across Europe, which has a mostly mountainous interior making overland travel difficult, they could be obtained more easily via maritime trading networks.

Working Model

Two approaches have been especially influential in the study of Bronze Age Mediterranean interaction: (a) *core-periphery*, and (b) *small world networks*.

Core-periphery: The core-periphery approach is a model derived from Immanuel Wallerstein's (1974) World-System Theory (WST) that focuses on modern trading systems and uses their directionality to identify areas serving as "cores," "peripheries," and "margins" in economic exchange. The original body of the theory has been refined in recent decades, with newer approaches—referred to as World-Systems Analysis (WSA)—highlighting the importance of "intersocietal interaction" when considering cultural processes (Hall, Kardulias, and Chase-Dunn 2011: 266; also Harding 2013; Kristiansen and Larsson 2005).

The archaeologist Andrew Sherratt (1993a, 1993b, 1994) has used WST to identify three broad cultural and geographical interaction spheres in the Bronze Age Mediterranean defined following Wallerstein's terminology (Fig. 3.1): (a) an urbanized Southwest Asia "core" with state-level organization where consumption and redistribution took place; (b) an Aegean "periphery" which acted as an intermediary between east and west in the movement of raw materials and manufactured goods; and (c) a central and western Mediterranean "margin" where resources were extracted and processed for shipment. Long-distance contact was based on directional exchange-cycles, with materials traveling mostly eastward and innovations westward (Sherratt and Sherratt 1998).

Small world networks: In recent papers, Dawson has drawn on Sherratt's work to study Mediterranean Bronze Age interaction from a network perspective (Dawson 2021a; Dawson and Nikolakopoulou 2020). Her point of departure is the "margin" represented by island and coastal sites in the central Mediterranean, especially around Sicily, its smaller islands, and southern Italy, which were strategically located to initiate and maintain maritime networks.

Working Hypothesis

Using a network approach has made it clearer how communities on all sides may have taken part in the exchange. Furthermore, long-distance networks emerged gradually from earlier and smaller local networks, such as the ones connecting Sicily and its smaller islands to southern Italy or Italy and the Adriatic during the Neolithic and Early Bronze Age (Dawson 2021a).

Evidence and Analysis

Contact among communities on the Mediterranean Sea is largely inferred from the increasing quantities of imported pottery found throughout this period in the central Mediterranean. Since it is wheel-thrown, fired at high temperatures, and painted, Aegean-type pottery is easily distinguished from local *impasto* (handmade) pottery found in Sicily and southern Italy. The direct association of Aegean-type pottery with pottery from the Aeolian Islands at sites in Sicily and mainland Italy is evidence of the early involvement of these maritime communities in

	Sicily & its islands	Southern Italy	Sardinia	Malta	Aegean	Cyprus/ Levant	North Africa
Sicily & its islands	X	X	X	X	X	X	X
Southern Italy	X	X	X		X	X	
Sardinia	X	X	X		X	X	
Malta	X			X	X		
Aegean	X	X	X	X	X	X	
Cyprus/ Levant	X	X	X		X	X	
North Africa	X						X

Figure 3.5. Simplified matrix of contacts between the Mediterranean regions around 1500–1200 BC (adapted from Dawson 2021a: table 2). © Helen Dawson.

the exchange networks. Moreover, the classification of ceramics into imports, imitations, and derivatives shows the complexity of the interaction and how it served the interests of different communities.

This study uses the presence/absence of raw materials as well as material culture items/traits as evidence of contact between Sicily and the Aegean to build a network mapping the interaction. It includes data derived not only from pottery and metalwork but also miscellaneous items (figurines, cylinder seals, etc.). Each of her assembled datasets could be used to build a different but incomplete network, instead including all the data available in one graph leads to an approximation of cultural interaction at the inter-regional scale (Figure 3.5).

Evaluation

Dawson's network approach highlights that specific sites in the central Mediterranean may have acted as exchange hubs at an intra- and inter-regional level within an emerging "small world" network (Watts and Strogatz 1988). Island and coastal communities thrived during this period and were able to take advantage of their "in-betweenness" within this network with many hubs rather than a single center and short paths

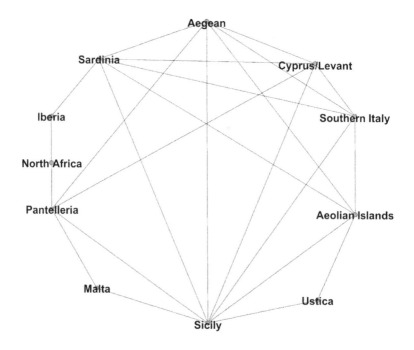

Figure 3.6. A Mediterranean Bronze Age "small world" network (adapted from Dawson 2021a: fig. 4). © Helen Dawson.

between most pairs of nodes (Figure 3.6). This period saw an increase in settlement numbers and their size in the central Mediterranean, a pattern that supporters of the core-periphery model have explained via a process of acculturation facilitated by the eastern traders. However, archaeological investigations have shown that proto-urban layouts and monumental funerary architecture at coastal hubs, such as Thapsos in Sicily, developed locally. Hence these hubs may have been gateways for innovation where external influences were locally mediated rather than introduced *tout-court* from the Aegean (Dawson and Nikolakopoulou 2020; Dawson 2019, 2021a, 2021c).

Discussion

If we compare these two ways of viewing Mediterranean Bronze Age interaction (Figure 3.7) following the scheme we explored earlier in

TWO MODELS of HISTORY	situational contingencies X_t	circumstantial contingencies Y	consequential contingencies X_{t+1}
Core-periphery	Bronze Age Near Eastern and Aegean state-level polities developed centralized power, economies, and religion	raw materials, especially metals, were not locally available and had to be obtained from elsewhere	communities in the central Mediterranean acquired greater complexity through their encounter with eastern traders (i.e. passive or one-sided acculturation)
Small-world network	Bronze Age coastal and island communities in the central Mediterranean were strategically located to exchange resources between east and west	traders from the eastern Mediterranean arrived in search of metals and offered other products in return	cultural change occurred on both sides of the Mediterranean as communities interacted (marginal communities also have agency)

Figure 3.7. Two models of history. © Helen Dawson.

the chapter (Table 3.1), their assumptions, premises, and conclusions are very different. The core-periphery model considers the core as the more dominant feature, culturally speaking, essentially taking a top-down approach, and treats the communities involved as well-defined (categorical) entities engaged in a polarized interaction; whereas the small network perspective focuses on the potential for those living in the margin to initiate change, taking a bottom-up approach (Dawson 2019; also Carter 2015 for a similar take on Iceland's "marginality" during the Viking period). By considering the many facets of these encounters (in a relational way), a network approach also illustrates how different communities located at opposite ends of the Mediterranean held different degrees of agency and ended up overlapping not just spatially but also culturally.

Which view of history of those described above is more accurate, and why does it matter? The way in which cores, peripheries, and margins are defined can vary depending on the information used, and on how we measure complexity and interaction. However, it is easier to view the Mediterranean as a connected space, a *mare nostrum*, bringing people together rather than separating them if we use small-world network models rather than core-periphery models (Broodbank 2013; Dawson 2021a). Why does this matter? At a time when migrant refugees are currently losing their lives at sea because of imposed political borders, understanding that the Mediterranean has long been a connected space is vitally important (Hamilakis 2018).

Why So Many Theories?

This sampling of the countless theories of history is just the tip of a proverbial iceberg. Why have so many theories been put on the table?

By dividing these fifteen examples—each stereotyped here in the simplest possible terms purely as a matter of convenience—into five types, we have focused on one of the key characteristics of theories in general, not just these in particular. To paraphrase the more formal definition of the word *theory* given at the start of this chapter, a theory is an explanation generally without the benefit of facts. By this we mean that although theories are sometimes inspired by what are commonly called facts, perhaps more often than not, they are (a) seemingly plausible claims based on (b) apparently reasonable assumptions about (c) what the facts would undoubtedly show us if (d) we had them to consult.

If this sounds too dismissive to you, consider the popularity throughout history of what are now being labeled on social media and elsewhere as *conspiracy theories* (Douglas et al. 2019). What is the difference between conspiracy theories and theories worth taking seriously? Some say what is needed when it comes to the former is increased news media literacy education. The difference between a good theory and a conspiracy theory, according to some commentators, is fairly straightforward. "Conspiracy theories are attempts to explain events or practices in terms of actors secretly abusing their power to accomplish their own goals" (Craft, Ashley, and Maksl 2017: 2). At least part of their success on social media is that unrelated and unresolved events and practices can be understood more easily when they are interpreted in the context of a compelling narrative that fits our personal beliefs.

However, saying that the antidote for misleading theories is something called literacy education is a narrowly focused solution to a much broader psychological issue. If believing conspiracy theories is the consequence of blindly accepting the truth of what we are being told because what we are hearing is in line with our biases and beliefs, how are we to avoid making the same error when it comes to what archaeologists, historians, and other scholars want us to take seriously . . . and accept?

Chapter Summary

In this chapter we have sketched five enduring (and debatable) types of theories about history related to the different types of networks we introduced in Chapter 1. We have also explored how these many theories have been proposed over the years as plausible answers to the simple yet provocative question *What is history?* While not exhaustive, the classification presented in the five tables in this chapter covers most of the key questions and types of answers put forward when attempting to reconstruct not just *what* happened in the past, but also *how* and *why*.

Sketched in this barebones fashion, we think it may be obvious that historical theories are often notably complicated ways of trying to resolve some of the most enduring questions about what it means to be human: Nature or nurture? Determinism or free will? Compulsion or choice? Psychological or social? Individual or group? And so forth.

We also think these five tables may make it more obvious why we have included Figure 3.3 in this chapter. As human beings, we are neither wholly controlled by the world around us, nor can we be held entirely accountable either for what happens or for what has happened in history. It depends on the kind of network we are dealing with.

To exemplify some of these questions, we considered two different models of history in the context of the Bronze Age Mediterranean, a time of increased demonstrable social interaction in southern Europe. Following the classification we proposed in this chapter, the small-world network way of viewing this interaction has a "participant" and *relational* character (Table 3.4), with communities at both ends of the Mediterranean being increasingly defined by their encounter; conversely, the core-periphery model could be considered as a "control/supply/production" type of history based on ideas of acculturation and grounded in categorical thinking (Table 3.6). Both allow for the fact that we humans have a certain degree of agency and are able to cooperate to get what we want.

People have always interacted with one another for a variety of reasons, and—in the context of this case study—their choices have contributed to what is effectively an ongoing process of "Mediterraneization," that is, the sharing of cultural traits across increasing distances over time (Horden and Purcell 2020; Morris 2003). It can be hard to distinguish archaeologically the agency of different communities over the *longue durée* of the Mediterranean (Braudel 1972–73); nonetheless, comparing these two ways of thinking about history also highlighted there is often more than one way to achieve the same result (formally called "equifinality"), and it can be difficult to unpack "motives" or "intentions" from presence/absence/abundance of material things alone.

Without belaboring the point, we hope what we have included in this chapter has shown why theories of history are *not* explanations.

Perhaps calling them educated guesses or informed suspicions would be going too far, but we are convinced that the only useful way to evaluate such claims about what happened in the past is to convert theories into models that lead to testable hypotheses—the issue we turn to in Chapter 4.

Key Points

1. Writing history worth reading means trying to answer the questions why and how as well as the important but often neglected one so what?
2. Relational models can be usefully classified into five basic categories: structural, functional, ecological, participant, and control (Figure 1.2).
3. These five classes of relational models differ in how prominently human agency is assumed to play a role in determining what is happening now and in the past.

CHAPTER 4

Modeling Theories

Since all models are wrong the scientist must be alert to what is importantly wrong. It is inappropriate to be concerned about mice when there are tigers abroad.

—George Box, "Science and Statistics" (1976)

Our goal here is not to undermine scientific efforts to understand human history, but to analyze how they are conducted, through which practices, using which tools and infrastructures, to understand how the outcomes are produced.

—Fujimura and Rajagopalan,
"Race, Ethnicity, Ancestry, and Genomics in Hawai'i" (2020)

In looking at Nature, it is most necessary to keep the foregoing considerations always in mind—never to forget that every single organic being around us may be said to be striving to the utmost to increase in numbers; that each lives by a struggle at some period of its life; that heavy destruction inevitably falls either on the young or old, during each generation or at recurrent intervals.

—Charles Darwin, *On the Origin of Species*, 1859

- What Is a Model?
- Modeling History
- Example: Explaining Human Diversity
- Chapter Summary
- Key Points

You have decided on a question about the past you want to resolve. You have convinced others, too, that this is a worthwhile question. Having a carefully researched answer might also help all of us better understand what it means to be human, and how we got to where we are today as a species. Moreover, you have a brilliant hunch about what the right answer may be. What is your next step?

What is needed at this point is what Richard Levins wrote about so insightfully during his career as an evolutionary biologist. He called them *models* in his classic 1966 paper on research strategies in population biology (see Chapter 1). Looking back on that same paper forty years later in 2006, however, he seemed to favor another way of making the same observation: "A theoretical enterprise explores reality through a cluster of abstractions that use different perspectives, temporal and horizontal scales, and assumes different givens" (Levins 2006: 741).

Call them models or call them clusters of abstractions, Levins remained insistent in 2006 that "since each model is partly false we need independent models to converge in on the truths we are looking for" (2006: 742). As we have said before, we agree with Levins.

Moreover, as the geologist T. C. Chamberlin did back in 1890, we would go further. Doing good research not only calls for what Levins called "independent models" because any given model is merely a useful simplification and, therefore, a deliberate fabrication. As Chamberlin argued long before Levins, we also need to use multiple models of what we are trying to fathom because the "mind lingers with pleasure upon the facts that fall happily into the embrace of the theory [we favor], and feels a natural coldness toward those that seem refractory" (Chamberlin [1890] 1965: 755).

Nobody has to agree entirely with Chamberlin's rather quaint way of saying that the human mind has "natural infantile tendencies" to acknowledge that it is easy to favor ideas we have invested a lot of ourselves in and a lot of our time researching and writing about. Yet it is not far-fetched to insist that models in the plural are needed not just because any given model is at best only a partial truth. We need them also because if we do not watch ourselves, we may come to think what we see as the best model of reality is not only *possibly* the right one, but *undeniably* so.

Accordingly, we agree with Levins and Chamberlin that when it comes to modeling the complexity of the world, the adage "the more the better" is worth honoring. We also believe how to put the verb "to model" into action is more challenging than some may think.

What Is a Model?

Like many ordinary terms adopted for academic purposes, the word *model* has many common meanings. In some contexts, for example, this word can mean *role model, exemplar, paradigm,* or *beautiful person* (Figure 4.1a). However, it can also refer to a *representation*, a simplified depiction of reality such as a map (Figure 4.1b); a *prototype, pattern, sample,* or *design* (Figure 4.1c); or a *characterization* setting out how you believe something works or happens (Figure 4.1d).

Generally speaking, however, it is the last of these four meanings that best matches what is involved in crafting historical and scientific models. In Chapter 1 we introduced some of the key ingredients we see as fundamental to model-making in both. Given his obvious commitment to mathematical modeling, Levins favored calling these ingredients the "variables and parameters of dynamic systems" (2006: 744). We are not similarly committed to the logic of systems modeling. Nor do we necessarily favor mathematics as the descriptive language of choice to model theories and suppositions. After all, as the physicist John R. Platt at the University of Chicago colorfully wrote in the journal *Science* back in 1964, many of the great issues of science are qualitative, not quantitative, even in physics and chemistry. Moreover, despite the continuing popularity of formal (and often elaborate) mathematical modeling (e.g., Friston 2008), "you can catch phenomena in a logical box or in a mathematical box. The logical box is coarse but strong. The mathematical box is fine-grained but flimsy. The mathematical box is a beautiful way of wrapping up a problem, but it will not hold the phenomena unless they have been caught in a logical box to begin with" (Platt 1964: 352).

Modeling History

Another way of asking what we have been calling the *so what?* question is to rephrase it as *what's the problem?* In this chapter, we have chosen three examples of model-building to illustrate how models can be constructed both logically and, when appropriate, mathematically. They are three different ways of trying to answer the same fundamental question about being human.

What is this question? Unlike, say, raccoons, chipmunks, zebras, or polar bears, our species is decidedly out of the ordinary both in its biology and its customary ways. Biologically speaking, all of us belong to

86 • Modeling the Past

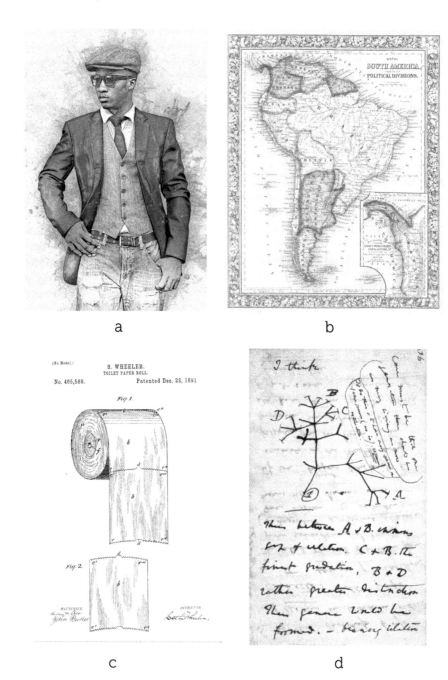

one and the same animal species, *Homo sapiens*. Yet at least to our own eyes, all of us do not look alike. How can this be?

Undoubtedly one raccoon can sort out who's who among the raccoons it comes across perhaps easily enough. People around the world, however, not only look *individually* different from one another, but also *collectively* different—so much so, that for many of us, it seems self-evident our species is biologically subdivided into separate and distinctively different human races each of which must have its own particular story. Is this true?

After discussing the details of these three models, we will illustrate why we favor the third strategy—network modeling—using human genetics data from islands in the southwest Pacific.

Example: Explaining Human Diversity

Problem Statement

1. What is the question being asked?

As the historian of biology Peter Bowler remarked years ago: "an evolutionary interpretation of the history of life on the earth must inevitably extend itself to include the origins of the human race" (Bowler 1988: 131). This is not an easy task. Ever since Darwin—in fact, since well before the publication of *On the Origin of Species* in 1859—the scientific world has been struggling with the paradox of human diversity. As a species, we are obviously diverse—at least outwardly—in our physical characteristics. Yet all of us belong to the same biological species, *Homo*

Figure 4.1. The word "model" can have different meanings. For example: (a) a *fashion model*; (b) a *representation* (a map of South America); (c) a *prototype* ("Toilet-paper roll." Seth Wheeler, Albany, New York. Specification included in Letters Patent No. 465,588, dated 22 December 1891); and (d) a *characterization* (a page in one of Charles Darwin's notebooks from July 1837 where he has sketched how he imagines species change over time, note the words "I think" at the top left). *Image sources*: (a) Pixabay, public domain, https://pixabay.com/photos/man-fashion-model-african-american-2961482/; (b) Rawpixel, public domain, https://www.rawpixel.com/image/2041627/vintage-world-map; (c) Seth Wheeler, Public domain, via Wikimedia Commons, https://commons.wikimedia.org/wiki/File:Toilet-paper-roll-patent-US465588-0.png; (d) Charles Darwin, public domain, via Wikimedia Commons, https://commons.wikimedia.org/wiki/File:Darwin_Tree_1837.png.

sapiens. Setting aside more fanciful accounts about space aliens and the like, three different sorts of historical models dominate the field of likely explanations for this seemingly paradoxical reality.

2. Why is this question important?

Common sense and science alike are grounded in human experience. These two complementary ways of understanding the world and our place in it, however, are often in conflict. The issue of global warming shows that when this happens, the simplicity of most down-to-earth commonsense explanations can make it difficult to win people over to the complexity and uncertainties of most scientific arguments.

History testifies to how difficult it can be for all of us to get our heads around the fact that just as networks are not real things but only abstract models of complex reality, neither are what our brains seem almost predisposed to categorize as "peoples," "populations," "races," and the like (Ackermann, Athreya et al. 2019; Fujimura and Rajagopalan 2011, 2020). Resolving the paradox of human diversity might not put an end to racial prejudice and strife, but at least having a good answer might make it harder to defend such harmful attitudes and abuses.

Current Theories

3. Background information

The idea that isolation and diversity somehow go hand-in-hand may not be a straightforward example of categorical thinking, but nevertheless, this is an idea based on the same basic assumption that something is what it is because it exists first and foremost as such apart from other things (Grinnell 1974). Despite how seemingly different they may appear to be, the first two of the three models discussed in this chapter both assume that isolation is a precondition for things that were originally the same to become different. However, in the first model—*The Creation Story*—isolation is a given (literally), but it is not the real explanation for human diversity. People are different now because God, in his anger, made us speak different languages and leave our original shared homeland (as well as the Tower of Babel which was under construction there) to end up at the far corners of the globe. The second—*Ancestry*—which is nowadays the model most favored by many scientists, although decidedly biblical in some of its basic assumptions, invokes isolation of one kind or another as a necessary contingency for biological divergence to occur. The third model—*Social networks*—is a network model that sees human diversity as an example of what has been called "the strength of weak ties."

> Within the new empirical sphere of human otherness that gradually emerged with the Expansion of Europe [after 1492], typology, explanation, and meaning were long constrained by an underlying "monogenetic" paradigm derived from the Bible . . . . Within the underlying biblical paradigm, the original categories of human taxonomy were "tribes" or "nations" whose primary differentia were linguistic, and whose relationships could be reconstructed historically in a genealogical tree with three main branches—the descendants of Shem, Ham, and Japheth.
> —George Stocking, "Bones, Bodies, Behavior" (1988: 4)

4. What are some of the possible explanations?

A. *The Creation Story:* Race and categorical models of human diversity

According to the Western chronological tradition derived from the Bible, we are all descended from a single, divinely-created, couple whose offspring degenerated both physically and culturally as they traveled—or were driven—away from the Tower of Babel through inhospitable environments toward the farther corners of the earth (Stocking 1988: 4). This biblical diaspora resulted in the races that common sense still tells us our species is obviously subdivided into today.

> **Genesis 11: 1-10** (King James Version)
>
> **1** And the whole earth was of one language, and of one speech.
>
> **2** And it came to pass, as they journeyed from the east, that they found a plain in the land of Shinar; and they dwelt there.
>
> **3** And they said one to another, Go to, let us make brick, and burn them thoroughly. And they had brick for stone, and slime had they for morter.
>
> **4** And they said, Go to, let us build us a city and a tower, whose top may reach unto heaven; and let us make

X_t	(1) the origin of our species in one place and at one time; (2) later population growth; (3) dispersal away from our species' place of origin (The Garden of Eden in the Book of Genesis, or somewhere in Africa according to most scholars today)
Y_1	(4) resulting geographic isolation; (5) subsequent genetic adaptation to differing local environments leading to . . .
X_{t+1}	(6) social isolation and tribal warfare
Y_2	(7) further population growth and dispersal leading to . . .
X_{t+2}	(8) subsequent admixture and introgression between previously isolated populations

Figure 4.2. Although the details may differ greatly, the biblical and modern scientific accounts of human origins are similar in their fundamental assumptions about human behavior. For the notation used, see Chapter 1, Proposition 1.4. © John Edward Terrell.

us a name, lest we be scattered abroad upon the face of the whole earth.

5 And the LORD came down to see the city and the tower, which the children of men builded.

6 And the LORD said, Behold, the people is one, and they have all one language; and this they begin to do: and now nothing will be restrained from them, which they have imagined to do.

7 Go to, let us go down, and there confound their language, that they may not understand one another's speech.

8 So the LORD scattered them abroad from thence upon the face of all the earth: and they left off to build the city.

9 Therefore is the name of it called Babel; because the LORD did there confound the language of all the earth: and from thence did the LORD scatter them abroad upon the face of all the earth.

10 These are the generations of Shem: Shem was an hundred years old, and begat Arphaxad two years after the flood.

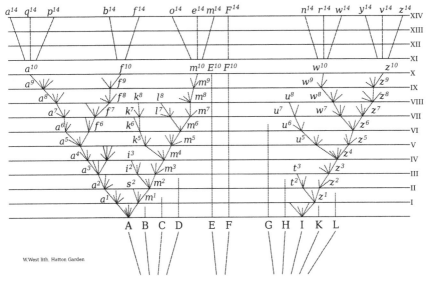

Figure 4.3. Darwin's own pictorial model of what he called "the great Tree of Life" (Darwin 1859: 130). As he explained: "The accompanying diagram will aid us in understanding this rather perplexing subject. Let A to L represent the species of a genus large in its own country; these species are supposed to resemble each other in unequal degrees, as is so generally the case in nature, and as is represented in the diagram by the letters standing at unequal distances.... The intervals between the horizontal lines in the diagram may represent each a thousand generations; but it would have been better if each had represented ten thousand generations.... Thus the diagram illustrates the steps by which the small differences distinguishing varieties are increased into the larger differences distinguishing species" (1859: 116–17, 120). Illustration by Charles Darwin, SVG file by Inductiveload, public domain, via Wikimedia Commons, https://en.wikipedia.org/wiki/File:Origin_of_Species.svg.

B. *Ancestry*: Population models in evolutionary biology

The idea has long been part of conventional Western thought that all of us "belong to" or are "members of" different and enduring ancestral social groupings, or "populations," that can be studied scientifically as corporate individuals having ancestors, descendants, relatives, and patterns of hierarchical descent—an idea that helps cement the commonsense wisdom based on their appearance and differing customs that people obviously come in fundamentally different kinds, types, or races (Fujimura et al. 2014; Terrell 2013a: 138).

92 • Modeling the Past

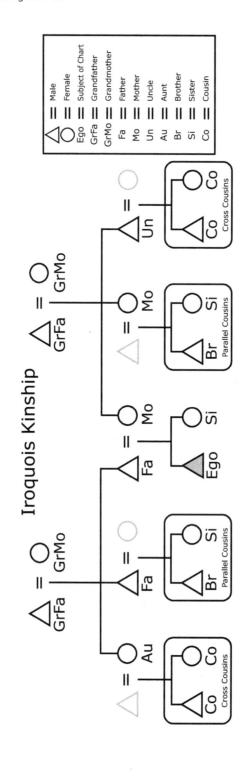

Figure 4.4. Graphic of the Iroquois type of kinship terminology system (one of six main systems commonly recognized by anthropologists). Source: Fred the Oyster, CC0, via Wikimedia Commons, https://commons.wikimedia.org/wiki/File:Iriquois-kinship-chart.svg.

Possibly the most famous and undoubtedly the most influential structural model of evolutionary history is the sole illustration Charles Darwin included in *On the Origin of Species*, a model he labeled as "the great Tree of Life" (Figure 4.3). Despite its obvious simplicity, this model is still popular today for mapping ancestry and biological divergence not only *between* species but *within* species (Figure 4.4).

Darwin himself knew that his now famous diagram is an imperfect way of modeling evolution by means of natural selection (1859: 118–20; Alter 1999). Nonetheless, as the historian Peter Dear has remarked, Darwin's model has made it possible for biologists ever since 1859 to have their cake and eat it, too. They can write about species in what is now referred to as "ecological time" as if they are categorically real entities that are taxonomically stable (Carroll et al. 2007). Yet they can also champion the reality of long-term speciation—historical descent with modification—in "evolutionary time" (Dear 2016: 14).

Another way of talking about what Peter Dear means by having your cake and eating it, too, is to say that when evolutionary biologists write about human variation, they commonly treat the individuals included in their samples as if they actually belong to reproductively isolated species-like human groupings even though as scientists they may be willing to acknowledge that the people in their samples have not actually been "drawn from" known and documented reproductive isolates. This sleight of hand, so to speak, is achieved by using the seemingly technical and unprovocative word "population" instead of the word "species"—which would give away the artifice of such a claim (Gannett 2003, 2013).

We suspect that using the word *population* instead of *species* (or *race*) is often not a conscious ploy and deliberate substitution. Perhaps ideally this word may refer to recognizable breeding units (i.e., bounded gene pools), but in practice, it is difficult if not impossible to show that the individuals being "sampled" biologically who live in a given hamlet, village, town, or city anywhere on earth truly "belong to" some sort of bounded community that has persisted as a biologically closed phenomenon for even a generation or two. As the famous geneticist Cavalli-Sforza and his colleagues acknowledged in *The History and Geography of Human Genes* in 1994, it is basically impossible to give an operationally useful definition of "a population unit that is panmictic and receives specified proportions of migrants from other specified populations" for reasons "similar to those that make it difficult or impossible to define races" (Cavalli-Sforza, Menozzi, and Piazza 1994: 21; also Bateman et al. 1990; Cavalli-Sforza et al. 1990; Templeton 2019). In short, human populations are not something you should go looking for in the real world. And good luck if you try.

Therefore, even if you are willing to accept that different species are real enough biologically speaking to study as "reproductively isolated" evolutionary units that may over the course of time—as Darwin wrote—grow more unlike one another through "descent with modification," it is not self-evident that however you decide to define them, *populations* are species-like enough in their isolation from one another to have ancestors and lines of descent (see also Chapter 2).

C. *Social networks*: Social cooperation and network modeling

Biologists are not alone in writing about human diversity as if we all live in isolated species-like populations. Not all that long ago, anthropologists were similarly intent on modeling the "kinship systems" of social entities called "societies" on the questionable assumption that at least in so-called primitive or egalitarian communities, the primary dimension of social organization and daily life has obviously been biological relatedness (Godelier 2010; Terrell and Modell 1994). From a relational network perspective, however, it is now often popularly acknowledged that everybody on Earth is linked with everyone else, at least broadly speaking, by "six degrees of separation" (Travers and Milgram 1969). Consequently, despite what conventional wisdom has long told us, we do not really live in separate, well-defined "populations," "races," "communities," or "societies." Instead, we are tied in countless ways with others of our kind in relational ways that can reach far and wide.

Working Models

5. Which do you think is the most plausible one?

A. *Races and categorical modeling*: Unlike books on ancient history published centuries ago, the Creator as an active force in the world is generally absent from modern modeling of our past as a species. Scientists today accept the monogenic unity of humans (most of us do nowadays), and favor an African origin for *Homo sapiens*. Nineteenth-century polygenists did take the alternative position that human races are actually different biological species, each descended from its own Adam (Stanton 1960), but no one advocating for such modeling is taken seriously nowadays by the scientific establishment (Marks 2021). However, although the word *race* is carefully avoided, it is arguable that modern molecular genetics research on ancient DNA, for instance, is motivated by the same aims (Wade 2014) as such notable nineteenth-century classics as James Cowles Prichard's *Researches into the Physical History of Man* (1813), and Robert Gordon Latham's *The Natural History of the Varieties of Man* (1850): (1) proving the unity of the "human race," and (2) tracing the history of the "out of Africa" diaspora of what some still refer to as the world's "regional populations" (what plain folks still call races), and others speak of as "major ethnic groups" (Cavalli-Sforza et al. 1994; Reich 2018).

B. *Populations and structural models*: Many geneticists, anthropologists, archaeologists, linguists, and others continue to make use of the conventional folk assumptions that human races are historically real subdivisions of our species (although nowadays, as just noted, the favored terms may be *groups, populations, lineages, tribes*, and the like), and observed similarities between such supposedly valid entities must either be traits inherited from the same common ancestor in the past, or are more recent traits shared through *admixture* (also called *introgression*) between previously isolated populations (see also Chapter 2). The model favored by those who hold such a view of human diversity and social life has long been the image Darwin favored (Figure 4.3): the image of a family tree, dendrogram, or cladogram showing separate cultural traditions as "limbs" branching off from a common "root" or "trunk" (Alter 1999; Bouquet 1996; Hoenigswald 1987). Alternatively, those who favor a less rigid view of human history are instead likely to say that the patterning of human biological history is more like a trellis, lattice, or reticulated graph (Figure 4.5) showing many local populations linked together by cross-cutting ties of contact, diffusion, borrowing, and human movement—a characterization that an older generation of scholars likened to a woven textile (Dixon 1928: 269–72, 284–85; Templeton 1998).

C. *Social cooperation and network models*: Evolutionary biologists commonly assume that genetic isolation is a precondition for the evolution of new species by means of natural selection despite the fact that natural selection presupposes that competition rather than isolation drives biological evolution. The geneticist Sewall Wright, however, famously tackled the issue of what exactly is isolation decades ago using simple problem-oriented mathematical models depicting how isolation might lead to genetic divergence significant enough to result in speciation.

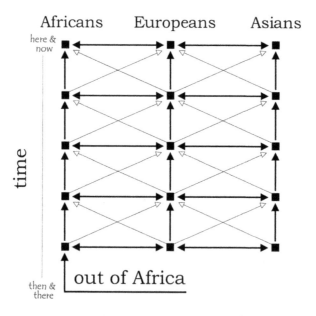

Figure 4.5. The trellis model of recent human evolution. Under this hypothesis, *Homo erectus* dispersed out of Africa and established populations in Africa and southern Eurasia, as indicated by the small squares. These populations were interconnected by gene flow so that there were no evolutionary sublineages of humanity or independent evolution of various "races." Arrows with heads on both ends indicate gene flow among contemporaneous populations, and arrows with single heads indicate lines of genetic descent (adapted from Templeton 1998: fig. 3). © John Edward Terrell.

The mathematical models Wright developed were of two kinds: island models and isolation-by-distance models. As he wrote in 1943 about the first of these: "The simplest model is that in which the total population is assumed to be divided into subgroups, each breeding at random within itself, except for a certain proportion of migrants drawn at random from the whole. Since this situation is likely to be approximated in a group of islands, we shall refer to it as the island model" (Wright 1943: 114). He is equally well known, however, for his mathematical treatment of the "effect of isolation by distance in a continuous population in which there is only short range dispersal in each generation" (Wright 1943: 136).

In a much-cited paper published in 1973, the sociologist Mark Granovetter tackled the same issues Wright had modeled, and he similarly took it more or less for granted that limited mobility can lead to local differentiation. He asked, however, how our interactions in small groups—and the fact that our most active social ties may be with others who are more or less geographically and socially nearby—can nonetheless lead to such large-scale phenomena as diffusion, social mobility, political organization, and far-reaching social cohesion (1973: 1361).

His solution to the enigma of how local events can have more distant outcomes, and by extrapolation, also lead to the paradox of human diversity, was to build on the likelihood that many of us—indeed, most of us—have what he has labeled as "weaker ties" connecting us both directly and indirectly with others of our kind farther away and outside the range of our normal daily lives, our everyday routines.

In both Wright's island and isolation-by-distance models, the ties involved are simply the movement of genes (and at least temporarily the individuals carrying them) from one place to another. In Granovetter's social network modeling of what is involved, however, the ties can be of many kinds.

Here is Granovetter's basic definition of what he means by the strength of a tie in social network modeling: "Most intuitive notions of the 'strength' of an interpersonal tie should be satisfied by the following definition: the strength of a tie is a (probably linear) combination of the amount of time, the emotional intensity, the intimacy (mutual confiding), and the reciprocal services which characterize the tie" (1973: 1361).

Given this working definition, he was not altogether clear in his 1973 article about where to draw the line between ties that are weak and those that are strong. A decade later Granovetter addressed this ambiguity head on. He tells us that "our acquaintances (*weak ties*) are less likely to be socially involved with one another than are our close friends (*strong ties*)" (1983: 201). This makes it perhaps clearer that he is referring to not only one's own personal ties with others, but also the general cohesiveness of the social worlds we participate in as individuals (1983: 201).

How important is it to have weak as well as strong ties with others? As Granovetter explains: "social systems lacking in weak ties will be fragmented and incoherent. New ideas will spread slowly, scientific endeavors will be handicapped, and subgroups separated by race, ethnicity, geography, or other characteristics will have difficulty reaching a *modus vivendi*" (1983: 202).

Now according to him, some of the payoffs for having weak ties outside your own immediate and strongly connected social group are these: adroitly negotiating weak ties can enhance your cognitive flexibility, improve your job mobility, and give you greater access to new ideas and information. Moreover, studying weak ties can help us understand more clearly how "large numbers of individuals, most of whom have never been in contact with one another," nevertheless are able to sustain common understandings and shared meanings "as in the example of youth culture" (1983: 215).

By the latter example, he means how effectively weak ties can communicate ideas and attitudes to those who are socially distant and even unknown to us. Granting that this is so, do we need to have a name or label—say, the word "culture"—for the widely distributed common understandings and meanings attributable to the sharing of weak ties?

The anthropologist Maurice Godelier has insisted that the difference between a community and a society is that "the criterion of a society is sovereignty over a territory" (Godelier 2010: 7). This may be so, but what then is a community? As he uses the word, this term is more or less synonymous with the expression "ethnic group," which he defines as a set of local groups in a region claiming to have a common origin, "a 'community' of culture and memory." Again, perhaps so, but such a definition seemingly overlooks or intentionally departs from the conventional belief that ethnic groups are biological real social phenomena. They are not just make-believe things or social categories.

> ❖ **community** [kuh-myoo-ni-tee] *noun*: a group of people living in the same place or having a particular characteristic in common.

There is no agreed upon term for the non-random local clustering of human ties in otherwise extensive social fields or networks. Granovetter himself has used the expressions "group," "social group," "subgroup," "local group," "small group," "face-to-face group," "interest group," "clique," and so forth.

Despite what Godelier has written, we favor using the word "community" with the understanding that "communities" come in many sizes, are open-ended rather than closed, and are ever-changing in who may be engaged with others "within them" at any given time.

6. How can you model this particular explanation so that it can be evaluated?

Although some have tried to do so, seeking tangible evidence supporting the biblical account of human origins is beyond the practical scope of science. However, as models of history rather than true historical

	BIOLOGICAL ANCESTRY	SOCIAL NETWORKS
X_t	The many hundreds of languages spoken today in the Pacific are classified by linguists as either *Papuan* or *Austronesian* (Gray et al. 2009; Pawley 2007)	Although people are good at drawing lines between themselves and others, we are also good at crossing the lines we draw. The barriers of gender, class, religion, ethnicity, national origin, and the like we erect are neither stable nor insurmountable (Godelier 2010; Watson 1990).
Y	Austronesian languages were brought to the Pacific by a racial migration out of Taiwan that started around 5,000 years ago and finally reached the Bismarck Archipelago around 3,400 BP (Bellwood and Dizon 2005)	People have many and at times seemingly unpredictable reasons for seeking and maintaining cooperative social ties with others of their kind near and far (Terrell and Terrell 2020).
X_{t+1}	The distribution and relationships of languages in the Pacific reflect the ancient racial history of this part of the world (Friedlaender et al. 2008).	The distribution of biological and cultural similarities among communities on the islands in the southwest Pacific reflects isolation-by-distance constrained by social ties and local geographic realities (Terrell 2010).

Figure 4.6. The situational X_t, circumstantial **Y**, and consequential X_{t+1} contingencies of the two models of why people in the Pacific are as diverse as they are in their ways, languages, and physical appearance.

accounts, *The Creation Story* and the *Ancestry* model are so similar that evaluating them both against the model that we have called *Social networks* can be done by seeing how successfully these models can be mapped using actual data, and then evaluating what the results look like. As we noted earlier, the data we will use is derived from recent efforts by several scholars to use the apparent biological diversity of Pacific Islanders to write their ancient history for them.

Working Hypotheses

7. What is the working hypothesis derived from your model that you want to explore?

  A. *Situational contingencies*: In human genetics, treating isolation by distance as a global parameter unstructured by the realities of human mobility and the variable contingencies of social interaction

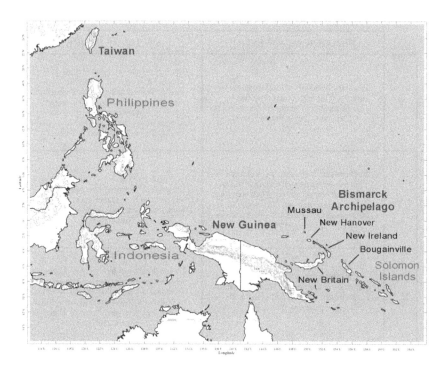

Figure 4.7. Map of the Pacific showing places included in the study. (*Source:* Terrell 2013b: fig. 2.7.) © John Edward Terrell.

can lead to underestimates of the extent to which social ties and connections may be constrained not just by geographic contingencies such as distance, resource availability, ease of access, and the like, but also by the social experiences and motives of those involved (Terrell 2013a: 136–37).

B. *Circumstantial contingencies*: Despite popular wisdom, the evolutionary theory of inclusive fitness (Hamilton 1964), and the claim made in evolutionary psychology that we are an inherently aggressive species that is ready, willing, and able to engage in social conflict and open warfare (Lopez 2017), people actually have many and at times seemingly unpredictable reasons instead for seeking and maintaining cooperative social ties with others of their kind near and far (Terrell and Terrell 2020). Furthermore, despite what conventional wisdom and the Book of Genesis alike tell us, language is a tool for social interaction, not an isolating mechanism (Terrell 2001a; see Chapter 7, this volume). Where there is a will to

communicate, people will find a way to do so, including learning other languages, and working toward mutual comprehension.
C. *Consequential contingencies:* The current distribution of genetic and cultural similarities among people in local communities in the Southwest Pacific reflects isolation by distance constrained by social ties and geographic realities far more than by ancestral descent and social (and genetic) isolation.

Evidence and Analysis

8. A step-by-step description of the evidence needed to evaluate these hypotheses.

The evidence available has been presented elsewhere (Terrell 2010), and will only be briefly summarized here.

A. *Biological information*: In 2007 and 2008, three studies by the same research team were published (Friedlaender et al. 2007, 2008; Hunley et al. 2008) on autosomal genetic variation and mitochondrial DNA diversity among people in forty-one localities on Bougainville Island in the northern Solomon Islands and on several of the islands located to the northwest in the Bismarck Archipelago (Figure 4.7). The authors of these studies reported that genetic variation among these islanders appears to be organized, or structured, geographically by variables they label as *island, island size/topography,* and *settlement location* (specifically, coastal *versus* inland). They also inferred that some of the genetic differences they had sampled in these residential communities are ancestral traits marking the migration trail some scholars have long believed the ancestors of the Polynesians took as they purportedly traveled all the way from somewhere in Asia or Island Southeast Asia to the archipelagoes of Fiji, Tonga, and Samoa ~5,000–3,000 years ago.
B. *Geographic information*: Geodesic distances among the localities sampled genetically.
C. *Social information*: In lieu of more specific social information, the assumption is made that nearest neighbors residing in different communities (localities) generally have stronger ties with one another than they do with more distant individuals and localities.
D. *Network mapping of the information in these published reports*: Figure 4.8 is a network mapping of the genetic variation reported

102 • Modeling the Past

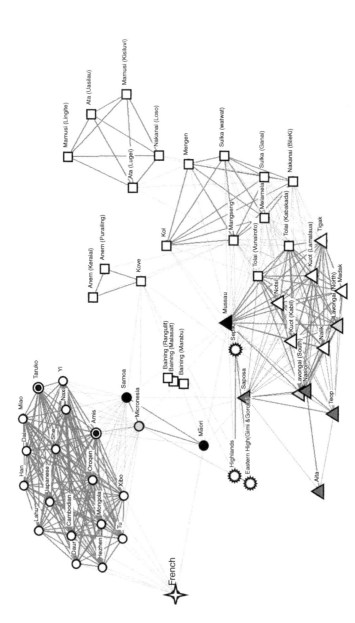

Figure 4.8. *Network mapping* of the localities included in the genome scan (see Terrell 2010 for details). Mapping derived from the mean assignment probabilities reported by Friedlaender et al. (2008). coded by geographic location. Open circles = Asia; target circles = Taiwan; open cross = Europe; black circles = Polynesia; gray-filled circles = Micronesia; open squares = New Britain; gear-toothed circles = New Guinea; dark gray triangles = North Solomons; open triangles = New Ireland; light gray triangles = New Hanover; black triangle = Mussau. (*Source:* Terrell 2013b: fig. 2.8.) © John Edward Terrell.

Modeling Theories • 103

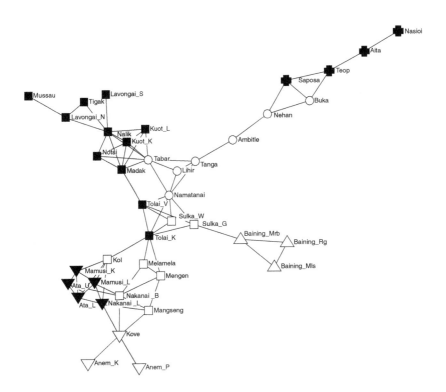

Figure 4.9. Nearest-neighbor structuring of interaction among the localities represented in the genetic study when the threshold geographic distance is 118 km or less (the minimum distance linking all of these localities into a single network) and the "resistance," or "friction" is adjusted for inland travel (here open-circle nodes represent locations *not* represented in the study; see Terrell 2010 for details). (*Source*: Terrell 2013b: fig. 2.9.) © John Edward Terrell.

for these localities. This mapping shows how this measure of human diversity in this area of the Pacific is patterned by geography.

E. *Network mapping of the localities included in this analysis*: Figure 4.9 is a mapping of the expected geographic ties among places in the northern Solomons and the Bismarck Archipelago when the distance threshold is set at 118 km or less—the minimum geodesic distance linking all of these localities into a single hypothetical network. The coding of the localities reflects genetic similarity when the similarity threshold for cluster membership is set at >0.80 (clustering breaks down when the threshold is higher than this). Note that there are six discernible clusters at this level of reported genetic similarity.

104 • Modeling the Past

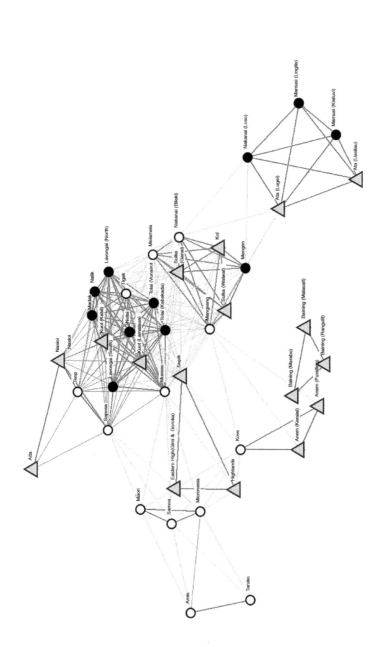

Figure 4.10. Network mapping of only the Pacific Island populations in the genome scan (Taiwan included) derived from mean STRUCTURE assignment probabilities (Pritchard et al. 2000) when K=10 reported by Friedlaender and his colleagues (2008), coded by language affiliation (black circles = Austronesian; gray triangles = Papuan; open circles = Austronesian [AN] languages whose speakers have an Austronesian signature >0.04). (*Source:* Terrell 2013b: fig. 2.10.) © John Edward Terrell.

F. Network mapping of the results of this analysis: As discussed in Chapter 2, it is commonly said that a racial migration out of Taiwan or thereabouts ultimately led to the Austronesian settlement of Polynesia (Pugach et al. 2018). However, what the authors in these three reports label as the "genetic signature" of this migration is demonstrably widespread throughout this region (the open circles in Figure 4.10). Furthermore, even the localities exhibiting this "signature" are otherwise often genetically quite similar to their neighbors who evidently lack it. Moreover, this supposedly Taiwanese signature is no more prevalent in Taiwan than it is today elsewhere in the southwest Pacific.

Since these three reports were published, further evidence suggests that this signature first arose somewhere in the Bismarck Archipelago, and later in the Holocene was carried at various times and in various ways both westward to some parts of Island Southeast Asia and eastward into Polynesia (Soares et al. 2011).

Evaluation and Discussion

9. How does this new evidence support or refute your working hypothesis?

It has long been assumed that the ancestors of the Polynesian (Austronesian) speakers on islands east of the Solomons Archipelago were the tail-end of a racial migration that started somewhere in Asia and finally reached what we now call *Polynesia* thousands of miles away to the east thousands of years ago. We will not argue further the case against this historical scenario here (see Terrell 2013a), and note only that as mapped in Figure 4.10, what is known about the geographic distribution of what these authors see as the genetic signature of this migration offers no obvious support for such an historical reading of the evidence considered.

10. How would additional research narrow the field of likely solutions?

The hypothesis that the geographic patterning of genetic diversity reported among the localities in these three studies best fits isolation by distance constrained by social networks and landscape geography could be strengthened considerably by the inclusion of detailed information about the social ties involved.

	Creation story	Ancestry	Social networks
X_t	Once upon a time, everybody on earth spoke the same language and were one people	Formerly people lived in isolated populations, each of which was genetically distinct in one or more characteristic ways	We are an obligate social species, and all of us are connected with one another in many different ways
Y	Then they began to build a city and a tower to make a name for themselves lest they become scattered all over the face of the earth	For various reasons, people eventually began to move around from population to population	Although most of the time we deal socially with the people we know really well, occasions arise when we connect with people we otherwise rarely encounter
X_{t+1}	God came down and confounded their language so they could not understand one another, and then He scattered them all over the earth	Therefore, both individuals and populations today are genetically admixed, which confounds the evidence of their original ancestry	Through these less frequent ties, we are socially connected with people all over the earth

Figure 4.11. The situational X_t, circumstantial Y, and consequential X_{t+1} contingencies of the three models discussed in this chapter.

Chapter Summary

In this chapter, we have modeled the same research question in three differing ways (Figure 4.11). *If all of us belong to one and the same biological species, why do we not all look alike?*

Although answering this question by referring to events that supposedly happened in the past, The Creation Story is at best a barebones historical model. According to the Book of Genesis and what its interpreters tell us, we are all "descendants of a single family" that after the Flood was "divided by language at the tower of Babel, and had thence degenerated both physically and culturally during the ensuing four millennia as they moved—or were driven—through inhospitable environments toward the farther corners of the earth" (Stocking 1988: 4).

Like this biblical counterpart, *Ancestry* models of history assume—as Darwin famously did—that "descent with modification" from a common ancestor explains much of the diversity of the Earth's species, past and present, including our own species, *Homo sapiens sapiens*. However, here as in so many other ways, Darwin knew the limitations of his own theory. As he wrote about variation in nature at the opening of the second chapter in *On the Origin of Species*: "every naturalist knows vaguely what he means when he speaks of a species. Generally the term includes the unknown element of a distinct act of creation. The term 'variety' is almost equally difficult to define; but here community of descent is almost universally implied, though it can rarely be proved" (1859: 44). The prior (and often unchallenged) assumptions of *common origin*, *isolation*, and *lineal descent* are fundamental to ancestry models of history.

Using network mapping and published information about autosomal markers sampled in forty-one communities in the southwestern Pacific, the third model we have considered in this chapter has examined whether *ancestry* (as defined above) or *isolation by distance* constrained by geography and nearest-neighbor social ties better describes the patterning of contemporary genetic diversity (as sampled) among places in this part of the world. Based on the available information, the latter interpretation would appear to be the most likely one.

We have not introduced these three ways of modeling human diversity to convince you that one of them is better than the others, although we obviously think so. Instead, we have pulled them apart, so to speak, to show you the steps we have found useful when we are trying to turn ideas about the past into working models.

Key Points

1. Models in the plural are needed not only because any given model is at best only a partial truth, but also because if we are not careful, we may think what we see as the best model is not just possibly the right one, but undeniably so.
2. People around the world not only look individually different from one another, but also collectively different—so much so, that to many of us, it seems self-evident our species is biologically subdivided into separate and distinctively different human races, each of which must have its own particular story.

3. Resolving the paradox of human diversity may not put an end to racial prejudice and civil strife but understanding why we do not all look alike may make it harder to defend such harmful attitudes and abuses.
4. Comparing the working assumptions of two or more models can be done using this simple template we use in this book (Figure 4.12).

	Model 1	Model 2
X_t	The initial (situational) contingencies assumed to be active in the first models being evaluated	The initial (situational) contingencies assumed to be active in the other model being evaluated
Y	The contingencies (circumstances) that may have altered the initial situation assumed in this model	The contingencies (circumstances) that may have altered the initial situation assumed in this model
X_{t+1}	The expected consequences of these assumed changes	The expected consequences of the changes assumed in this model

Figure 4.12. A simple template for comparing two or more models specifying the situational X_t, circumstantial **Y**, and consequential X_{t+1} contingencies thought to be involved.

CHAPTER 5

Developing Hypotheses

Although Bayes' Theorem, the fundamental core of Bayesian inference, was developed in the eighteenth century, it was only in the 1990s that the scientific use of Bayesian statistics increased significantly. Since then, Bayesian statistics has become fundamental to the scientific endeavor in general and increasingly common in anthropological and archaeological science.
—Erik Otárola-Castillo and Melissa Torquato, "Bayesian Statistics in Archaeology" (2018)

In brief, I argue that Holocene foragers across Europe adopted Neolithic things and techniques in many ways and for many widely differing reasons. Similarly, where the Neolithic was borne by the movement of peoples, such movements took many forms and had many differing social motivations.
—John Robb, "Material Culture, Landscapes of Action, and Emergent Causation" (2013)

- Bayes' Theorem
- Bayes' Theorem and History
- Using Bayes' Theorem
- Baseline Plausibility Analysis
- Quantitative Baseline Analysis
- Subjective Baseline Analysis
- Example: What Can DNA Tell Us?
- The "Why?" Question
- Three-Factor Contingency Analysis
- Chapter Summary
- Key Points

No modern historian would claim witches can fly, people can change themselves into animals and then back again, or kingdoms fall because of unfavorable heavenly alignment of the planets. Our understandings of physical reality rule out these possibilities. To appear to be taking them seriously would undermine the plausibility of everything else said along with them. But what about less doubtful explanations and events? How do you draw the line between what is an impossible claim, and what is at least a plausible hypothesis?

More to the point of this chapter: (a) once you have a theory in mind you want to evaluate, and (b) you have modeled this theory well enough to see how it might play out in reality, (c) how do you decide whether the implications of how you are modeling your theory—popularly called the *hypotheses* you have drawn, deduced, or derived from what you are suggesting—are (d) worth the time, labor, and funding needed to decide whether (e) your theory is more than just the fanciful product of wishful thinking or an overworked imagination?

Although much has been written about statistical probability, surprisingly little has been codified about how to propose and evaluate hypotheses despite the enduring interest of philosophers in what are the proper characteristics of a good argument. The economist Bart Nooteboom years ago offered one of the few explicit definitions of plausibility that we are aware of: "We consider a proposition plausible when it is well connected with available knowledge, when it is in agreement with categories of perception and thought, with observations and theories that merit our belief" (1986: 221). As he suggested, without first assessing the plausibility of a hypothesis, it is unclear how seriously anyone should listen to evidence seemingly in support of what is being proposed.

This may be easy to say, but how is this to be done? Some would suggest that sooner rather than later it is time to turn to statistics. Specifically, to Bayes' Theorem.

Bayes' Theorem

According to the statistician Regina Nuzzo, many nowadays are saying that rather than using conventional probability statistics to evaluate the credibility of hypotheses and research findings, it is better to adopt methods that "take advantage of Bayes' rule: an eighteenth-century theorem that describes how to think about probability as the plausibility of an outcome." Importantly, a "Bayesian framework makes it comparatively easy for observers to incorporate what they know about the world into their conclusions, and to calculate how probabilities change as new evidence arises" (Nuzzo 2014: 152).

Being able to do so readily is a key component of investigative historical research. It is no surprise, therefore, that according to Erik Otárola-Castillo and Melissa Torquato (2018) in an overview article, Bayesian statistical methods are being increasingly used in archaeology and anthropology. These methods are derived from Bayes' Theorem (Barnard 1958; Edwards, Lindman, and Savage 1963) which states that the probability of an event **H | E** happening *P* **(H)** is conditional on its relationship *P* (**E | H**) × *P* (**H**) to one or more other events *P* (**E**).

$$P (H \mid E) = P (E \mid H) \times P (H) / P (E)$$

What does this string of probabilities mean? Key in this mathematical expression is what the term *conditional* means. Classically, a *conditional statement* is one having the formal structure "if **p,** then **q**" in which **p** is called the hypothesis, and **q** is the conclusion (usually written as **p ⟶ q**). A *causal conditional statement* is one in which it is asserted that "if *x*, then *y*," where *x* is held to be the cause of *y*. Bayes' Theorem, on the other hand, is about *conditional probability*. As Otárola-Castillo and Torquato explain, conditional probability is "the probability of an outcome given that another outcome has already occurred" (Otárola-Castillo and Torquato 2018: 441). In other words, what is the probability of something given that you *already know something else related to it*?

Rather than calling this "conditional probability," we prefer the expression *contingent probability*. We favor these words because we think they capture more clearly the relational interdependence of things and events without needing to claim that the relationship is unidirectional or solely causal.[1]

Bayes' Theorem and History

It has long been conventional in the academic world of Western scholarship to say that science is about data, measurement, sampling, and statistical probability with the goals of explaining and predicting. In contrast, philosophy, history, and the rest of the humanities are said to be about ideas, logic, creativity, and critical reasoning.

In recent years, there has been much discussion about the relative merits of science and the humanities as ways of understanding the world and coping with its challenges. Regardless of the merits of this continuing debate, the strength of Bayes' Theorem lies in how it makes use of what we already know about the world when we are trying to decide how much confidence we should have in how we think the world works.

There are well-developed mathematical ways (and supporting open-source computer software) in science and engineering employing Bayesian logic to construct dynamic Bayesian networks (DBNs) for research and computer applications in speech and language processing, bioinformatics, activity recognition, and time series application (e.g., Bilmes and Rogers 2015; Stephenson 2000). Although it might be argued that what we are calling dynamic relational analysis is an application of dynamic Bayesian network modeling (Murphy 2002) to the study of history, this would be misleading for several reasons including:

1. Although history can be seen as a developmental process of the general form

$$X_t + Y_1 \longrightarrow X_{t+1} + Y_2 \longrightarrow X_{t+2} \qquad \text{proposition 1.4}$$

   the assumption that history is a sequential or developmental process, stochastic or otherwise, is not fundamental to our implementation of Bayes' Theorem.
2. Furthermore, the focus of DYRA is not on trying to predict the probability of a transition and resulting state. As Larissa Albantakis and her colleagues have remarked: "even with detailed knowledge of all circumstances, the prior system state, and the outcome, there often is no straightforward answer to the 'what caused what' question" (Albantakis et al. 2019: 2 of 48). Even when history is being studied as a sequence of related events, there may be little reason to calculate their probability of occurring (unless there is some doubt about whether they actually happened!). Instead, what is being explored is why the transitions that did take place happened, not how likely it is that they had happened.
3. In the study of history, statistical sampling is difficult and often impossible, a fact of life that severely limits the usefulness of representational mathematical statements, however stochastic or deterministic.
4. Instead of focusing on statistical modeling and prediction, DYRA is a research strategy that combines Bayes' Theorem with historical information and plausibility modeling to develop and evaluate alternative explanations for known or reconstructed historical conditions and events.

Said simply, therefore, DYRA is a strategy for implementing Bayes' Theorem and network modeling in the study of history where the state transitions are already reasonably well known, and the goal isn't calculating—as in DBN modeling—their likelihood, or probability, but pinning down the contributing causes and conditions. That is, the contributing contingencies.

Using Bayes' Theorem

Here is an example of how Bayesian analysis can be used to explore the contingent probability of a hypothesis about relational information (data) without assuming that the relationship being investigated is solely causal.

Given available data, it looks like there may have been a connection—at any rate, here is one plausible hypothesis—between old age and death in 2020 caused by the SARS-CoV-2 coronavirus without assuming that old age causes the disease called COVID-19, or alternatively that this disease magically causes old age. Using language Thomas Bayes himself might have favored, can we take for granted that those who were infected with this virus were at greater risk of dying if they are sixty years of age or older?

Here is the relevant historical and statistical information. Between 18 March and 26 June in 2020 during the coronavirus pandemic in Wisconsin, there were 26,747 confirmed infections and 766 of these individuals died. The unconditional probability that any given infected individual had died was $P(\mathbf{H}) = 766/26,747 = 0.0286$ (which is the statewide average death rate among those infected), or roughly 3 percent of those testing positive for coronavirus. It is also known that 669 of these deaths occurred among the 1.4 million people sixty years or older, who are roughly 24 percent of Wisconsin's population of approximately 5.8 million. Therefore, given what is known, the mortality rate among those over sixty years of age attributed to coronavirus infection is actually closer to 88 percent (Figure 5.1). Clearly, old age was a decided risk factor.

What does this example show us? As the coronavirus pandemic spread around the world in 2020, it became apparent early in the year that older people were at greater risk of becoming severely ill and possibly dying. These Wisconsin data lend support to this theory. There does appear to be a strong contingent relationship between becoming infected and dying if someone is sixty years old or older. But note this is all these data suggest.

BAYES' THEOREM: The probability of an event [$P(H|E)$] happening is contingent on its relationship [$P(E|H) \times P(H)$] to one or more other events [$P(E)$].

IF: $P(H|E) = P(E|H) \times P(H) / P(E)$

GIVEN:

Number of people in Wisconsin at the time: ~5,822,434
Number of senior citizens 60 years old or older: ~1,391,738
Number of confirmed cases of COVID-19 during this period of time: 26,747
Total number of deaths among these cases: 766
Number of seniors among those who died: 669
Probable number of seniors over 60 among those infected: ~6,392

THEN:

$P(E)$ = Probability someone infected had died: 766/26,747 = 0.0286 = ~3%
$P(H)$ = Probability someone was a senior: 1.4/5.8 million = 0.2390
$P(E|H)$ = Probability someone over 60 had died: 669/6,392 = 0.1046
$P(E|H) \times P(H)$ = 0.1046 x 0.2390 = 0.0250
$P(H|E) = P(E|H) \times P(H) / P(E)$ = 0.1046 x 0.2390 / 0.0286 = 0.8741 = probability someone who died was old

---

Figure 5.1. Using Bayes' Theorem to determine the probability that someone sixty years of age or older in Wisconsin died between 18 March and 26 June in 2020 after becoming infected with the coronavirus. © John Edward Terrell.

Among the seven known coronaviruses that can infect people, the types labeled as severe acute respiratory syndrome (SARS-CoV) and Middle East respiratory syndrome (MERS-CoV) had also by then been associated with severe complications, notably acute respiratory distress syndrome, multiorgan failure, and death, especially in individuals with underlying comorbidities and old age (Garnier-Crussard et al. 2020).

Yet here is the main point. Identifying a highly plausible contingent relationship during the first half of 2020 between dying and old age among people in Wisconsin who had become infected with the coronavirus explains nothing. It could even be argued that saying people then were dying due to "severe complications" also explains nothing, even if adding the further information that SARS-CoV and MERS-CoV can lead to acute respiratory distress and multiorgan failure hints at how COVID-19 can lead to death.

Although this is just one example, this may be enough to convince you that Bayes' Theorem can at least sometimes be a good way to decide whether to spend time, effort, and research funding on finding out how credible hypotheses may be. Yet there are obvious limitations. What if your hypotheses are only hunches, and you have no data whatsoever to plug into Bayes' formula? What if there is no obvious way to count or measure something that your hypothesis suggests may be involved?

Baseline Plausibility Analysis

Although it may not always be possible or even wise to measure or count things to decide whether a hypothesis should be taken seriously, what is important about Bayes' Theorem is the logic at the heart of this proposition, not the mathematical formula widely used to model it.

The human brain is a highly sophisticated pattern recognition device. Although some would debate the observation, most of what human beings are capable of doing is learned over time as they live and breathe (Terrell and Terrell 2020). What this means is that we are all fundamentally Bayesian learning machines. We are able to survive as well as we do precisely because we are constantly updating our prior baseline knowledge about the world—in Bayesian jargon, our *"Bayesian prior distributions"*— in light of our new experiences to fashion (hopefully) better memories (some of which are the memories called "habits") to help guide us through life. Again, in Bayesian jargon, in that secret cranial vault on top of our shoulders, we are all constantly revising our brain's "Bayesian posterior distributions."

If so, then how can knowing that the brain is a Bayesian machine help us decide whether to investigate a hypothesis we have derived from how we have modeled a theory we are exploring? To see how, let us first go back to the Wisconsin data we just analyzed, and put Bayes' Theorem to work using the same information arrayed this time more simply in a 2×2 table (Hashemi, Nandram, and Goldberg 1998). Then we will offer you other ways to use Bayes' Theorem that are less dependent on having quantitative data available to analyze and evaluate.

Quantitative Baseline Analysis

Otárola-Castillo and Torquato are not alone in saying that using Bayesian logic and methods in archaeology can not only help those writing about history incorporate prior knowledge about what happened into their theories, models, and hypotheses, but can also be a way to update

116 • Modeling the Past

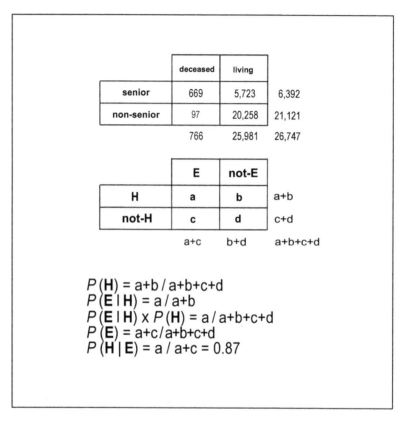

Figure 5.2. Bayes' Theorem modeled as a 2×2 contingency table of the COVID-19 data previously analyzed (Figure 5.1.) © John Edward Terrell.

what they are writing in light of new evidence (Otárola-Castillo and Torquato 2019: 442). Although they also suggest Bayesian methods are mathematically and computationally challenging, this need not necessarily be so.

In Figure 5.2, we use the quantitative data associating COVID-19 with old age to illustrate (*top*) the basic logic (*bottom*) of this way of thinking about the likelihood of our suppositional claims. Note that the likelihood of the association between dying and old age among people in Wisconsin who had become infected with the coronavirus ($P[H \mid E]$), which we have previously determined using the complete formula, as being roughly 87 percent is simply the ratio of the number who died who are old divided by the total number of deaths ($P[H \mid E] = a / a + c = 669/756 = 0.884$). The real challenge, therefore, is not the mathematics, but rather how to apply Bayesian logic when the facts available cannot be easily reduced to numerical figures.

Subjective Baseline Analysis

In what is perhaps one of the most famous articles in the last century on the psychology of decision-making, Daniel Kahneman and Amos Tversky (1973) explained how easily the human brain is able to make judgments about reality that unfortunately are insensitive to the reliability of the evidence available and the prior probability of the claims being made, in violation of the logic of statistical prediction. Said less formally, they have shown how easy it is for all of us to make irrational decisions.

Also back then, the renowned philosopher of science Karl Popper argued that to cope with how readily we can stumble in this naive way, we must accept that merely piling up more and more evidence seemingly supporting our ideas, our hypotheses, our view of the world, does not invariably lead to the truth. Instead, what we must do is winnow down the number of possible hypotheses by discarding those that can be shown to be wrong. Furthermore, we must be careful not to accept hypotheses as worthy of serious consideration simply because they have (so far, at any rate) not been *falsified*—a word which has now become almost indelibly associated with Popper and his way of deciding whether a theory should be ranked as scientific (Popper 1962: 33).

Why is such caution necessary? Because regardless of how watertight a scientific theory or hypothesis seems to be given the current evidence in its favor, there is always a chance that new discoveries will come along and cast a long shadow across the credibility of its claims.

Not everyone accepts Popper's insistence that science is not about trying to establish whether theories are true, but is instead about seeing if they can be falsified (Gardner 2001). In keeping with Bayesian logic, however, as Kahneman and Tversky underscored in their famous article, it is generally better to say that science is not so much about trying to confirm the truth or falsity of our theories and hypotheses, but rather about trying to decide how seriously we should attend to the claims, hypotheses, and theories being put on (or in!) the table for serious consideration and study.

This is where Bayesian logic comes into play. If we accept the premise of relational thinking that things, people, and events are what they are because of how they are interconnected and interdependent, then what is at issue in doing science is not only whether there is evidence for or against some idea, claim, or theory. What must also be evaluated is how far *other lines of evidence* support the probability of what is being primarily considered. Said another way, *given what we know about the world in addition to the particulars we are attending to, how plausible are the inferences and conclusions we believe we can reasonably make?*

> ❖ Adoption of the Bayesian outlook should discourage parading statistical procedures, Bayesian or other, as symbols of respectability pretending to give the imprimatur of mathematical logic to the subjective process of empirical inference.
> —Ward Edwards, Harold Lindman, and Leonard J. Savage (1963: 240)

As we have just seen using quantifiable information about old age and the risk of dying if you have come down with COVID-19, weighing the impact of other contingencies can change the likelihood of a hypothesis. But can Bayes be helpful if the information available is not quantifiable? Fortunately, the answer is yes. Here is an elementary example of how to use Bayesian logic even when quantitative information is all or mostly lacking.

Example: What Can DNA Tell Us?

Archaeologists have been excavating on islands in the southwest Pacific for a long time, particularly since World War II. Only rarely, however, have they recovered intact human skeletal remains. You can imagine, therefore, how surprising it was several years ago for archaeologists and others excavating on the island of Efate in the Vanuatu archipelago (which is in the Pacific 7,250 km southeast of the Asian mainland) to discover an intact ancient cemetery dating back to ~3,000 years ago. Unexpectedly, most of the surviving skeletons had had their skulls removed and taken somewhere else not long after burial. Five human skulls, however, were recovered during excavations at this ancient site. Three of these had been placed on the skeletal chest of the same person (whose own skull, however, had been removed and was missing; Valentin et al. 2010, 2016).

It proved to be possible to extract sufficient intact human genetic material ("ancient DNA") from four of these skulls (Lipson et al. 2018; Spriggs and Reich 2020) to determine that all of them were the skulls of individuals whose forerunners, genetically speaking, most closely resembled the genetic diversity of people today living in Island Southeast Asia (ISEA) rather than in the New Guinea region (NGR) despite the fact that the latter lies geographically between ISEA and Vanuatu (see Chapter 2).

These laboratory findings were soon widely publicized both in the academic and the popular press as a major historical discovery. Recently the archaeologist Matthew Spriggs and the geneticist David Reich asserted in forceful words what they see as the significance of this "now irrefutable evidence" for the first arrival of people in Vanuatu's ancient past:

> The ancient DNA research program in Vanuatu has also been significant for archaeology beyond its specific findings concerning the history of the Pacific Islands. It exemplifies a major theme that has emerged from the whole genome ancient DNA revolution in the last few years, which is that large-scale movements of people—involving population turnover and major admixture—have played a key important role in a number of important shifts in material culture that are evident in the archaeological record. (Spriggs and Reich 2020: 631)

Optimism of this sort, however, was soon challenged by others working in the Pacific largely on the grounds that it would be imprudent to claim too much about the past based on such a small sample of individuals, especially since they had been recovered from the same cemetery, and therefore might all have been closely related to one another. This caution is in keeping with Kahneman and Tversky's insistence that rational decisions have to be based on reliable evidence.

Statistically speaking, this cemetery is a "single event," and we have no way to judge how representative this cemetery is of what was happening in this part of the world three thousand years ago. As Stuart Bedford, one of the archaeologists who made this discovery, acknowledged in 2018, "different things may have been happening in different parts of the Vanuatu archipelago, with its 82 inhabited islands that stretch over 1000 km" (Bedford *in* Bedford et al. 2018: 206).

Perhaps more to the point, the suggestion that knowing the genetics of such a small number of individuals is sufficient justification for claiming there was an ancient human diaspora (Skoglund et al. 2016), "colonizing migration" (Bedford in Bedford et al. 2018: 206), or "migration stream" (Spriggs et al. 2019: 53) seems more intuitively pleasing than statistically robust (Christophe Sand in Bedford et al. 2018). Less charitable critics have suggested this interpretation is also more bibli-

$$0 \cdot 1 \cdot 2 \cdot 3 \cdot 4 \cdot 5 \cdot 6 \cdot 7 \cdot 8 \cdot 9 \cdot 10$$

—scale of your confidence in the contingencies being considered—

Figure 5.3. A simple way of recording how much confidence you have that a contingency may have contributed to a change or changes in the past over time and space. © John Edward Terrell.

cal than credible. How likely is it really that these particular individuals collectively represent a great historical movement of people in some way comparable, say, to the exile of Jews from the ancient Kingdom of Judah by the Babylonians in the sixth century BCE?

What has been generally overlooked, however, is what Kahneman and Tversky also advised. *Making rational decisions calls for paying attention to the prior probability of the claims being made.*

In this regard, two observations about these Vanuatu crania can be noted immediately from a Bayesian (rather than a Babylonian) point of view. First, the hypothesis about the past being offered—that this cemetery shows us the first diasporic movement beyond the Solomons of a singularly and clearly identifiable group of people from ISEA—has been framed as *binary*. It is being suggested *either* these early settlers on Efate were related to people in ISEA, *or* to people long resident then in NGR. Given this simple binary characterization, the unconditional probability that these few individuals or their forebears had sailed away from either one or the other of these two "source areas" three thousand or so years ago is statistically just the flip of a coin: 0.5 ISEA vs. 0.5 NGR.

Second, is there also some way to estimate the probability that people living then in one or both of these two parts of the southwestern Pacific had the voyaging technology needed to sail to Vanuatu successfully three thousand years ago? We cannot directly quantify these probabilities. It is necessary instead to make a *subjective estimate* of what they might be. One simple way to do so is to make use of the kind of subjective scale commonly used in healthcare settings (Figure 5.3).

Given what was discussed in Chapter 2 about the introduction of outrigger sailing technology into NGR around 3,500–3,300 years ago by people whose predecessors had once lived somewhere in ISEA, a reasonable subjective guess would be that everyone three thousand years ago in NGR whose ancestors had originally come from ISEA probably knew how to make and sail ocean-going outrigger canoes. However,

	sailing canoe	Efate	
Southeast Asia	10	5	15
New Guinea	1	5	6
	11	10	21

$P(H) = a + b / a + b + c + d = 0.71$
$P(E \mid H) = a / a + b = .67$
$P(E \mid H) \times P(H) = a / a + b + c + d = .48$
$P(E) = a + c / a + b + c + d = .52$
$P(H \mid E) = .91$

Figure 5.4. A subjective baseline analysis using Bayes' Theorem of the likely association between being able to sail successfully to Efate in Vanuatu, and the assumed ancestry of those found buried in a cemetery there. © John Edward Terrell.

Geoffrey Irwin and Richard Flay (2015: 435) have presented several lines of evidence and argument for thinking that between approximately 1300 and 1000 BCE, sailing from place to place in NGR led to innovations in ocean navigation that opened routes out to places such as Vanuatu beyond the Solomons. In other words, it would probably be an oversimplification to assume that anyone from ISEA would have immediately known *how* to negotiate seasonal weather changes, for example, strategically enough to venture out on return voyages, at least over distances greater than those they had previously experienced in ISEA or in NGR (Chapter 2).

Hence a reasonable subjective claim would be that the probability that there were people living in NGR three thousand or so years ago who could have sailed as far as Vanuatu would be something like $P(H) = 0.90$. On the other hand, while it seems likely that at least some local communities in NGR by then had learned from their ISEA neighbors how to make and sail ocean-going canoes (see Blust in Bedford et al. 2018: 207; see also Blench 2014), the odds of their being able to do so by then are probably lower. Our own subjective estimate is that this probability is only about $P = 0.10$.

What then can we say about the contingent probability that the first settlers to reach Vanuatu were probably people closely related genetically to folks in ISEA or NGR? Entering these subjective estimates into a Bayesian statistical model (Figure 5.4), it is obvious that discovering that these several now long dead individuals on Efate may have had distant kin living somewhere in ISEA is exactly what archaeologists and others should have been expecting all along. Yet even so, this new ancient DNA (aDNA) information adds little if anything to the seemingly ambitious further claim that these few individuals had been part of a great "diaspora," "colonizing migration," or "migration stream" of biblical proportions that had been launched for some reason from a point of departure—a "homeland" comparable, say, to the Kingdom of Judah—located somewhere in ISEA.

Historically, therefore, little if anything new has actually been learned from this admittedly new and novel biological information about the history of the Pacific. In light of the apparent odds being so strongly in favor of a connection with ocean-going settlers in NGR whose predecessors had come from ISEA, it would surely be far more informative, historically speaking, if this biological evidence had instead suggested more strongly than it does (Matisoo-Smith in Bedford et al. 2018) that their ancestors were actually people long resident in NGR, perhaps even living there before the end of the last Ice Age.

In any case, using Bayesian logic, it is apparent that seeing the arrival in Vanuatu of adventurous souls three thousand years ago as evidence for a major diaspora out of ISEA seems to be making a lot out of little.

The "Why?" Question

Not everyone would agree with our baseline analysis of the historical significance of a small number of skulls from an ancient cemetery in Vanuatu. Quite correctly, critics of this analysis might say that the only contingency we have weighed is *how* people back then could have sailed all the way to the island of Efate. Given that the remains of more than one hundred individuals were found by archaeologists in this cemetery, both males and females, it does seem subjectively improbable that this was simply the final resting place of those who had accidently voyaged off course so far from wherever it was between NGR and Vanuatu they had come from. And yes, using Bayesian logic to try to answer only the *how?* side of their story entirely ignores the question *why?*

The obvious reason why we have not tried to guess subjectively what their motivations may have been is that there would seem to be no sure way to guess what their reason, or reasons, might have been. Given the number of people in that cemetery, it does seem likely whatever these motivations were, there must have been collective agreement by however many had actually been the ones to risk their lives on the open sea to get there in the first place. Nonetheless, it is a mystery to us why the archaeologist Matthew Spriggs is by no means the only one to say that their eventual pioneering landfall at Efate must have been not only an agreeable outcome, but also self-evidently the sign of a "large-scale movement of people."

Unlike the flight of refugees from ancient Judah in the sixth century BCE, no one has suggested that those traveling down the hypothesized ancient "migration stream" running all the way from ISEA to Vanuatu and islands even farther out in the Pacific were on the move for only a few years or decades from start to finish. Most who have written about this purported migrational pathway have accepted that it took thousands of years for people to get from ISEA to NGR, and then hundreds of years more to reach Vanuatu and other islands and archipelagos even farther east in the Pacific as far as Western Polynesia (Lipson et al. 2018; Summerhayes 2019). If so, then voyaging from *Point A* (somewhere among the islands of Southeast Asia) to *Point B* (far away in the archipelago now called Vanuatu) *could not have been undertaken by the same people*. Why assume, therefore, that over the course of thousands of years everyone involved shared one and the same intent and purpose, or that they even imagined that they were on an intentional (and directional) migration from Point A to Point B with the same aims in mind and motivated by the same desires and reasons? It seems far more likely that the circumstantial contingencies ($Y_1, Y_2, \ldots Y_n$) that ultimately led to the settlement of Vanuatu were several, even many, and undoubtedly diverse.

If so, then how is the word "migration" (Koikkalainen and Kyle 2016) appropriate for such a lengthy slice of time? Why is this the proper labeling for what evidently happened three thousand and more years ago? Using this word in archaeology without making it clear what it is intended to mean reduces it to being little more than a black box theory—a shallow claim turning good questions into misleading answers that prematurely may even seem to be suggesting no further inquiry or research is necessary.

> ❖ **black box theory**: "A black box is a fiction representing a set of concrete systems into which stimuli (S) impinge and out of which reactions (R) emerge. The constitution and structure of the box are altogether irrelevant to the approach under consideration, which is purely external or phenomenological" (Bunge 1963).

In philosophy and semantics, classic examples of such pseudo-explanations would be the claim that we sleep because of a *somnolent factor*, and we misbehave because we are *bad* or *sinful*. Invoking the word "migration" without explanation is equivalent to saying that something falls to the ground because it is heavy.

Although we can only guess why people finally opted to abandon their homes and risk their lives on the open sea, there are two contingencies behind the decision to do so that seem likely, at least subjectively speaking. First, although there is a possibility that scouting parties may have sailed beyond the Solomons (Chapter 2) in advance and had returned home safely to report on what they had discovered (Irwin 2008; Irwin and Flay 2015), it seems more than probable that at least the first of those making the long voyage to Efate had no real clue where this island was located or even that it existed. Nor could they have known what they would find there. Second, although it is possible most of the people buried in that ancient cemetery may have been born on Efate (Bentley et al. 2007), it seems likely that more than one voyage from wherever home was located to this new settlement may have been involved.

Three-Factor Contingency Analysis

Although perhaps it would be unwise to rule out entirely the role of chance, it would be difficult to argue that human choice was not part of what happened there in the Pacific three thousand or so years ago (Avis, Montenegro, and Weaver 2007; Irwin and Flay 2015). But did they do what they decided to do because they *wanted* to or because they *needed* to? Were the voyages that ultimately carried people beyond the Solomons mostly a matter of choice or necessity?

Another way of asking this same question about the past is to ask what was the likely role of *human agency* in what was happening in the Pacific back when Vanuatu was first colonized (Robb 2010; Wurzer, Kowarik, and Reschreiter 2015)? Said less dramatically perhaps, to what extent do we need to include in our historical theories, models, and hypotheses the contingencies we are calling *intentional* and *purposeful* (Figure 1.2)?

One way to subjectively assess the need to include human agency as a contingency behind what happened in the past is to use a scale like the one just used earlier in this chapter (Figure 5.3). Given this scale, it is at least possible to estimate the strength of the various likely contingencies involved by reducing them all to three complementary dimensions,

Developing Hypotheses • 125

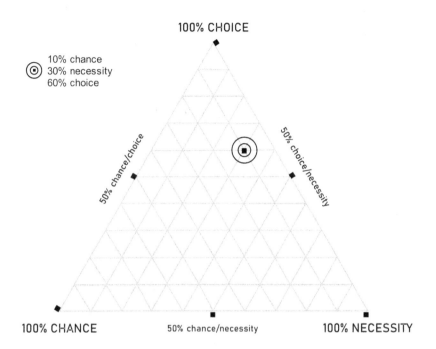

Figure 5.5. A three-dimensional ternary graph mapping the combined probability that certain species of plants and animals were transported to islands east of the Solomon Islands as provisions to be consumed on the voyage there and also to recreate once ashore the subsistence practices that had been used "back home." The dimension labeled **CHANCE** refers to the likelihood from 0 to 100 percent that what happened was *random and unpredictable*; **NECESSITY** shows how *fixed and predictable* this cargo of selected species may have been; and **CHOICE** indicates how arbitrary and unpredictable it was. © John Edward Terrell.

or axes, each with a probability range of 0.00 to 1.00: *chance, necessity,* and *choice* (Figure 5.5).

❖ Historical Explanation

Although understanding what has happened in the past can be challenging and difficult, the contingencies involved may often be usefully resolved by graphically reducing them to three factors (or proportional determinants) that taken together add up to 100 percent (Figure 5.5). Two of these dimensions are chance and necessity

(Monod 1971). The third is control—the power to influence or direct people's behavior or the course of events.

Here is an example of what we are suggesting. Archaeologists have been saying for years that to be able to colonize the islands of the Pacific east of the Solomons successfully, it was necessary for people to take with them what they would need to survive not just on the trip but also in their new island homes. Why? Because the farther an island in the Pacific is away from Asia, the more ecologically "impoverished" and biologically "depauperate" are its natural (biotic) resources. Therefore, it has been conventional wisdom in Pacific archaeology for decades that would-be colonists sailing beyond the Solomons to colonize new places to live needed to take with them the "biotic and cultural components necessary to recreate in each new island precisely the kind of managed landscape they had just left behind" (Kirch 2000: 109).

As a biogeographer's rule of thumb, there is sound ecological evidence supporting the generalization that islands are increasingly depauperate the further away they are from source regions (continents, say) of new species. However, enough is now also known about the archaeological record, for example, of the islands in the Kingdom of Tonga 9,000 km from Asia to be able to say that the first human settlers there around 2,850 years ago feasted far and wide off the natural abundance of these previously untouched natural habitats—so much so, that the archaeologist Les Groube in the 1960s theorized that the first colonists did not even need to be agriculturalists. Instead, he argued, they could have survived as "strandlopers" living off the natural goodness of these islands, particularly their rich marine and avian diversity (Burley, Horrocks, and Weisler 2020; Groube 1971).

From a Bayesian perspective, therefore, the suggestion that people back then in the Pacific somehow knew from the start that it would be necessary for them to transport to new places the landscapes they were accustomed to living on back home is questionable however appealing such a theory may seem. Rather than assuming that the first colonists who reached, say, Vanuatu or Tonga knew in advance that it would be necessary and strategic for them to carry in their canoes the species of plants and animals they and their descendants would eventually need to survive there, it is statistically more probable that people took with them simply what they wanted to be sure to have on the dinner table, so to speak, in their new homes (Koikkalainen and Kyle 2016). Hence, using the three-dimensional graphic framework shown in Figure 5.5, perhaps we should give *chance* a fairly low probability (0.10?), and then on the premise that people are not necessarily fools, perhaps give *necessity* a higher probability (0.30). But on the assumption that these early pioneers were not clairvoyant, it seems most probable that they simply took with them what they wanted "just to be sure" (say, 0.60) rather than what they knew they would undoubtedly need.

In other words, although it sounds reasonable to argue that it was *necessary* for colonists to transport the landscapes they cultivated back home and knew how to exploit, a more likely baseline assessment would be that they did so mostly, if not entirely, as a matter of *control* over the choices they would have once they came ashore wherever they finally opted to do so.

Chapter Summary

A good hypothesis is one that offers a plausible explanation for a phenomenon, event, or an observed relational pattern over time and space. Bayes' Theorem can be helpful when you want to sort out hypotheses that should probably be taken seriously from those that may well be a waste of time, effort, and research funding.

While it is not always possible to quantitatively estimate the prior probability of an hypothesis, the logic at the heart of Bayes' Theorem can nonetheless be a useful way to evaluate hypotheses subjectively as to their potential for further study.

Key Points

1. If we accept the premise of relational thinking that things, people, and events are what they are because of how they are interconnected and interdependent, then what is at issue in doing science is not simply whether there is evidence for or against some proposition. What must also be evaluated is how far other lines of evidence support the probability of what is being primarily considered.
2. Making rational decisions calls for paying attention to the plausibility—the prior probability—of the claims being made.

3. When including the contingency of human agency in our theories, models, and hypotheses, care must be taken not to assume a greater and more deliberative role for human behavior and decision-making than is likely or necessary.

Note

1. You have perhaps already seen that Propositions 1.1 and 1.2, first introduced in Chapter 1, are an alternative way of notationally stating Bayes' Theorem.

CHAPTER 6

Gathering Information

> How odd it is that every one should not see that all observation must be for or against some view, if it is to be of any service.
>
> —Charles Darwin's letter to Henry Fawcett, 18 September (1861)

> In the beginning I couldn't see anything. Luckily, I started deciphering, and from very tiny shards I began to piece it together. None of the literature could help me. I had to make my own way, little by little. Later on I became passionate to find more.
>
> —Marija Gimbutas (quoted in Marler 1996: 45)

- Interpretation or Explanation?
- Big Data and the Elephant
- The Neolithic Revolution?
- The Elephant in the Room?
- Example: The "Neolithic Revolution" in Europe
- Three Kinds of Evidence
- Three Kinds of Data
- Chapter Summary
- Key Points

In a famous letter thanking a young economist named Henry Fawcett for taking up the "cudgels in defence of the line of argument in the *Origin [of Species]*," Charles Darwin was blunt about saying why blindly gathering information without a clearly defined objective is futile:

> About 30 years ago there was much talk that Geologists ought only to observe & not theorise; & I well remember some one saying, that at

this rate a man might as well go into a gravel-pit & count the pebbles & describe their colours. How odd it is that every one should not see that all observation must be for or against some view, if it is to be of any service. (Darwin 1861)

While we agree with Darwin, we also think saying this skirts the issue of how to decide *what* to observe—what needs to be collected as evidence—"for or against some view."

Interpretation or Explanation?

If Francis Bacon was on the right track back in the seventeenth century (Chapter 1) when he wrote that truth is the daughter of time, not authority, then history might be likened to someone with a shady past. If left on their own, they will reveal nothing. If asked directly, all they will be willing to say is this: what do you need to know?

Resolving this question is more challenging than commonly acknowledged. Archaeologists, for instance, during their excavations often find far more not just in quantity but also in kind than they need to have in hand to honor the research goals detailed in their grant proposals and previous research publications. This may be one reason why many archaeologists, when asked, are likely to say that they are trying to *interpret* what they are finding historically, although sometimes they may use the word *explain* to mean more or less the same thing. But interpretation is not just an alternative word for explanation.

> ❖ **interpretation** [in,tərprə'tāSH(ə)n, ɪn,tərprə'teɪʃ(ə)n] *noun*: the action of explaining the meaning of something.
>
> **explanation** [,eksplə'nāSH(ə)n, ɛksplə'neɪʃ(ə)n] *noun*: a statement or account that makes something clear.

In *Writing the Past: Knowledge and Literary Production in Archaeology* (2018), Gavin Lucas describes how archaeologists in the English-speaking world today have been struggling to turn what they find into dependable knowledge about the past. The disagreements arising have often been intense. Furthermore, the clashes over method and theory are not over. As he has observed: "In the wake of debates in archaeology during the 1980s and 1990s one can no longer entertain any

	WHAT ?	WHY ?	HOW ?
CATEGORICAL THINKING	✔		
RELATIONAL THINKING	✔	✔	
MODEL BUILDING	✔	✔	✔

Figure 6.1. *Categorical thinking* accepts that what something is like is both self-evident and predictable; *relational thinking* assumes instead that things are the way they are because they are connected with, linked to, etc. other things; *model building* is the effort to connect the evident "what?" with the most probable "why?" © John Edward Terrell.

naivety about archaeological knowledge as an untroubled road to the truth about what happened in the past" (2018: 3).

As he goes on to note, however, at the present time debate about the hows and whys of turning archaeological finds into credible historical knowledge has all but ceased. Nowadays, attention is more often than not focused on methodological issues. What might still be called archaeological theory is being glossed as "the theory of interpretation" (2018: 24)—which he describes as what needs to be done to decide "which of two or more explanations best accounts for the data" recovered archaeologically (2018: 54). If we have any quarrel with this assessment, it would be that we do not see the aim of archaeology as simply to account for—or interpret—what archaeologists recover from the past. Instead, we think the goal of archaeology is to contribute material evidence that can help answer—and explain—not only what happened in the past, but also how and why (Figure 6.1). And yes, also why we should care.

Big Data and the Elephant

In this chapter we want to underscore three points. First, simply having enough "data" to do a statistical analysis, even a Bayesian analysis, is not the high road to truth. Evidence—even what is now being billed as "big data" (Hariri, Fredericks, and Bowers 2019)—does not interpret itself. Hence even under the best of circumstances, the "prior probabilities" that are the hallmark of Bayesian statistics are actually just the results of previous experience, conventional reasoning, and prior statistical analyses aimed at uncovering how the world apparently works.[1]

Second, merely getting more of the same data for or against this or that view of what may have happened in history does not necessarily improve the level of confidence we can have in the results we may be getting. A classic example of the truth of this observation is what Copernicus did when he challenged the commonsense Ptolemaic model of the (then) known universe with the decidedly counterintuitive claim that the sun, not the earth, is at the center of our planet's solar system (see Figure 3.2). For thousands of years before Copernicus, mathematically inclined astronomers had been getting what to them seemed to be quite reasonable astronomical results despite the fact that they were taking it for granted that the Earth, not the Sun, is at the center of all that is going on around them. The evidence against this traditional geocentric belief seemed to most working astronomers then to make absolutely no sense at all.

Third, as the old parable "The Blind Men and the Elephant" tells us, gathering evidence for or against what is being proposed is not just a matter of how much evidence you have for or against what you are saying. Your argument can be much improved, much strengthened, *by gathering other kinds, or lines, of evidence*. As the influential philosopher of science William Whewell (1794–1866) wrote persuasively in the nineteenth century, when our ideas, hypotheses, and conclusions reached on the basis of one type, or class, of evidence work well also for other sorts of evidence, they have a "much higher and more forcible character" (Whewell 1840, vol. 2: 230).

Whewell coined the phrase "consilience of inductions" to describe this use of different lines of supporting evidence (Fisch 1985). "*The Consilience of Inductions* takes place when an Induction, obtained from one class of facts, coincides with an Induction, obtained from another different class. This Consilience is a test of the truth of the Theory in which it occurs" (Whewell 1840, vol 1: xxxix).

Our favorite example of why consilience is important is the parable we have just mentioned: "The Blind Men and the Elephant." Here is one version of this famous old fable graphically illustrating both how relying on only one sort of evidence can be misleading, and also how challenging it can be to see what different lines of evidence may have in common (Râmakrishna 1907: 28–29):

Gathering Information • 133

Figure 6.2. "The Blind Men and the Elephant." *Source*: Illustrator unknown, public domain, via Wikimedia Commons, https://commons.wikimedia.org/wiki/File:Blind_men_and_elephant.png.

> Four blind men went to see an elephant. One touched a leg of the elephant and said: "The elephant is like a pillar." The second touched the trunk and said: "The elephant is like a thick club." The third touched the belly and said: "The elephant is like a huge jar." The fourth touched the ears and said: "The elephant is like a big winnowing-basket." Then they began to dispute among themselves as to the figure of the elephant. A passer-by, seeing them thus quarreling, asked them what it was about. They told him everything and begged him to settle the dispute. The man replied: "None of you has seen the elephant. The elephant is not like a pillar, its legs are like pillars. It is not like a big water-jar, its belly is like a water-jar. It is not like a winnowing-basket, its ears are like winnowing-baskets. It is not like a stout club, its trunk is like a club. The elephant is like the combination of all these." In the same manner do those sectarians quarrel who have seen only one aspect of the Deity. He alone who has seen God in all His aspects can settle all disputes.

This is just one of the popular versions of this parable. Despite their differing details, however, most versions reach the same resolve. It is easy to be fooled into believing we know the Truth even though all we have in hand, so to speak, is only a piece, one part, of what we need to know to "settle all disputes."

We also like to use this parable, however, to talk about a different but related resolve. Why do these blind men all think they are talking about the same thing even though what they have in hand comes across to them as so very different? To invoke another popular saying, why do they all believe there is "an elephant in the room" even if they cannot see it for what it is?[2]

Case in point: why do many scholars believe there was a great turning point in human history called the "Neolithic Revolution" even though what this might have been can seem so different depending not only on the historical evidence in hand but also on the sorts of evidence being gathered?

The Neolithic Revolution?

It has long been seemingly self-evident to many scholars of deep time and ancient history that something genuinely important in the past—something quite revolutionary—happened after the end of the Pleistocene around eleven thousand or so years ago. When it came to putting food on the table, people began to focus their efforts not just on hunting down animals or gathering "wild" vegetables, fruits, and the like wherever they could be found. Instead, people around the world began to specialize on what they were taking and eating by investing time and effort on species that they could effectively control and in other ways, too, manage well and then reliably exploit (Terrell et al. 2003).

The evidence used to support this claim of a "Neolithic Revolution" has varied depending on the antiquity and locale where the evidence has been gathered, and it has also long been accepted in archaeology and the study of ancient history more generally speaking that all of us once upon a time made our way through life as "nomadic hunter-gatherers" living in small egalitarian "tribes." It was only during this revolution in the waning years of the last Ice Age that we began to change our ways, take up husbandry and agriculture, settle down, and start living in ever growing settlements now popularly called "cities." Today it is also said that this allegedly important transitional event happened more than once and in more than one place on earth.

Without repeating what has previously been said elsewhere at some length (Terrell et al. 2003), it can be argued, however, that exploiting differing species as foods or raw materials calls for differing skills depending on the species in question and the circumstances under which they are being taken. In some situations and for some species, the tactics used are mainly behavioral—people adjust, or adapt, their own actions to fit the behavior and circumstances of the species they are using. Under other circumstances and for other species, the skills and tactics used may call for greater environmental preparation or manipulation. Therefore, instead of trying to distinguish people today and those in the past as either hunter-gatherers or agriculturalists—or foragers and farmers—it makes more sense to define human subsistence behavior as a relational matrix of species and harvesting tactics, that is, as a "provisions spreadsheet."

The Elephant in the Room?

Despite the argument that human subsistence behavior has always been situational, circumstantial, and varied, the following example based on archaeological research in the Mediterranean and continental Europe shows that archaeologists and other scholars of the past for generations have agreed almost unanimously that they are all "touching" the same thing—not the proverbial elephant, of course, but rather something comparably large and powerful that was revolutionary—despite the obvious differences in the evidence being gathered concerning what people were doing and eating in the past.

It may not be a universal human failing, but despite all their accumulated evidence *for* such a proposition—such a "beast"—it is both scientifically and historically unwise to overlook and pay too little attention to evidence *against* what Darwin called a "view," and we have been calling instead theories, models, and hypotheses. Yet, as Terrell and his colleague John Hart observed years ago, when looked at closely, hunting and foraging are not as different from farming as popularly believed. Farming, too, is a hazy category that covers a diverse range of human behaviors and relationships with other species. As they concluded:

> Once it is accepted that people throughout history have been exploiting not only a few but, in fact, many kinds of plants and animals in varying ways and to varying degrees—only some of which might now be described as "true domesticates," then both in effect as well as in practice *Homo sapiens* has been domesticating not just a few species for untold years but entire landscapes for the provisioning of food, useful materials, and shelter.... [Therefore,] the real challenge is developing ways of improving how successfully archaeologists can use what they discover to learn about what people in the past were actually do-

ing on the landscapes they inhabited to put food on the table and a roof over their heads. (Terrell and Hart 2008: 331)

What then was really happening as the Pleistocene was drawing to a close? More to the point of this chapter, how can you tell when differences in the historical evidence you are gathering are probably telling you, nonetheless, the same thing?

Example: The "Neolithic Revolution" in Europe

Problem Statement

Nobody doubts that certain foreign species of plants and animals began showing up in the European archaeological record starting ~9,000 years ago (Shennan et al. 2013; Fuks and Marom 2021). There is archaeological evidence, for example, that three exotic plant species—emmer (*Triticum monococcum*), einkorn (*T. dicoccum*), and barley (*Hordeum vulgare*)—were being cultivated as food by ~5500 BC as far west in Europe as the Iberian Peninsula and in the Maghreb. Animal domestication (sheep, goat, and cattle) is attested in central and northern Europe by ~4000 BC.

It is now generally believed that these species were introduced from southwest Asia over the course of several centuries by people traveling through central and northern Europe along the Danube and Rhine river valleys, and across southern Europe along a maritime route from the Levantine coast to Anatolia, via the islands of Cyprus and Crete towards the central Mediterranean and further west into Iberia and the Maghreb (for rates of spread, see Figure 6.3).

Did the arrival of these species along with the foreign subsistence strategies they witness—commonly called "farming" and "husbandry"—radically change the course of history in Europe? If so, given the ecological and geographic diversity of the European subcontinent (i.e., the genuine diversity of the *situational contingencies* of daily life prior to the introduction of these new species), was the impact (the *consequential contingencies*) of these species also variable?

Current Theories

Over fifty years ago, Ammerman and Cavalli Sforza (1971) postulated that there had been a gradual movement by Neolithic colonists from southwest Asia into Europe averaging a rate of advance of about one kilometer per year. Using newer archaeological data (e.g., the spatial distribution of sites, their size, and associated radiocarbon dates), their "wave of advance" theory has since then been refined and remodeled not as a gradual transition from hunting and gathering to farming and husbandry, but rather as an arrhythmic "jump dispersal" or "leapfrogging" human advance; that is, in all likelihood there were periods of rapid local population growth and settlement expansion alternating with periods of prolonged stasis (e.g., Shennan et al. 2013)—a punctuated rather than a smooth process of population growth and expanding settlement (Fiedel and Anthony 2003; Guilaine 2013; Zilhão 2001).

Both of these theories assume that new species of plants and animals (along with the associated cultural practices) began showing up in Europe after the Pleistocene not because people in Europe were cultivating new social and economic ties with people elsewhere who were already exploiting these species, but instead through the actual resettlement (or "migration") of newcomers from southwest Asia—a region long identified by archaeologists and others as an "early cradle of domestication" following the "ex oriente lux" ("light from the Near East") model of cultural diffusion (Childe 1925).

How important is it to know historically how these new species and their associated economic practices first reached Europe? How diverse was their impact on the ways and means of life in this part of the world?

Working Model

Given current knowledge, it is widely assumed that foreigners migrated into and through Europe at least in the early phases of the period commonly referred to as the "Neolithic" (starting in southeastern Europe ~7000–6000 BC). It is also assumed that there was at least some engagement between incoming farmers and local hunter-gatherers (Shennan et al. 2013: 2), followed by the subsequent adoption by the latter (often called "cultural diffusion") of the recently introduced foreign species and associated practices.

This historical scenario is supported by recent biological studies that have identified genetic links between individuals found at archaeological sites in southwest Asia and the modern populations of Cyprus and Crete (Fernández et al. 2014), as well as genetic similarity between Mediterranean and Central European early farmers with those of Greece and Anatolia (Hofmanová et al. 2016).

Early coexistence between local hunter-gatherers and resettled farmers with subsequent adoption by the former of farming and herding as a way of life has also been inferred using archaeological and

138 • Modeling the Past

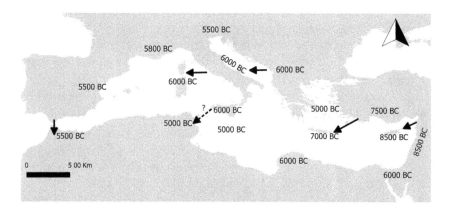

Figure 6.3. Approximate dates of the earliest Neolithic sites on the Mediterranean islands and adjacent coasts with main sea crossings (from Dawson 2021b: 93). © Helen Dawson.

environmental data from sites attesting to mixed subsistence strategies—farming as well as hunting-gathering—such as those that have been excavated in the Alps, Central Iberia, the Atlantic coast of France and Portugal, Belgium, the Netherlands, Scandinavia, Britain, and Ireland (Robb and Miracle 2007).

Furthermore, local adoption is also supported along the southern shore of the Mediterranean where the earliest domestic crops in the Egyptian and Sudanese Nile Valley and the northern coast of Morocco are dated to the sixth millennium BC (Lucarini and Radini 2021: 70). Domesticated animals—notably caprines (*Ovis aries* and *Capra hircus*) and some cattle (*Bos taurus*)—had already reached Egypt ~6200 BC, centuries before the main domesticated plant species. Although caprines have no local wild ancestors and therefore must have been introduced from southwest Asia, wild cattle (*Bos primigenius*) did occur in Egypt so that local domestication as well as introduction are both a possibility there (Linseele 2021: 60).

In a recent article, Dawson (2021b) draws on data from 150 Mediterranean islands to discuss what may have been the contingencies leading to the patterning that has been found in the first human colonization (and sometimes abandonment) of these islands during the Neolithic—and the possible role of these same contingencies in the spread of farming into the lands bordering the Mediterranean, as well (Figure 6.3). The available data generally support a migrationist model with limited evidence for local adoption. The key points in Dawson's model are:

1. A general westward maritime expansion can be traced on the basis of the available dates from Neolithic sites from the coast of southwest Asia, via Cyprus, Crete, the Balkan and Italian peninsulas and islands, the French and Iberian coasts and islands, finally reaching the Moroccan and Tunisian coasts of North Africa from the western side.
2. A maritime coastal movement of settlers from place to place would have been easier than if they traveled westward inland through the often-rugged interior reaches of the lands bordering the Mediterranean.
3. The islands may have represented an attractive option for incoming farmers in terms of freely available space, stop-over places, and desirable resources (e.g., raw materials such as obsidian).

Evidence and Analysis

The earliest permanent settlement of the Mediterranean islands is largely a Neolithic phenomenon, except for the largest islands which were inhabited earlier. Thus, the first human settlement of Cyprus, some 80–90 km from the southern coast of Anatolia, occurred in the 11th millennium cal BC, but this island's first Neolithic sites date to ~9000–8500 cal BC (Dawson 2014: 139–45). A similar scenario applies to the island of Crete. People were living there as early as the Mesolithic (~9000 cal BC), but the island was apparently abandoned only to be recolonized by Neolithic groups around 7000 BC. Concerning the smaller islands, the remains of sheep, goat, and poorly fired pots at Sidari on Corfu dating to ~6500 cal BC have been found directly above an earlier shell midden, but it is unclear whether this evidence represents a case of the local adoption of Neolithic traits, or their subsequent introduction (see Leppard 2022). A stratigraphic gap is reported on Kythnos, Lemnos, and Ikaria, which when taken together points to a widespread phase of abandonment followed by recolonization (Dawson 2021b: 87–89).

Moving westward, the large islands of Sardinia, Corsica, and Sicily were also inhabited prior to the Neolithic (see Dawson 2014: 83–90, 95–101; Dawson 2021b: 90). At Grotta Corbeddu in Sardinia, the start of the Early Neolithic (Layer 1) is dated ~6000 cal BC but this evidence is separated by a lengthy gap from the end of the Mesolithic (top of Layer 2) dated ~7000–6500 cal BC. A similar gap can be seen at several sites in Corsica and is thought to represent a prolonged phase of abandonment followed by recolonization (Dawson 2021b: 87).

Most small islands of the central and western Mediterranean still lack evidence of pre-Neolithic activity (Dawson 2014: 122), and on present knowledge the majority were settled for the first time during the Neolithic, starting ~6000 cal BC. The Dalmatian Islands, a vast littoral archipelago hugging the Croatian coast, are an exception, as they were attached to the mainland during the last glacial maximum and their occupation continued following their insularization, ~8500–6000 cal BC (Dawson 2014: 119–22). A mixed economy of hunting-gathering and Neolithic traits is attested at Vela Špilja on the island of Korčula in Croatia (Pilaar Birch 2018), and this evidence is generally interpreted as support for the idea that the people involved were local hunter-gatherers who had adopted Neolithic traits and practices.

Sicily stands out among all the Mediterranean islands with its continuous occupation record and supports the possibility of coexistence between hunter-gatherers and early farmers and partial adoption by hunter-gatherers of Neolithic practices. The Grotta dell'Uzzo (Uzzo Cave) in northwestern Sicily has yielded an uninterrupted stratigraphic sequence spanning the Mesolithic and Neolithic transition. Evidence has been recovered for hunting, fishing, and the introduction of domesticated crops, a rare example of occupation continuity spanning this critical transition in the Mediterranean region. A recent genome-wide and isotopic study of nineteen individuals from Grotta dell'Uzzo by van de Loosdrecht et al. (2020) suggests that this site was occupied both by people long resident on the island and newcomers. Two individuals dating to around 6050–5850 cal BC when the earliest pottery occurs at this site apparently had different diets. One of them consumed a large proportion of freshwater protein, in line with the subsistence practices of hunter-gatherers elsewhere in the Mediterranean; the other—although of the same evident genetic ancestry—had a more terrestrial-based ("farming") diet with very low levels of animal protein. The authors of this study thus hypothesize that some hunter-gatherers living at this site had adopted Neolithic practices.

Discussion

Given the archaeological evidence just reviewed, it would seem obvious that Neolithic ways and means reached almost all of the Mediterranean through migration rather than by local adoption. As a rule, the arriving Neolithic colonizers evidently targeted islands that were within one day's reach from the mainland (50 km or less) with the exception of large islands such as Cyprus and Crete; modeling the speed of the spread in some areas required maritime jumps of up to 150 km (Fort, Pujol, and Vander Linden 2012), although more distant or smaller islands often underwent multiple colonization and abandonment events (Dawson 2014). The abandonment evidence from the smaller islands across the Mediterranean also supports a punctuated pattern of population movement and settlement relocation.

Therefore, with the exception of Sicily and the Dalmatian Islands, where there is some evidence of coexistence between hunter-gatherers and farmers indicating possible local adoption of Neolithic traits, it is now generally accepted that incoming farmers from southwest Asia introduced this new way of life to the Mediterranean islands, in line with most of Europe. Yet how reliable is such an explanation? What is this "Neolithic" that we are "touching"—to borrow from the allegory of the blind men and the elephant? Both of the leading theories of the early Neolithic in Europe (above) are basically similar in their major assumptions about the past. But was the history of Europe after the end of the Pleistocene really this predictable, this straightforward?

❖ Theories about the European Neolithic

1. **situational contingencies**—until the introduction of certain key species from southwest Asia, Europe and the Mediterranean were undomesticated ("wild") landscapes (but see Terrell et al. 2003).
2. **circumstantial contingencies**—either through local borrowing ("adoption") or foreign population expansion ("migration") that began in southwest Asia, new species and their associated subsistence practices spread widely through this region of the world, more or less swiftly, more or less continuously.
3. **consequential contingencies**—these newly introduced species and practices, by radically improving the chances of human survival in Europe, led to local population growth and local settlement expansion.

To answer this obviously important question, it is necessary to consider how the archaeological data now available were collected and why. There is a fundamental methodological issue at stake here having to do with the comparative archaeological "visibility" of incoming Neolithic farmers and local hunter-gatherers. While European farmers lived in settled villages and built permanent structures, evidently European hunter-gatherers had a largely mobile lifestyle based around seasonal camps that have as a rule left behind only ephemeral archaeological traces. Consequently, the archaeological record is surely biased towards the recovery of Neolithic remains. Hence our earlier observation should be rephrased as follows: "The earliest permanent settlement of the Mediterranean islands is *on current evidence* largely a Neolithic phenomenon, except for the largest islands which were inhabited earlier."

Furthermore, while those who were farmers back then apparently favored living on the fertile loess plains of the European subcontinent that were suitable for agriculture, hunter-gatherers apparently favored places on the landscape (some would call them "ecological niches") offering plentiful terrestrial and marine resources. As a matter of fact, targeted field surveys, such as those that have been done over the last decade in the Aegean islands, have successfully located pre-Neolithic sites by focusing research on specific areas of the landscape that would have provided such resources. Therefore, the apparent lack of pre-Neolithic occupation on the islands may well just be a sampling error due to a field research bias favoring the more visible, that is, Neolithic, archaeological record.

The inference that some places where people had been living as hunter-gatherers were abandoned prior to the Neolithic is also open to question. In Dalmatia, for example, there is continuity at specific sites and erosional discontinuity at others, which may have removed evidence of interaction (Mlekuž et al. 2008). At a number of sites, the 2-σ calibrated age ranges of the radiocarbon dates for the latest pre-Neolithic and earliest Neolithic occupations overlap, so that the existence of a gap is less certain. Moreover, the gaps observed at different sites are not contemporary, and a number of sites exist with undated Late Mesolithic–Early Neolithic sequences, so that abandonment on a regional scale cannot be easily proven (Mlekuž et al. 2008: 400–1).

A second issue is more conceptual and relates to how we make sense of change occurring over long periods of time. How can we make sense of a phenomenon of elephantine proportions (to go back yet again to the parable) that took some four thousand years to take hold across the whole of Europe? It is worth remembering that the term "Neolithic" is basically just a convenient shorthand for multiple contingencies leading along different paths. Although still widely referred to as a "revolution" in human history (Childe 1937), already in 1975 Graham Clarke dismissed Childe's Neolithic and Urban revolutions as existing "in our thoughts" rather than in prehistory (quoted in Greene 1999: 97).

It is tempting to draw arrows in time and space linking the inception of farming, which provided sufficient resources for sizable communities to settle permanently for the first time, to the subsequent emergence of urbanized state polities a few millennia later in the Bronze and Iron Age. This linear and teleological narrative of continuity and change punctuated by significant technological revolutions is largely derived from a nineteenth-century evolutionary model known as the "three-age system" in European prehistory that greatly oversimplified the past (Trigger 1989: 73–79).

Despite this, the popularity of this concept has endured, as have other similar "revolutions" in archaeology, such as the "Broad Spectrum Revolution" (Flannery 1969), the "Secondary Products Revolution" (Sherratt 1981) and the "Human Revolution" (Collins 1976; Mellars and Stringer 1989; see Chapter 7, this volume). The idea that such "revolutions" have actually happened is often inspired by historical events, such as the Industrial Revolution, that make events that took place long ago more relatable, being closer in time to us (see Table 3.4 on how scientific theories develop) (Trigger 1980).

Three Kinds of Evidence

Inspired by Darwin and the parable of the blind men, when gathering evidence and getting ready to analyze what we have in hand, the four of us try to keep in mind that evidence can be used in these three differing ways:

1. **Evidence for**—As just discussed, currently there seems to be substantial evidence in favor of the idea (with some notable exceptions) that foreigners from the east introduced what archaeologists have long called the "Neolithic way of life" to the Mediterranean and the European subcontinent. Yet, as we pointed out in Chapter 5, caution is required when equating the quantity, and even the quality, of available evidence with certainty and the "Truth." Who doubts that if these legendary blind men had all been touching the trunk of the elephant, they would have all agreed that they were touching, say, one of the pillars of a substantial building.
2. **Evidence against**—According to the philosopher Karl Popper, as we noted in Chapter 5, the best way to evaluate scientific claims is not to look for information proving hypotheses (or

theories) to be right, or true, but instead for evidence showing them to be wrong—and therefore, no longer ideas we need to take seriously. There is danger, however, in accepting too readily a lack of contrary evidence as support for what may appear to be a sound and perfectly logical conclusion. Believing something to be true because it has not been shown to be false is a risky proposition. Arguing in favor of something based on the lack of contrary evidence in Latin is called *argumentum ad ignorantiam*. A traditional version of the same observation is the old aphorism "absence of evidence is not evidence of absence." As we have just pointed out, although the weight of the current evidence supports the theory that farming as a way of life became widely spread in Europe long ago through the agency of people moving in who were already farmers, this "grand narrative" risks overlooking the possibility that there has simply not been enough research in the right places showing this theory about the past is ignoring evidence supporting the coexistence of alternative processes.

3. **Other evidence**—In some versions of the parable about the elephant, when they discover they do not agree on what they are touching, they come to blows. Some versions also tell us how their disagreement is resolved less dramatically. Someone who can see the whole elephant for what it is comes to their rescue. In recent years, new analytical technologies—such as remote sensing, X-ray fluorescence (XRF), and inductively coupled plasma mass spectrometry (ICP-MS)—have added new kinds of evidence that can be used to build more robust arguments for or against theories about what happened in the past much like the blind men in some versions of the fable who finally start talking civilly to one another, and are then able to piece together what it is they are actually touching.

Archaeology is arguably going through a "third revolution" (Kristiansen 2014) as Big Data, quantitative modeling, stable isotope analysis, and aDNA data are questioning current knowledge and pushing for new theories and hypotheses about what the archaeological record may be showing us. At the same time, these new developments are helping scholars test and, in some cases, revive older theories (or aspects thereof).

A notable example is Marija Gimbutas's Kurgan hypothesis which linked the spread of Indo-European languages to the migration of horse-riding herders (referred to as the "Yamnaya" people) from the Steppes into Europe at the start of the Bronze Age (Gimbutas 1997). Genetic studies support population movement into Europe from the Steppes at this time (Haak et al. 2015), though this phenomenon was likely on a smaller scale to the mass migration originally envisaged by Gimbutas and by paleogeneticists more recently (Furholt 2017).

Three Kinds of Data

Not only can the same evidence be used in these three differing ways, but what is available may be telling us different things about history and how the world works depending on how we see it fitting into the ideas, theories, and the like we are trying to evaluate. In keeping with Proposition 1.2:

1. **Situational data**—Given what is now known about the subsistence practices of people in Europe and the Mediterranean during the Pleistocene and for a long time thereafter, archaeologists and others should be careful how they use explanatory terms such as "adoption" or "replacement" to explain changes in the archaeological record. Not everyone in Europe prior to the "arrival of the Neolithic" was living under the same conditions and dealing with the same situational contingencies.
2. **Circumstantial data**—Scholars using words such as "migration," "invasion," and "colonization" may sound like they know what they are talking about, but what is needed is evidence in hand about the actual contingencies leading to what evidently happened in history. What did hunter-gatherers actually do when they "adopted" foreign species and practices? Why did anyone bother to "migrate"? What would the evidence look like if it can still be found?
3. **Consequential data**—We are also convinced that care must be taken to avoid assuming that despite situational and circumstantial variation in the contingencies people in the past were dealing with, the consequences were not only predictable, but usually the same. As recent demographic modeling now suggests, enough is now known to be able to say that population growth throughout the Mediterranean and the European subcontinent has not been uniform, continuous, or entirely predictable.

Chapter Summary

The quotations by Darwin and Gimbutas at the start of this chapter illustrate two more or less different ways to do science: (a) one way is to start with a question and a hypothesis, and then collect information accordingly (following a hypothetico-deductive method); (b) the other is to collect and score the data to find a meaningful pattern that can in turn be used to formulate a hypothesis (following an *inductive* method). Clearly, even in the latter case, what constitutes a "meaningful" pattern is based on prior assumptions, observations, and ultimately hypotheses, but these are not always fully acknowledged.

Both approaches are widely used in archaeology and may be more or less suitable depending on the research problem being studied. Either way, we stress the need to make prior assumptions and baselines explicit and to formulate questions that can clearly frame and guide new research.

Data collection is thus never an aimless exercise, since it is always informed by prior assumptions that are based on our previous observations and experience (bias), undeniably influencing our data sampling strategies (we collect the data that "matter"). Testing prior assumptions or refining existing hypotheses is often done by running models using larger datasets, as new evidence becomes available, but in fact can be done much more effectively if the models are tested on different datasets or by comparing the results of different models on the same datasets.

The parable of the blind men and the elephant underscores that while we may be right about something, we may be missing out on important information that would let us make sense of the full historical picture (in this case, hunter-gatherers are underrepresented in the archaeological record, and new more targeted research may begin to correct this bias).

Although we suspect some would criticize us for promoting such elementary cautions, we know from our own research that the obvious is often not seen, and it never hurts to pay attention to the lessons that parables can teach us. Here then are two key points we try to remember when we are looking for new evidence favoring (or refuting) an idea, hypothesis, model, or theory about the past.

Key Points

1. Charles Darwin and the Gravel Pit. It is important to gather evidence not only for our ideas, but also against them.
2. The Blind Men and the Elephant. It is possible to be right about the evidence you have in hand but wrong about what it means. Therefore, avoid looking for only a single line or type of information when you are gathering evidence for or against what you see as the most likely explanation for what happened in the past.

Notes

1. Prior probabilities are those derived from evaluating the situational contingencies of the phenomena under consideration.
2. In some versions of this parable, the blind men believe they are touching different animals although they are all touching the same one (Griffiths 1991: 46–47).

CHAPTER 7

Analyzing Data

The likelihood principle emphasized in Bayesian statistics implies, among other things, that the rules governing when data collection stops are irrelevant to data interpretation. It is entirely appropriate to collect data until a point has been proven or disproven, or until the data collector runs out of time, money, or patience.

—Ward Edwards et al.,
"Bayesian Statistical Inference for Psychological Research" (1963)

Supporting a research hypothesis against all competing rival hypotheses which explain a given effect is not something significance testing can help with. Such support (a.k.a., scientific support) is gained only after meticulous theorizing, sound methodology, and numerous replications lead to diverse, corroborating evidence demonstrating the effect in a variety of situations.

—Charles Lambdin, "Significance Tests as Sorcery" (2012)

There is not just one knowledge but multiple knowledges where multivocality is a virtue, not an obstacle. At the same time it is probably fair to say that most archaeologists nonetheless still hold some conviction about the verisimilitude or truthlikeness of their accounts: one can never be sure it was like this, but here is a plausible possibility at least.

—Gavin Lucas, *Writing the Past* (2018)

- Typological Analysis
- Statistical Analysis
- Social Network Analysis (SNA)
- Dynamic Relational Analysis (DYRA)
- Example: Language, Material Culture, and Society
- Chapter Summary
- Key Points

The history of early astronomy as a mathematical science is a story that should not be forgotten by anyone who is about to analyze the information they have gathered—"their data"—with a particular research aim and question in mind. Years ago, for example, the astronomer Owen Gingerich wrote about those in Ancient Greece who went against conventional wisdom and good common sense to argue that the Earth goes around the Sun, not the opposite (Gingerich 1973). He made it clear that Copernicus had known their arguments, and he had said so in his famous book *De revolutionibus orbium coelestium* (*On the Revolutions of the Heavenly Spheres*) first published shortly before his death in 1543. Gingerich, however, felt called upon to write about astronomical knowledge and mathematics before Copernicus because some would insist that Copernicus is given too much credit for getting us to accept the seemingly counterfactual truth of the heliocentric model of our solar system.

We bring up this well-known chapter in the history of science to underscore what we see as a vital point. Although often associated only with the second century AD Greco-Egyptian astronomer Claudius Ptolemy, others scholars, too, had labored diligently long before Copernicus was born to perfect the mathematical accuracy of the common sense idea that the Sun goes around the Earth, and the planets likewise follow suit . . . despite the fact—as Copernicus and a few others realized—this model is utterly wrong.

What do we see as the moral of this story? The accuracy with which a mathematical model fits the data you have in hand is not proof that the model you are working with is correct.

As Gingerich recounted in 1973, this moral was not lost on those who were involved in the publication of *De revolutionibus* in 1543. The author of this book's anonymous introduction (which was not written by Copernicus but by the Lutheran theologian, Andreas Osiander) used this moral, so to speak, to defend Copernicus against the accusation of apostasy that Galileo had to contend with nearly a century later during his famous trial in 1633. Here, in part, is what Osiander tells us in his introduction:

> Since the novelty of the hypotheses of this work has already been widely reported, I have no doubt that some learned men have taken serious offense because the book declares that the earth moves; these men undoubtedly believe that the long established liberal arts should not be thrown into confusion. But the author of this work has done nothing blameworthy. For it is the duty of an astronomer to record celestial motions through careful observation. Then, turning to the causes of these motions he must conceive and devise hypotheses about them, since he cannot in any way attain to the true cause.... The present author has performed both these duties excellently. For these hypotheses need not be true nor even probable; if they provide a calculus consistent with the observations, that alone is sufficient.... Now when there are offered for the same motion different hypotheses, the astronomer will accept the one which is the easiest to grasp. (quoted in Gingerich 1973: 515)

Needless to say, we ourselves do not endorse the idea that the decisive criterion for favoring one hypothesis over another should be its simple intelligibility. But note the assertion being made. A hypothesis evidently does not have to be "true" to be useful. Although this may sound a lot like an early version of what Richard Levins later wrote about the role of hypotheses in science (see Chapter 1), this defense of the heliocentric model goes well beyond what Levins has written. There is a decided difference between saying a hypothesis does not have to be true to be useful and a hypothesis is not true—Heavens, no!—but is nonetheless useful.

No wonder, therefore, Isaac Newton in 1713 made his now famous remark *Hypotheses non fingo* ("I feign no hypotheses") when he was explaining how his theory of gravity was more than a hypothesis. As the historian of science I. Bernard Cohen concluded about this controversial remark:

> Newton was willing to propose hypotheses to be tested or to be used tentatively until proved or disproved—even though they were never to be *called* hypotheses if Newton could help it. Above all, even if Newton did " frame " more than an occasional hypothesis or two to be tested by experiment, or to be used without proof *pro tempore*, he wanted to make it perfectly clear in the General Scholium of the *Principia* that he was not (to use the language of the *Opticks*) one of those "later

philosophers" who indulge in the practice of "feigning hypotheses for explaining... things." (1962: 388)

In other words, just like the old saying "the proof of the pudding is in the eating," so too, for Newton and for the four of us writing this book, a hypothesis is only useful if it leads to the analysis and evaluation of relevant and thoughtfully gathered data.

Typological Analysis

In Chapter 2, we proposed ten steps to follow when you are doing historical research (or almost any other kind of scholarly investigation). We have now reached steps eight to ten. In this chapter, we briefly review four ways to analyze information about the past to learn what may have been the contingencies leading to the patterning of history over time and space. Then, once again, we offer you an example illustrating how we ourselves do so. We begin with typological analysis.

- **Problem statement**
    1. What is the question being asked?
    2. Why is this question important?
- **Current theories**
    3. Background information
    4. What are some of the possible explanations?
- **Working model**
    5. Which do you think is the most plausible one?
    6. How can you model this particular explanation so that it can be evaluated?
- **Working hypothesis**
    7. What is your working hypothesis derived from this model, and what do you expect your data will show you given this proposition?
- **Evidence and analysis**
    8. A step-by-step description of the evidence available and the analyses done.
- **Evaluation and discussion**
    9. How does this new evidence support or refute your working hypothesis?
    10. How would additional research narrow the field of likely solutions?

Archaeologists for generations have been dividing up—classifying—what they find into different kinds, or *types*, of things and events with or without the help of modern statistics. They have also been arguing probably for just as long about how best to do *typology* (Lyman 2021). We have little to say in this book about types and typology beyond noting that just about everything Richard Levins wrote about models and model-building applies equally well to defining types and constructing typologies. We want to emphasize, however, that like models and model-building, types and typologies are more than merely useful. They are essential tools for thinking about and trying to understand—and explain—what happened in the past. We also want to repeat what every good archaeologist knows. Don't become too attached to your analytical tools.

> ❖ **type** [/tīp/ /taɪp/] *noun*: a category of people or things having common characteristics.
>
> **typology** [/tī'pälǝjē/ /taɪˈpɑlǝdʒi/] *noun*: a classification according to general type, especially in archaeology, psychology, or the social sciences.

What archaeologists have long called a "culture" is an example of this kind of data analysis. A definition of what is a *culture* found on the Internet does a good job of saying what this word means to many archaeologists:

> An archaeological culture is a recurring assemblage of types of artifacts, buildings and monuments from a specific period and region that may constitute the material culture remains of a particular past human society. The connection between these types is an empirical observation. But their interpretation in terms of ethnic or political groups is based on archaeologists' understanding and interpretation, and is in many cases subject to long unresolved debates. The concept of the archaeological culture is fundamental to culture-historical archaeology. ("Culture" 2022)

This definition makes it clear that typological analysis can be a useful way of summarizing what has been found at archaeological sites of approximately the same age in more or less the same part of the world. Yet calling something, say, "Lapita culture" (Spriggs 2011) or "Linearbandkeramische Kultur" (Gronenborn 2007) can easily take on a life of its own. Instead of simply being a handy way to recognize the apparent commonalities of things, places, and times that seem real enough to

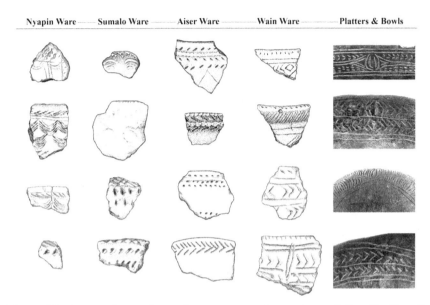

Figure 7.1. A ceramic typology—the sequence of ware types defined by Terrell and Esther Schechter for the Aitape coast of northern Papua New Guinea starting around 2,000 years ago (Nyapin Ware) (Terrell and Schechter 2007: fig. 21). © Cambridge University Press, reproduced with permission.

call for explanation, such labels are not explanations. If care is not taken, they can delude us into thinking we know more than we actually do about what, how, and why things happened in the past (see Figure 3.1).

To give an example, while most archaeologists these days recognize that "pottery types" are just useful analytical abstractions—and not what the philosopher Immanuel Kant called a *Ding an sich*, a "thing-in-itself"—there is still significant debate about how real or abstract are the various types of human beings that have long been classified as such by paleoanthropologists (Ackermann, Baiz et al. 2019; Athreya and Hopkins 2021). There continues to be, for instance, a great deal of both scientific and public fascination with the so-called Neanderthals who lived in Europe and parts of central and southwest Asia during the extremely cold and variable Middle Pleistocene period (around 130,000–30,000 years ago), and who had physical characteristics indicating they were biologically adapted for survival under such harsh living conditions (Bruner and Manzi 2006: 23).

Scientists in the nineteenth and twentieth centuries grappled with the question of whether Neanderthals were different enough from us—who, unlike them, are usually classified as "modern humans"—to be labeled as a distinct species or subspecies in the genus *Homo* (Trinkaus and Shipman 1993). Most scholars today still see them as such (and classify them as *Homo neanderthalensis*). They continue to debate how advanced or "primitive" were their cognitive abilities, lifestyles, conceptions of the world, and even whether they had a sense of humor (Wynn and Coolidge 2011).

Nowadays, however, there is new genetic and archaeological evidence suggesting that the cognitive and behavioral differences among the "ancient humans" living in different parts of Eurasia and Africa during the Pleistocene were far less clear-cut than long supposed (Green et al. 2010). There is evidence, therefore, that instead of classifying them as a different species or subspecies, the Neanderthals show us that during the Middle Pleistocene our species (*Homo sapiens*) was simply once morphologically far more diverse than we are today.

Many questions regarding their behavior and even what finally happened to them—for instance, were they completely replaced by people who looked more like all of us, or do Neanderthals still "live on" in our modern gene pool?—become less meaningful if we accept that classifying people as "Neanderthals" is just a clumsy way of talking about the genetic mosaic of our human diversity back then.

❖ Suggested Reading

>Adams, William Y., and Earnest W. Adams. 1991. Archaeological Typology and Practical Reality: A Dialectical Approach to Artifact Classification and Sorting. Cambridge: Cambridge University Press.
>
>McKern, W. C. 1939. "The Midwestern Taxonomic Method as an Aid to Archaeological Culture Study." American Antiquity 4: 301–13.
>
>O'Brien, Michael J., and R. Lee Lyman. 2003. Cladistics and Archaeology. Salt Lake City: University of Utah Press.

Statistical Analysis

The now familiar phrase "data analysis" may conjure up thoughts of rigorous statistical testing showing whether one way of explaining something of interest is more likely, or probable, than some other way. If you have studied statistics, you may also be familiar with what is called "null hypothesis significance testing," or NHST.

NHST is a way of doing statistics that was mostly the brainchild of Ronald Fisher and Karl Pearson, two British scientists who were both fervent eugenicists. They developed their now widely used statistical methods in large measure to show unmistakably that there are major racial differences within our species that education, equal opportunities, and fair treatment cannot overcome (Clayton 2020).

Central to NHST is the assumption—formally referred to as the "null hypothesis" (H_0)—that a dataset (or "sample") taken ("drawn") from a randomly varying larger "population" (or "sampling universe") should differ only randomly. Hence an observed deviation from randomness can be used to support the likelihood that the difference observed may actually be meaningful rather than simply haphazard (Box 1976; Hubbard 2004).

How meaningful? Typically, this is done by calculating a *p-value*, "which is the probability of obtaining the results in hand, assuming that the statistical null hypothesis is true in the population" (Lambdin 2012: 74). However, as Charles Lambdin has lamented: "The most common and destructive delusions are, in my opinion, that *p* values somehow tell you (a) the odds your data are due to chance, (b) the odds your research hypothesis is correct, (c) the odds your result will replicate, and (d) the odds the null is true" (2012: 74; see also Valeggia and Fernandez-Duque 2021).

❖ The proper use of a p value is to assist in deciding whether the probability is in fact 100 percent that your results are due to chance. Perhaps then the best wording for a low p value is simply to state: "Assuming my results are due to chance, my obtained mean difference is very unlikely. Therefore chance may not be the culprit. Now it is up to me to employ other methods to determine what that culprit might be."
—Charles Lambdin (2012: 75)

NHST has been adopted in many fields as the gold standard for evaluating whether a particular contingency, or variable, has explanatory power. That said, however, many researchers both today and for decades past have challenged the usefulness of NHST, arguing that deciding which p-values and significance levels to use are arbitrary rather than objective choices. Furthermore, as the admonishment "correlation does not equal causation" underscores, it is not good enough to find that there may be differences among whatever is in the samples you have "made," or drawn. No amount of significance testing can ever tell

156 • Modeling the Past

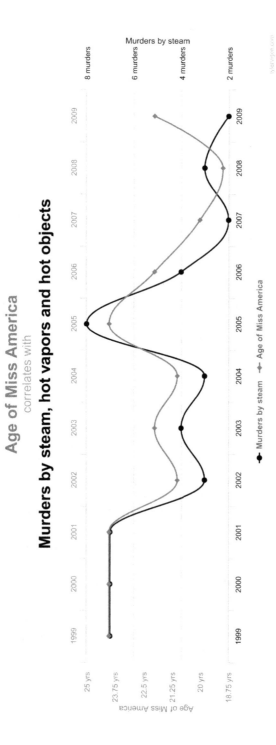

Figure 7.2. Age of Miss America and the number of murders by steam, vapors, and hot objects in the United States between 1999 and 2009. These two values are about 87 percent correlated. *Image source:* Tyler Vigen, CCBY 4.0, https://tylervigen.com/spurious-correlations.

you *why* you are seeing the differences you are uncovering in the dataset you are analyzing (Fiedler 2011).

To give an example, the age of the person each year voted as Miss America and the number of murders by steam, hot vapors, and hot objects in the United States has been said to be about 87 percent correlated between 1999 and 2009 (Figure 7.2). Even if this result looks significant, would anyone really believe there is a significant relationship among these contingencies? Most sensible people would reject such a conclusion simply because it seems ridiculous based on our general (prior) understanding of the world around us.

Do not get us wrong. Just as typological analysis can be a helpful way to sort through the evidence you have in hand, so too, statistical analysis can be a useful way to assess whether the evident similarities and differences being seen are likely to be informative enough to be worth spending more time and effort trying to make sense of what your evidence is all about. But as critics of NHST have long said loud and clear, statistics do not give anyone answers, just reasons (or not) to continue looking for answers to what, so to speak, is on the table.

Moreover, as George Bakan cautioned back in 1966, and to repeat something we have already said: "We must overcome the myth that if our treatment of our subject matter is mathematical it is therefore precise and valid. Mathematics can serve to obscure as well as reveal." Referring specifically to Bayesian statistics (see Chapter 5), he added that if anyone "reads some of the material on the Bayesian approach with the hope that thereby he will find a new basis for automatic inference," then his cautionary words have misfired, and his readers "will be disappointed" (Bakan 1966: 436).

❖ Suggested Reading

> Carlson, David L. 2017. Quantitative Methods in Archaeology Using R. Cambridge: Cambridge University Press.
> Drennan, Robert D. 2010. Statistics for Archaeologists. New York: Springer.
> Shennan, Stephen. 1997. Quantifying Archaeology. Iowa City: University of Iowa Press.

In this book, we have been advocating for using Bayesian statistics in the study of history chiefly as a way of "putting your cards on the table," that is, as a way of making it clear, first, what you see are the main contingencies that should be addressed to resolve the question you are asking, and second, how you think those contingencies bear on one another, how they "go together" (see Chapter 5 and Figure 5.5).

Social Network Analysis (SNA)

NHST generally also requires that observations (i.e., "data") be "independent" of one another—in other words, that the outcome of one observation, say of obtaining heads or tails when flipping a coin, has no influence on the next observation, that is, whether the next flip comes up heads or tails. Social network analysis (SNA) emerged as a set of methods in part due to the fact that studying social life means collecting data that are intrinsically *not* independent. In other words, the observed "state" of one individual (whether they smoke, like a particular kind of music, and so forth) is likely to be at least in part contingent on the behavior of people they regularly associate with.

In principle, therefore, it would seem that SNA should be an ideal set of theoretical propositions and methods for doing the kind of analysis we have been proposing in this book. As we have noted previously, however, there are important limitations to SNA methods that make them less suitable for answering questions about why and how things happened in history.

As elementary as the distinction may seem, one of the important differences between relational analysis in SNA and that done in dynamic relational analysis (DYRA) turns on the distinction between *position* and *location*. In SNA, the position of a social actor can be analyzed using a variety of statistical algorithms that try to capture such properties as (1) the **density** of the network under consideration, i.e., how many of the *possible* connections, ties, links, etc. there *actually* are among the nodes—the people and places—involved; (2) the **path length** between specific nodes (people, places) in a network, i.e., how many steps (links, ties, etc.) are there between them; (3) the **diameter** of the network being studied, i.e., the *shortest path* between the two *most distant* nodes in the network; and (4) the relative positional **centrality** or **marginality** of different nodes (people and places) in the network, and so on (Brughmans and Peeples 2020).

Therefore, SNA can be seen either as (a) an exploratory form of analysis for evaluating the likelihood that positionality matters, that is, where you happen to be relative to other people can help account for some of an observed outcome of interest; or (b) as an explanatory model that assumes positionality is the primary and most significant cause of what is being observed.

For example, by focusing on where different actors were located within the global financial system, SNA has been used to model and explain why the 1998 Asian financial crisis remained a localized phenomenon, but the 2007–2008 US mortgage crisis a decade later sparked a worldwide financial meltdown. Why? Apparently because many US banks and lenders had become far more centrality positioned (i.e., better connected) by the later 2000s than Asian banks had been in 1998, and their failures sparked a cascade of defaults and other problems on a global scale rather than a regional one (Oatley et al. 2013). To offer yet other examples, SNA has been used to analyze power grid failures (Buldyrev et al. 2010), disease propagation (Jolly et al. 2001), and the structure of scientific collaborations (Newman 2001).

As discussed in Chapter 1, archaeologists, too, have used SNA to study the patterning of archaeological finds to see if they can use such material evidence to pin down the social and economic links between people and places in the past. For instance, Golitko and Feinman (2015; see Figure 7.3) have used SNA as a means of visualizing and modeling the distribution of obsidian (volcanic glass) at ancient sites in Mesoamerica on the assumption that the presence of obsidian from similar geological sources may indicate that there used to be significant social and economic ties between these settlement locations in the past. They argue that changes in how well-positioned different settlements were back then might account in part for why some ancient Mesoamerican cities flourished while others declined in size and were finally abandoned. Other archaeologists have similarly used the geographic distribution of ceramic styles to infer ties between communities, arguing that the evident patterning of such ties may reflect past ethnic and/or political organization (e.g., Hart and Engelbrecht 2012; Mills et al. 2013).

❖ Suggested Reading

> Borgatti, Stephen P., Martin G. Everett, and Jeffrey C. Johnson. 2018. Analyzing Social Networks, 2nd ed. London: Sage Publications.
>
> Knappett, Carl. 2011. An Archaeology of Interaction: Network Perspectives on Material Culture and Society. Oxford: Oxford University Press.
>
> Menczer, Filippo, Santo Fortunato, and Clayton A. Davis. 2020. A First Course in Network Science. Cambridge: Cambridge University Press.

160 • Modeling the Past

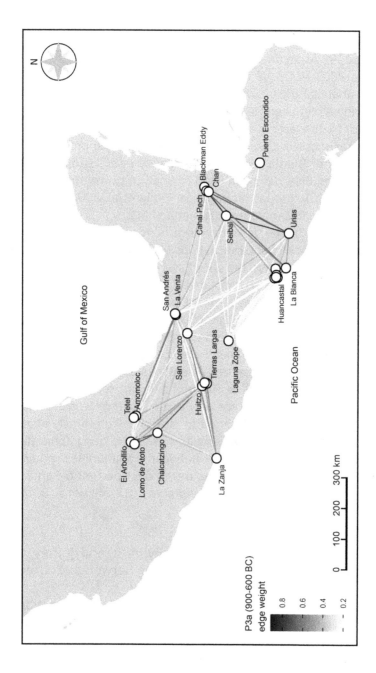

Figure 7.3. Settlements in Mesoamerica dated to between around 900–600 BC linked into a network based on presence of shared obsidian from different regional volcanic sources. The presence and weight (darkness) of ties are arguably proportional to the existence and intensity of likely economic and social engagement between these different locations. See Golitko and Feinman (2015) for more details. © Mark L. Golitko.

Dynamic Relational Analysis (DYRA)

The three kinds of analysis we have just briefly surveyed are grounded on the categorical assumption that things exist first of all on their own and may later become "tied together" in one way or another. This is so even for SNA which is usually seen as a type of relational analysis. Yes, in SNA it is the relative positioning of the nodes said to be in the network under study that is a prime interest, but therein lies the revealing qualification: "in the network under study." As we have said before, networks in SNA are generally treated as if they are "things" (e.g., "whole networks") made out of "things" (nodes) that have properties that are dependent on where any given node "in the network" happens to be "within the network."

In DYRA, on the other hand (as we have been saying repeatedly), relational analysis begins with a different basic, or core, assumption about the world and how it works. It is assumed that things and events have the character they have (or had) not just because of *what* they are, but also *how* and *why* they are interrelated. From this perspective, what is needed to analyze and try to understand what has happened in the past are the sorts of information—*situational, circumstantial*, and *consequential* data—that we have summarized in this book as Proposition 1.2:

$$P(X_t + Y) \longrightarrow X_{t+1}$$

Experience has taught us, however, that distinguishing among these three uses—note that we did *not* say "kinds"—of information is not always easy to do. Why not? Because these are not really *types* of information at all. For instance, what is a consequential contingency at one point in time (i.e., the outcome of an event) can later be a situational or circumstantial contingency. Since this may sound confusing, here is an example of what we mean when we say this can be so.

Example: Language, Material Culture, and Society

Problem Statement

Today the island nation of Papua New Guinea (PNG) is home to more than nine million people who are estimated to speak something like 850–1,000 different languages. Some of these languages have been classified by linguists as belonging to major language families—for instance, the Austronesian, Trans New Guinea, and Sepik language families. Other languages in PNG, however, are spoken by only a handful of small communities (Novotny and Drozd 2000). Some are spoken in only one or two (Foley 2000).

Some linguists say that PNG is the most *linguistically diverse place* on earth, although there are those who say this is not true and other places, too, are at least as diverse, if not more so—the huge continent of Africa being favored by some. Much depends on how you answer the question "What is a language?" and on how you go about counting them.

Regardless of whether you favor New Guinea or Africa, say, as the most linguistically diverse place on earth, why are so many languages spoken in PNG? What is the most likely historical explanation for such remarkable linguistic diversity?

These are not irrelevant questions. As we have previously said, social scientists (and other human beings, too) have long been taking it more or less for granted that distinct and enduring "groups," "ethnic groups," "populations," "races," and the like actually exist in the real world, and therefore, they can be used as the basic "units of analysis" in social, political, and economic research. It has long also been conventional wisdom that "different people speak different languages," and therefore, if you can unravel language history around the world, it should be possible to go a long way down the road toward understanding the history of the people speaking different languages. But is this true? Are language classifications used to map ethnic groups and their particular ways (and material things) historically realistic and reliable?

For generations, archaeologists have been analyzing and writing about what they have been finding using collective (and decidedly categorical) units of analysis variously labeled as *cultures, horizons*, and so forth (Gramsch 2015) on the assumption that such entities can be used to identify and map the many diverse ways that people have done things in the past—for instance, who they traded or married with, or how they organized themselves politically (Anthony 2007; Renfrew 1987).

However conventional and widely used such units of analysis have been in archaeology, nonetheless it has also long been commonplace to remind students that "pots aren't people." In other words, it is not a foregone conclusion that archaeological units of analysis defined using artifacts and other kinds of material traits can be used successfully to map the biological and social realities of people in the past. Is there any reason, therefore, to expect linguistic units of analysis to a better job of mapping history and social life?

Theory	situational contingencies (X_i)	circumstantial contingencies (Y)	consequential contingencies (X_{i+1})
natural state	climate and geography (geographic & spatial distance)	sorcery, warfare, and language (linguistic distance)	~ 850 languages
social use	climate and geography (geographic & spatial distance)	many reasons for engagement (social network distance)	~ 850 languages

Figure 7.4. Two possible ways of explaining language diversity in New Guinea, each of which highlights differently the contingencies which may have been involved. Lacking sufficient information about the frequency and impact of sorcery and warfare, the first theory uses the *linguistic distance* among communities as the key variable on the popular assumption that not speaking the same language isolates people from one another. In the second, the focus instead is on *social network distance* as a way of estimating how likely people are to be engaged with one another.

Current Theories

1. **"Natural state" theory** (Figure 7.4)—There are so many languages in Papua New Guinea because people there have not had the opportunity, need, or motivation to be in touch with people outside their own home community.

Elliot Sober (1980) has argued that one of the most enduring ideas in Western thought is the distinction commonly made between things that are "wild" and those that are tamed, cultivated, and under our control. He has noted, for example, that a key idea behind Aristotle's worldview is one that he refers to as Aristotle's natural state model. "Aristotle's hypothesis was that there is a distinction between the *natural state* of a kind of object and those states which are not natural. These latter are produced by subjecting the object to an *interfering force* . . . which prevent[s] them from achieving their natural state by frustrating their natural tendency" (1980: 360).

This was one of the prime assumptions of philosophical thought during the Enlightenment, the Age of Reason, in the seventeenth and eighteenth centuries (Batz 1974). Scholars then often took as their starting point a question that had been every bit as popular in ancient Greece and Rome: *What had life been like at the beginning of time when all of us were living in a "state of nature" prior to the development of such everyday civil institutions as marriage, property, the sovereign state, and the right of the few to rule over the many?*

What can be seen as a natural state theory of language and language history is often invoked to explain why this part of the Pacific has so many languages. Some of the key assumptions of this kind of explanation are these:

1. It is assumed that people living in the same place at the same time will all speak the same language.
2. When people leave and resettle elsewhere, they inevitably lose contact with those who remain back in their old home village.
3. With the passing of time, things inevitably change as people adjust to the environmental challenges and opportunities of where they are now living, and as they develop both new ways of doing things and new ways of speaking.
4. It is only natural, therefore, that social and geographic isolation may ultimately lead to diversity in language and material culture alike, such as that seen today in New Guinea.

Given such assumptions, explaining why something like 850 or more different languages (X_{t+1}) are spoken in PNG seems easily done. The historical explanation for such remarkable diversity often advanced in the popular press and frequently also in academic studies is not only the *situational argument* (X_t) that people there speak in so many different ways because New Guinea's challenging environment and rugged landscape combine to naturally isolate communities from one another. People there also rarely need to go beyond their own residential community because most of their needs can be met right at home. Furthermore, it is often assumed, as well, that there are *circumstantial contingencies* (Y) favoring social isolation: (a) sorcery and warfare have been endemic in many places in this part of the world, and (b) perhaps tautologically, the fact that people speak so many languages means language differences, too, have isolated communities from one another (Terrell 2001b).

2. **Social use theory** (Figure 7.4)—People do not need to speak the same language to be understood by and deal with one another. Just as there can be many reasons for engagement, so too, the outcomes of such involvement can be many and diverse.

Photos, GIFs, videos, cartoons, and the like on social media today are obvious proof that verbal communication—spoken or written—is not the only tool we all have available for social engagement and collective involvement. While no one doubts that any kind of miscommunication can lead to trouble, even disaster, it is not far-fetched to say that language diversity in a place like Papua New Guinea today is best seen—until it can actually be shown to be otherwise—as an epiphenomenon, a side effect, of how people there have been living their lives.

If so, then language diversity may perhaps be a phenomenon worth explaining, but not necessarily a reliable guide to human history. Contrary to what is often assumed (Gray, Bryant, and Greenhill 2010), it makes sense to ask instead (a) how do people in New Guinea communicate with other people when they do *not* speak the same language, and (b) has *not* being able to speak the same language had much of an impact on the lives of people there?

> ❖ **epiphenomenon** [-ˈnämənə] *noun, pl* epiphenomena: a secondary effect or byproduct that arises from but does not causally influence a process.

Working Model

It has been conventional wisdom that New Guinea was first settled long ago by different groups of people speaking different languages and making different kinds of things. In other words, some of the diversity evident in language and material culture on this island today and in the recent past should be credited to—apportioned to—primal differences in *ancestry*. However, it has also long been conventional to say that once people began moving out widely across this huge island seeking new places to live, they began to differ from one another both linguistically and in their ways of life. Why? Perhaps the most obvious explanation—*isolation*—may be at least partly true. Those who went away may have both lost touch with people back home where they had come from, and may have ended up in places where they were also isolated from other places. However, people moving to new places may also quickly become influenced by the new people they encounter, and their ways of doing things. Alternatively, people who move far away from their original homes sometimes do just the opposite—they stubbornly hold on to old ways of doing things, even as people from "back home" have moved on to new ideas and practices.

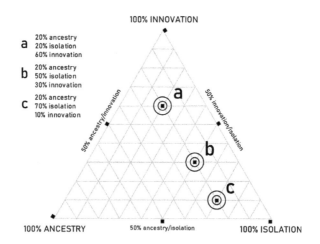

Figure 7.5. Apportionment of variation. How similar or different people and their ways of life happen to be in different (hypothetical) places on New Guinea labeled a, b, and c might be explained in three complementary ways: (1) how different their ancestors were (here ancestry as a contingency has been held constant at 20 percent in all three cases); (2) how isolated they have been from one another; (3) how innovative they have been in handling the challenges and opportunities of life in this part of the world. © John Edward Terrell.

It seems unlikely, therefore, that the diversity of New Guinea's languages can be explained by a single cause, variable, or contingency, or that the degree to which these contingencies are involved will always be constant across space and time (see Figure 7.5, for instance). Yet as Richard Levins advocated (see Chapter 1), it makes sense to start with one or two possibly casual contingencies to see how far we can get in the direction not only of a plausible, but perhaps even a robust explanation.

Working Hypothesis

Hypothesis 1—Given the first theory, variation in language and material culture in New Guinea is likely to be strongly correlated because of the inherently divergent local histories of people living in isolated communities.

Hypothesis 2—Given the second theory, variation in language and material culture may be strongly correlated in some places and at some times, but the correlations are more likely to be weak and contingent

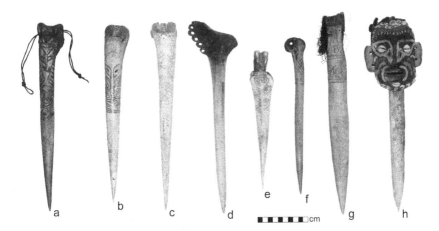

Figure 7.6. A selection of New Guinean bone daggers, showing a range of technological and stylistic possibilities. Each is grouped into a different "type" in our analysis. (a) Type 1: Juo, 1890s (© The Field Museum, Image No. CL0000_37842_Front_XMP2, Cat. No. 37842, photographer Sarah Rivers); (b) Type 2: Wewak, 1908 (© The Field Museum, Image No. CL0000_105422_Front_XMP2, Cat. No. 105422, photographer Sarah Rivers); (c) Type 3: Wewak, 1909 (© The Field Museum, Image No. CL0000_144772_Front_XMP2, Cat. No. 144772, photographer Sarah Rivers); (d) Type 4: Maipua, 1909 (© The Field Museum, Image No. CL0000_142484_Front_XMP2, Cat. No. 142484, photographer Sarah Rivers); (e) Type 16: Sissano, 1909 (© The Field Museum, Image No.CL0000_144974_Front_XMP2, Cat. No. 144974, photographer Sarah Rivers); (f) Type 17: Tarawai Island, 1908 (© The Field Museum, Image No. CL0000_148684_Front_XMP2, Cat. No. 148684, photographer Christopher Philipp); (g) Type 18: Tarawai Island, 1908 (© The Field Museum, Image No. CL0000_148524_Front_XMP2, Cat. No. 148524, photographer Christopher Philipp); (h) Type 20: Tambanum, 1976 (© The Field Museum, Image No. CL0000_278940_Front_XMP2, Cat. No. 278940, photographer Christopher Philipp).

on circumstances such as how people are actually engaged with one another socially, their particular circumstances (e.g., how mobile they are, what environments they live in, and vagaries of their particular histories), and so forth.

Evidence

Language—There is scholarly disagreement about how best to describe and classify language similarities and differences in New Guinea.[1] Linguists, however, commonly convert the patterning of such diversity into branching "trees" supposedly mapping the apparent divergence over time and space of a set of languages judged by linguists to all be "historically related." Whether such "family tree" models adequately portray the history of the people speaking (or who spoke) the languages included is debatable (Alter 1999; Bloomfield 1935: 310–20). However, such a mapping of linguistic diversity from place to place in New Guinea can be used as a working model of such variation.

Material culture—People on the island of New Guinea have long made and used many different kinds of things—for instance, pottery, stone tools, woven baskets, painted shields, net bags, bow and arrows, ritual paraphernalia, and so forth. Some of these things are (or used to be) made and used only in a few local communities; others are or were widely distributed across the island. In principle, one could choose to study any (or all) of these things (e.g., Welsch, Terrell, and Nadolski 1992), but for the present case study, we have chosen to consider only bone daggers (Figure 7.6) made from either the leg bones of cassowaries (large flightless birds related to African ostriches, South American rheas, and the emus of Australia), or human femora.

Although these daggers were being widely made on this island during the late nineteenth and early twentieth centuries, they are largely absent in the archaeological record. Many of them ended up in museum collections around the world as "ethnographic artifacts" (Newton 1989). The 827 daggers included in the analysis we are describing here came from 152 local communities spread across New Guinea where people speak languages of considerable variation and historical relatedness.

For analytical purposes, we have coded the stylistic variation displayed by these daggers (their stylistic "attributes") in several ways to document: (a) how these leg bones were modified to produce a pointed dagger-like end; (b) what decorative materials (feathers, beads, seeds, and so forth) were added to them; (c) whether and where designs were carved on them; and (d) what these designs seem to represent (geometric patterns, depictions of people or animals, and so forth).

Social networks—In addition to these bone daggers, the research being summarized in this chapter has also made use of what is known historically about how people on this island were engaged with one another socially when these daggers were manufactured. Why? Because New Guinea is anthropologically famous not just for its astonishing language diversity but also for the extent to which people there have been linked with one another in often quite elaborate relationships of exchange, friendship, marriage, and enmity (Golitko 2020). By combing through the available ethnographic literature, it has been possible to construct social network models of how people in different communities on the island historically have been dealing with one another over time and space.

Summary—Figure 7.7 summarizes the information gathered for this analysis of 1720 different local communities (including all 152 from which we have sampled daggers) across the island during the period 1890 and 1960. The ties (edges) shown linking these communities are those recorded for any type of reported social contact between these places other than hostile encounters. Technically the resulting network model shown in this figure is what in SNA analysis is referred to as "undirected" and "binary"—the links do not specify how frequently people from one community may have visited another community, how long they spent there, or what activities they engaged in once there.

Analysis

How can these several lines of information be analyzed to evaluate the relative plausibility of the two hypotheses under consideration? One way would be to use a typological approach—we could group our total sample of bone daggers into different types (akin to ceramic types traditionally used in archaeological cultural typologies), and then determine statistically how many of these dagger types are shared between the different communities included in the analysis. Such an approach assumes, however, that particular kinds of daggers exist, that people saw them as such, and then manufactured daggers in keeping with them.

In some known cases, this actually seems to be what people in this part of the world, as elsewhere, do. They may even buy whole "packages" of things, costumes, rituals, dances, and the like associated with particular kinds of ceremonial performances (e.g., Dobrin and Bashkow 2006; Roscoe 1989). Archaeologists typically use a metric called the Brainerd-Robinson coefficient to assess whether the "artifactual assemblages" found at different ancient sites are similar enough to label them as all as "belonging to" the same shared "cultural tradition" or type (see, for instance, Mills et al. 2013). This metric ranges between 0 (no shared types) and 200 (identical type frequencies). Using this coefficient, we have grouped the daggers included in this study into twenty-seven such types that reflect differences in technology and style (see Figure 7.6), although we do not know if the people who made them would recognize these types as more or less the same as the ones they may have actually had in mind.

Alternatively, we could instead quantify how similar or different are the particular characteristics, or attributes, of each of the daggers in our

170 • Modeling the Past

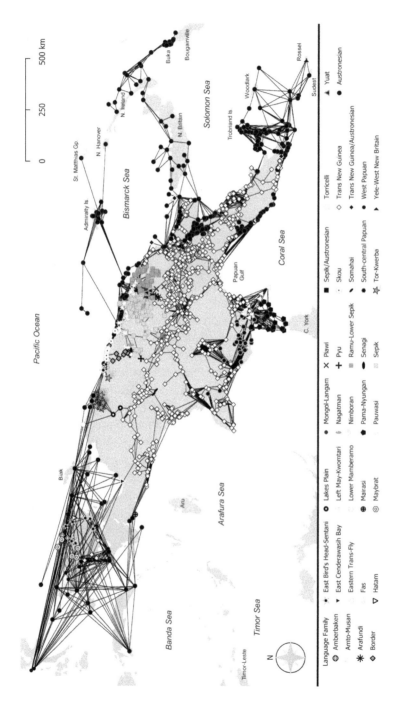

Figure 7.7. A social network model of 1,720 communities on and around the island of New Guinea during the period between 1880 and 1960 based on ethnographic sources, with language classification indicated (author's unpublished data). © Mark L. Golitko.

total sample. Such a detailed "attribute level" approach might be more appropriate if those making these daggers were given to "mixing and matching" the traits of the daggers they were creating. To make sense of such detailed information about each dagger, we could use a measure of similarity called the Jaccard index. After pairing each community in our sample with every other one in a 2×2 data table, this index uses only the number of attributes evidenced for one or both in each pair (i.e., shared absences are ignored) to calculate their "distance" apart from one another. This computed distance metric ranges from 1 (no shared attributes) to 0 (all attributes used on daggers in one community are present, as well, in the other).

Such analytical strategies may work well for studying material culture assemblages, but what about language? Assessing how similar or different the languages spoken are in any given pair of communities in the world is an immensely difficult task. Nonetheless, we could consider how extensively vocabulary words are shared between any given pair of communities in our study. Many historical linguists, however, argue that such an approach masks the true tree-like structure of language relatedness. Why? Because words can be too easily "shared" between people who actually speak historically unrelated languages.

Given that the first of our two models, however, assumes that language and material culture are likely to be strongly correlated due to how isolated communities have historically been on New Guinea, we used how historical linguists have categorized the "relatedness" of the many different languages that are (or were) spoken in the communities in our sample to calculate a "language distance" metric ranging from zero (people in that given pair of communities on our 2×2 table evidently spoke the same dialect of the same language) to 19 (linguists have decided there is no evident historical relationship between the languages being spoken in those two communities).

Finally, we needed a way of calculating how likely people residing in any two communities may have been in touch with one another and could have shared ideas, information, and social practices. One way to do this is to count the number of network edges that link the shortest routes between these many communities—a measure called *network distance*. However, realizing that real world geography still matters, we have elected to take into account also how long it might take to get from one place to another. We have weighted the calculated network distances by the actual geographic distance represented by each such network link to create a composite measure of *social/geographic distance*.

Additionally, we have also parsed our data by time—in this analysis, we have divided the daggers in our sample into those dating to between about 1880–1940, and those produced between 1945–2002 (few daggers were collected between 1940–45 during World War II)—to see if the changes that occurred on New Guinea during the twentieth century (including shifts in governance, population growth, integration into the global economy, and changes in transportation technologies, among many other historical contingencies) may have changed the relationship between language and material cultural variability.

There are of course other ways we could measure distance, language relatedness, or material similarity, and there are also other contingencies we could add to our analysis. In effect, each one of these ways of comparing our three lines of evidence could be considered a separate model with different built-in social, historical, and ecological contingencies that can be formally tested using a variety of network and other methods of analysis. No single test is likely to tell us everything we want to know, but by trying a variety of tests, we wanted to see how congruent—how consilient (see Chapter 6)—the results turn out to be so that we could assess whichever contingencies specified in the two hypotheses being discussed might have played a discernible role in patterning language and dagger variability.

Evaluation

While we have advocated in this book for a broad framework for analyzing contingencies between different lines of evidence, there are times and places where the formal mathematics of NHST or Bayesian analysis can come in handy when evaluating how seriously to take a particular result, or how heavily we should focus on a particular set of contingencies. We could, for example, calculate how strong are the correlations—ranging between 0 (no association or influence) and 1 (complete association)—among the contingencies under consideration to evaluate which, if any, of these correlations might be significant enough to warrant further study.

When we did this, we found that all three of our contingencies are associated with one another to some degree (Figure 7.8). Thus, both language and dagger variability are associated with social/geographic distance and with each other.

What this finding suggests is that variation of both kinds—in language and material culture—shows us the kind of patterning that statisticians and ecologists alike refer to as *spatial autocorrelation*. In this

	Typology		Attributes	
Analysis	1880-1940	1945-2002	1880-1940	1945-2002
net|language	**0.34** (p=0.001)	**0.37** (p=0.001)	**0.70** (p=0.0001)	**0.38** (p=0.0002)
language|net	0.07 (p=0.06)	**0.32** (p=0.001)	0.06 (p=0.17)	0.05 (p=0.37)

Figure 7.8. Results of Partial Mantel tests examining the degree of correlation between social/geographic distance (**net**, geographically weighted network distance), and language distance (**lang**), i.e., how similar or different any given two languages are among the communities for which daggers were sampled for this study. Tests were run using (a) dagger types, (b) the frequencies of the attributes exhibited by these types, and (c) when these daggers were made (Period 1: 1880–1940; Period 2: 1945–2002). The contingency listed first in each case (e.g., **net**) is the one being compared to dagger similarity, the second listed is the contingency that was held constant (e.g., language as in **net**|language). Tests with p-values below 0.05 (the value most commonly accepted as "significant" in studies employing an NHST framework) are indicated in bold and shaded. © Mark L. Golitko.

case, saying this means we need to keep in mind that how closely language diversity and material culture diversity are patterned in space and time may simply be alternative statistical ways of "saying" the same thing: people on this island who live nearer to one another are both more likely than not to make similar things *and* speak similar languages.

One way to explore statistically how robust this confounding explanation may be is to use the type of correlation analysis called the Partial Mantel test (Legendre, Fortin, and Borcard 2015) which is a way of estimating the degree of correlation between how variation is patterned in two sets of data (e.g., language and daggers) while controlling for the effect of a third source of variation (here, social/geographic distance). Figure 7.8 presents the results of running this test using our information on these three dimensions of observable variation both for types of daggers and for their specific attributes over the course of time.

What do these calculations suggest? For the earlier daggers in our sample, it looks like after controlling for language, up to ~70 percent of the attribute variability in these daggers could be accounted for by social/geographic distance, that is, how readily people back then were able to engage with one another. However, the association between attribute variability and social/geographic distance is less evident for daggers produced after World War II. While language still shows an association with attribute variation, we cannot rule out the possibility that if we had a different or larger sample of daggers, we might find that this association has gone away (i.e, the p-values would be above the selected cut-off value of 0.05).

Now if we assume instead that daggers are whole "packages" of stylistic and technological choices that can be classified into different types, the association with network distance and with social/geographic distance drops considerably, while language now appears to associate with the typological variation of the daggers in ways that are less likely to be simply a matter of chance (i.e., p-values are below 0.05). Even so, language tends to associate far less strongly with dagger production in the pre-World War II period than the period after, when language and social engagement are about equally associated with how people choose to make and decorate bone daggers.

Discussion

It would be all too easy to use these results to suggest that social engagement "causes" daggers to be more similar to one another between different communities, that people living on New Guinea freely mixed and matched the different attributes of their daggers, and that when considered this way, language has little or no influence on material culture. Alternatively, we might read our results as suggesting that daggers were conceptualized as "packages" of related technologies and motifs, and that as a result, we can demonstrate that social engagement and language both contribute to how similar or dissimilar daggers made in any two communities might be. Or, we could read these results as suggesting that how people conceptualized dagger production changed somehow during the course of the twentieth century in ways that made language a more meaningful correlate of how people manufactured these particular objects. For instance, we might hypothesize that the growth of the foreign art and tourist market after World War II made certain types of daggers more likely to sell and so those making them started to standardize their products to look more like those made by other people on the island, perhaps especially by those who also happened to speak in similar ways.

Our analysis suggests, however, that the contingencies influencing the manufacture of these items of material may have shifted over time,

Analyzing Data • 175

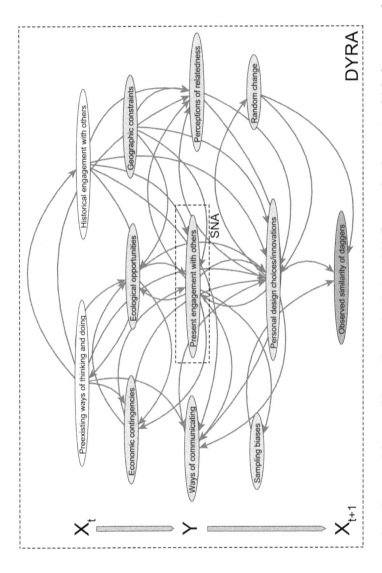

Figure 7.9. A mapping of some of the possible contingencies that could influence the degree to which daggers made in any two communities on New Guinea are similar to one another. If each line on this graph represents a possible historical contingency, then the analysis of dagger variability we present here has only weighed the strength of a handful of possible consequential contingencies. © Mark L. Golitko.

and hence we cannot simply assume that language has changed along with material culture variability over time in any straightforward or uniform way.

In any case, we think the results of this analysis can be used to caution against overly simple explanations. After all, we have only considered some of this island's many communities, and we have focused on only one of the many different kinds of things that people on New Guinea made in the late nineteenth and early twentieth centuries. Furthermore, there may well be other reasons for the statistical associations we have found in the data we gathered and analyzed for this study.

For example, we have only loosely addressed the situational contingencies of life before ca. 1880, when the oldest daggers in our sample were produced, which nonetheless are likely to have constrained what happened subsequently. People further back in the past may have engaged with each other differently, lived in different places, or even spoken differently. Additionally, even when someone is exposed to new ideas about how to make and decorate daggers, there is no guarantee that they will adopt these new ideas. And doing so may depend on how congruent a new idea or motif is with previous sets of symbolism and their associations (e.g., Roscoe 1989). While by no means exhaustive, Figure 7.9 presents an attempt to depict more broadly some of the contingent factors that might be included in subsequent models and analyses.

Chapter Summary

Models, as we have noted, are "useful" lies that give direction to data collection and evaluation. At best, we can gather information and evaluate patterning in our data in ways that make some hypotheses and their associated models and assumptions relatively unlikely to account for what we have observed and how things got to be that way. However, data collection and analysis will likely lead to a new set of questions, other hypotheses, and perhaps other models after we have ruled out those that have been found to be implausible. There is no single "correct" method for uncovering the set of contingencies that actually contributed to what happened in the past, and why things are the way they are now. However, a variety of methods exist that can help to evaluate particular statements about the past, and help us to decide which models and hypotheses are more or less plausible and consequential.

Key Points

1. We have presented several variant ways to analyze data to evaluate the plausibility of different historical models, including typology, frequentist statistics (Null Hypothesis Significance Testing), and positional analysis (Social Network Analysis). These approaches are valuable tools for testing how well what we have observed fits our hypotheses and models.
2. None of these approaches intrinsically tells you how or why something happened in the past. They are tools for evaluating how seriously to take a hypothesis or model in light of the data available.
3. It is always wise to remember that any given set of theories, models, and hypotheses will leave much unexplained. Therefore, the aim of research should be a better idea of what else needs to be investigated to have a more confident sense of what may have happened in the past.

Note

1. See, for instance: https://ethnologue.org/ and https://glottolog.org/.

CONCLUSION
So What?

Research is formalized curiosity. It is poking and prying with a purpose. It is a seeking that he who wishes may know the cosmic secrets of the world and they that dwell therein.

—Zora Neale Hurston,
Dust Tracks on a Road (1942)

Native tribes in New England today are a twenty-first century population with dynamic, modern cultures and exciting futures that in many ways will directly connect to a distant past. But in many ways they will morph into new cultural practices as native people, like all others, transform along the continuum that has defined all of humanity since deep time. The sooner archaeologists (and others) can see through the line that divides prehistory and history and recognize that this continuum is part of Native American history, too, the further our science will be.

—D. Rae Gould,
"Cultural Practice and Authenticity" (2013)

Although archaeology is a relatively new concept to the indigenous population of Vanuatu, recognition of the importance of this field and its contribution to the country's cultural heritage is slowly gaining momentum. The discovery of the Lapita cemetery at Teouma in 2004 and other findings from subsequent research projects have helped to shed light on the origins of the first settlers of Vanuatu and on the Pacific's history in general. Being a ni-Vanuatu archaeologist has helped me flesh out the stories that are told over the fire across the archipelago regarding our origins and our heritage.

—Edson Willie,
"A Melanesian View of Archaeology in Vanuatu" (2019)

- The Living Past
- How History Matters
- Historical Justification
- Historical Explanation
- Historical Foresight
- Historical Insight

Years ago, the science writer and anthropologist Misia Landau observed that writing about history is an act of communication that easily lends itself to storytelling since any set of events that can be arranged in a sequence can be told as a story (Landau 1984). Although most scientists may be keenly aware of how theories influence what they do, she felt they are generally less aware of how often scientific theories are basically narratives, however disguised they may be by the formalities of most scientific writing and publication. Perhaps chemists and physicists may not be as predisposed to use storytelling to report their findings and ideas, but certainly archaeologists, historians, and other social scientists have hardly been loath to do so. Indeed, nowadays some archaeologists are writing with approval about how the kind of knowledge they specialize in creating is a skillful, nuanced, and challenging form of literary production (Lucas 2018; see Chapter 6, this volume).

There is no use denying, therefore, that telling good stories can be a great way to communicate not just with the general public but also with our own immediate research colleagues. No doubt about it, what we have been calling theories and models of history can often be expressed as stories of one sort or another. Moreover, such stories can also be a genuinely creative and often extremely useful way to piece together new ideas and hypotheses (Terrell 1990).

In this book, however, we have endorsed a more formal way of putting ideas and information together in the quest for historical understanding. Although it is popular nowadays to equate scientific model building with mathematics and numerical analysis, we have advocated for an open modeling strategy that does not privilege any particular form of hypothesis development and data analysis. What we have emphasized is the value of using relational thinking and model building as a way of being honest about what is uncertain and perhaps still largely unknown about the past.

What we have not as yet said much about is why doing archaeology and writing about history are worthwhile. What are some of the reasons for doing archaeology? What are the rewards of taking history seriously—which after all is something that more than a few would say is just about "stuff" that is over and done with, and about people whose time has come and gone? So why bother with the past?

The Living Past

Cynics and misanthropes contemplating the human condition may willingly endorse the claim made by the French writer Jean-Baptiste Alphonse Karr in 1849 that *plus ça change, plus c'est la même chose* ("the more things change, the more they stay the same"). History shows us clearly enough, however, that change happens. Yet it is also true that "starting all over again from scratch" is not the way the world works (Monod 1971: 154). Instead, the past continues to play an active and ever-present role in our lives through our laws and social conventions, the physical and environmental legacies of our previous acts and decisions, our genetically inherited biological characteristics, our acquired habits both good and bad, our memories, regrets, and feelings of guilt, and yes, even in our efforts to blame others for our own mistakes.

As we have been saying repeatedly in this book, knowing not just what happened in history but also how and why can shape how we see ourselves, how we understand others, and what we think it means to be human. In this last chapter, therefore, we want to explore with you what we see are three prominent ways in which knowing what happened in the past is much more than just an entertaining way of passing the time and having something to do—in other words, *so what*?

How History Matters

Figure 8.1 is our somewhat fanciful way of illustrating—and thereby, we hope, anchoring in your mind's eye—these three ways in which history matters and must be taken seriously. The left-hand panel is our version of the famous optical illusion called the Rubin's vase ambiguous face. This rendering of that illusion deliberately asks you to see not only a central shape resembling a black vase, but also two mirror images of Charles Darwin's face in profile. As such, this particular rendering is far from a perfect illusion—it is likely your eyes may pay more attention to Darwin looking at himself than to the central vase—but we have opted to draw the illusion this way to demonstrate the point we want to make.

Conclusion • **181**

Figure 8.1. (a) Charles Darwin's face in profile is used here to evoke the optical illusion known as a "Rubin's vase ambiguous face" (Eagleman 2001) to show how looking at the past solely from our own point of view may create the illusion we are seeing more about how things used to be than we actually are (Julia Margaret Cameron, public domain, via Wikimedia Commons, https://commons.wikimedia.org/wiki/File:Charles_Darwin_by_Julia_Margaret_Cameron_2.jpg); (b) another famous optical illusion, this one drawn by William E. Hill in 1915, depicting two faces in profile—one is the left profile of a young woman, the other an older woman—showing how different initial impressions can lead to strikingly different observations (W. E. Hill, public domain, via Wikimedia Commons, https://www.loc.gov/resource/cph.3b45252/ and also https://en.wikipedia.org/wiki/My_Wife_and_My_Mother-in-Law); (c) Medieval sculpture of Janus, the Roman deity with two faces who was the god of gates, doorways, transitions, beginnings, and endings, and who is used here to show how the study of history is not only about the past but also the future (Nicola Quirico, CC BY-SA 4.0, via Wikimedia Commons, https://commons.wikimedia.org/wiki/File:Maestro_dei_Mesi,_Ianus_-_January,_detail,_Museo_della_Cattedrale.jpg). Composite figure: © John Edward Terrell.

It is far too easy for us all to see the past as simply mirroring and thereby reinforcing our own experiences, our own opinions, our own way of seeing things.

Belittling history this way keeps us from learning anything new from history about how the world works. Even more pernicious, this way of seeing the past can be used to justify and codify our own ideas, our own beliefs, our own convictions unjustly and at times harmfully. We explore this theme more fully in the next section, "Historical Justification."

The central panel in Figure 8.1 is a copy of the equally famous optical illusion called "My Wife and my Mother-in-Law" also known as the "Young Girl–Old Woman Illusion." This fanciful illusion graphically depicts how the past can look different depending on your point of view, and—in the context of this book—why it is so important to model the past in multiple ways as advocated by the biologist Richard Levins. We discuss this theme in the section that follows titled "Historical Explanation."

Finally, the third panel, the one on the right, depicts the Roman god Janus, the god of gates, doorways, and transitions. In the next to last section of this final chapter, "Historical Foresight," we offer you some of the reasons we are convinced the study of history can help all of us face and confront what lies ahead for all of us.

Historical Justification

Despite the popular sentiment that history is just about things, people, and events that are over and done with, it is common knowledge that the past is often invoked to justify what people are doing, or want to do, in the here and now or down the road. Three examples should suffice to confirm how often the past is not merely prologue—as William Shakespeare told us in *The Tempest*—but is widely used by those who are currently among the living to argue for or against all sorts of aims and activities however humdrum, practical, or grandiose.

1. **Repatriation.** On 16 November 2021, a delegation of officials from the Muscogee (Creek) Nation met with University of Alabama administrators to press for the return of nearly six thousand remains and artifacts from Moundville Archaeological Park. "We were forced to cede our treaty lands, but we never ceded our rights to our intellectual property or the remains we left behind," said RaeLynn Butler for the Muscogee Nation. "At this point, our patience has been taken advantage of." As reported on the web by a local media outlet: "The remains found at Moundville predate some of the modern tribes that have claimed them, complicating the process of repatriation." Although forced out of Alabama in the 1830s and now headquartered in Oklahoma, "the tribe still has deep ties to an area near Wetumpka known as Hickory Ground, a political and spiritual center before the tribe's removal." Muscogee Principal Chief David Hill is reported to have said: "We don't want to be a dog and pony show. Why do they need all these items in the museum? It's never too late to do the right thing. That's all we want. Just return them back" ("Repatriation" 2021).

2. **Decolonization**. Although the word *decolonization* may be favored today as the right way to say it, there is now wide recognition that the history of European global adventurism, subjugation, exploitation, and often genocide since 1492 has left an indelible scar on the social fabric, well-being, and prosperity of millions around the world ("Decolonization" 2020). As the archaeologist Stephen Acabado at the University of California in Los Angeles has written:

   > Philippine history textbooks and history curricula reflect the glaring absence of Indigenous Philippines in our historical narratives. Perhaps, it is part of the response to the need to define what is Filipino. However, it neglects the dynamic ways in which Indigenous groups responded to the pressures of colonization. Most importantly, the Philippines may have gained its political independence, but the colonial experiences of Indigenous Filipinos endure. (Acabado 2021)

   As an example of how pervasive the colonial legacy still is in his homeland, he points to the myth-like status of the "waves of migration" theories learned by students in the Philippine elementary and high school educational systems (see Chapter 2). As an archaeologist from the Philippines, Acabado is using archaeology and local community knowledge (and expertise) to document the deep history of the Philippines, and thereby also bring into focus the genuine diversity of local ways and means popular throughout this archipelago of 7,600 islands, around 2,000 of which are today inhabited. To paraphrase Acabado's own words, he and his colleagues are using the archaeological record to push back against foreign models of the past in the Philippines, and to give voice instead to Indigenous histories that deepen the connectedness of people in the archipelago to the land and their global neighbors.

3. **Racism**. In Chapters 2, 4, and 7 as well as elsewhere in this book, we have used archaeological approaches to the past to question the racial migration models of history in the Pacific and elsewhere that Acabado refers to. Without repeating what has already been said, it is clear that archaeology often can make direct and telling contributions addressing the naive and prejudicial assumptions fundamental to institutionalized racism and pseudoscientific racial typologies (Fujimura and Rajagopalan 2020; Reece 2019).

Historical Explanation

As first discussed in Chapter 1, our answer in this book to the question "What is history?" rests on an elementary dynamic proposition about how the world works:

$$P(X_t + Y) \longrightarrow X_{t+1} \qquad \text{Proposition 1.2}$$

To repeat what we have said before, this statement implies that understanding the sequential pathway leading from a prior situation X_t to a later one is conditional on the probability P that an intermediate set of contingencies Y has contributed to the observed or hypothesized outcome X_{t+1}. Although we have not said so until now, this probability statement can be interpreted as a working definition of Bayes' Theorem.

As we wrote in Chapter 5 when we were discussing Bayesian probability and the evident connection between old age and death caused by COVID-19, it would be conventional to label what in this proposition is called the intermediate set of contingencies Y as the cause or causes of the shift over time from a prior situation to one that follows. We favor instead, however, using the expression *contingent probability* over the word *cause* because we find that these two words more effectively capture the dynamic relational interdependence of things and events without having to claim that the specific contingencies Y under study are or were solely necessary and sufficient to bring about the posited historical change from X_t to X_{t+1}.

Furthermore, as we said in Chapter 5, the human brain (and undoubtedly the brains of other animal species) can be thought of as a sophisticated *pattern recognition device*—a Bayesian learning machine—that we use to constantly update our working impressions of the world—what are popularly called *memories, habits,* and *opinions*—derived from our ongoing experiences as living, breathing human beings.

As we first discussed in the opening of this book, and then brought up again several times thereafter, the patterns—the apparent generalities—that our brains are predisposed to "find" outside the confines of their boney shells serve us as the mental categories into which we slot new experiences and concerns—more often than not without having to think too carefully about their "goodness-of-fit," as statisticians would say it.

Perhaps for this reason, historical explanations for what may have happened in the past are often categorical rather than relational. They often have the logical form **X | not X** rather than the relational specifications $X_t + Y \longrightarrow X_{t+1}$. Here are three examples of such categorical explanations that have long been popular in anthropology and archaeology.

> ❖ From the earliest traceable cosmical changes down to the latest results of civilization, we shall find that the transformation of the homogeneous into the heterogeneous, is that in which progress essentially consists.
> —Herbert Spencer,
> "Progress: Its Law and Causes" 1857

1. **Origins and diversity.** As we remarked in Chapter 4, one of the enduring assumptions of much of Western historical scholarship has been the idea that our diversity as a species can be mapped, or reconstructed, historically as a genealogical "family tree," the trunk of which was rooted in one specific place on earth, and the branches of which are the separate races or populations that have changed and grown apart from one another over time. From a biblical perspective, the trunk of this tree—the "center of origin" of our species—was in the Garden of Eden. Nowadays, it is more conventional to say instead that our species got its start somewhere in Africa and only later "branched out" from there. However, from the research perspective of DYRA, there is no reason to assume we haven't always been a diverse species. If so, then the outstanding question is *why aren't we now more diverse than we are?* Having better historical answers to such a question has bearing on how we understand and cope with social, economic, and political issues such as race and racism, hatred, and the dehumanization of those we see as "too different" for us to care about them as equal to ourselves.

> ❖ As we see in still existing barbarous tribes, society in its first and lowest form is a homogeneous aggregation of individuals having like powers and performing like functions: the only marked differentiation of function being that which accompanies difference of sex. Every man is a warrior, fisherman, toolmaker, builder; every woman performs the same drudgeries; every family is self-sufficing, and, save for purposes of aggression and defence, might as well live apart from the rest. Very early, however, in the process of social evolution, we find an incipient differentiation between governing and the governed. Some

kind of chieftainship seems almost co-ordinate with the first advance from the state of separate wandering to that of a nomadic tribe.

—Herbert Spencer,
"Progress: Its Law and Causes" 1857

2. **Urbanism and inequality.** According to the archaeologists Douglas Price and Gary Feinman: "The study of inequality is essentially a concern with the evolution of human society and in fact is a predominant issue in recent considerations of social evolution" (Price and Feinman 2010: 1). Defining inequality as unequal access to goods, information, decision-making, and power, they have acknowledged that social inequality is "a characteristic of virtually every society on earth today and its history goes back thousands of years" (2010: 2). However, often fundamental to their way of modeling history is the assumption, also shared by philosophers during the Enlightenment (Terrell 2015), that originally all human communities were small-scale and egalitarian.

If this prior assumption is granted, it can be argued that it has been only been since the end of the last Ice Age that the growth of inequality—which Price and Feinman say may be defined as our human ability to make and exploit categorical status distinctions—became a ruling characteristic of human politics, economics, and social life. Why? The most widely accepted explanation has long been that the primary cause was the dramatic increase in the size and density of human settlements during the Holocene, specifically following the onset of farming and animal domestication (Strassberg and Creanza 2021).

Since it has so often been taken for granted (i.e., categorically assumed) that inequality was not characteristic of our dealings with one another until quite recently (Graeber and Wengrow 2021), tracking down its causes has been a major research theme in the practice of archaeology, especially in North America. However, as Price and Feinman wrote in 2010, "we still do not know precisely when or why this principle became dominant, or how it operated in the past. How was inequality expressed in the past? Were there different trajectories to hierarchy?" (2010: 2).

❖ Hereby it is manifest, that during the time men live without a common Power to keep them all in awe, they are in that condition which is called Warre; and such a warre, as is of every man, against every man. For WARRE, consisteth not in Battell onely, or the act of fighting; but in a tract of time, wherein the Will to contend by Battell is sufficiently known: and therefore the notion of Time, is to be considered in the nature of Warre; as it is in the nature of Weather.
—Thomas Hobbes, *Leviathan* 1651

3. **Violence and warfare.** One topic that is almost always guaranteed to attract the attention of both scholars and the general public is whether humans are innately violent. Steven Pinker (2011) has argued that the archaeological record supports the assertion that warfare is innate in our biology, with governments serving to curtail our innate drive to engage in violent acts. This belief that humans are naturally violent is found in many books written by non-anthropologists. Often, like Pinker, these popular writers point to the archaeological record to support this assertion (Ferguson 2013).

As one example, Marta Mirazón Lahr and her colleagues (2016) have reported on Nataruk, Kenya, a ~10,000 BP site located along the banks of what would have then been a lagoon. Of a dozen individual skeletons found there, ten show signs of lethal violence. They argue "the deaths at Nataruk are testimony to the antiquity of intergroup violence and war" (Lahr et al. 2016: 397). This interpretation, however, has been criticized by Christopher Stojanowski and his colleagues (2016), who argue instead that the burials at this site are not contemporaneous, and that much of the observed cranial damage is not consistent with blunt force trauma, which is the physical evidence used by Lahr and her team to infer that these individuals had been killed during a warfare attack.

Both this case and that of Jebel Sahaba (a ~13,400 BP site in Sudan which also shows signs of evident violence; Crevecoeur et al. 2021) are often touted as examples of humans having a deep history of violence and an innate tendency to warfare. Yet these two sites are not that old compared to the entire arc of human evolution, and human history did not start in the Late Pleistocene.

Since we are predisposed as human beings to look for patterns, sites like these two may seem to be convincing evidence that engaging in interpersonal violence and warfare are truly ancient characteristics of our species. It would seem wise to remember, however, that archaeological sites that lack possible evidence suggesting interpersonal violence and maybe warfare may not attract as much public (or possibly even scholarly) attention or research funding.

Historical Foresight

Chance and Necessity (*Le Hasard et la Nécessité*) by the biochemist and Nobel Laureate Jacques Monod is a best-selling book we highly recommend despite the fact it was published over half a century ago; it is not shy about presenting technical information on the basic mechanics of biological evolution. Chapter by chapter, Monod lays out how the history of life on earth is an ever-changing dialogue between the senseless "chance" creation of purely random biological variation at the molecular level, and the absolute "necessity" of repeating over and over again *via* reproduction, sexual or otherwise, what has been prescribed in the DNA recipe for life called the genome. Or said another way, because no organism lives forever, "history matters" precisely because the essential historical patterning encoded in every genome must be repeated, generation after generation, for the very survival of life on earth.

> ❖ **chance** [CHans / tʃæns] *noun*: the probability of something happening.
>
> **choice** [CHois/ /tʃɔɪs] *noun*: an act of selecting or making a decision when faced with two or more possibilities.
>
> **necessity** [nəˈsesədē / nəˈsɛsədi] *noun*: the fact of being required or indispensable.
>
> **random** [ˈrandəm/ /ˈrændəm] *adjective*: made, done, happening, or chosen without method or conscious decision.

However, like the Roman god Janus, there is more to life than simply what has happened in the past that must be repeated in the future if life is to go on from one generation to the next. Life is not just a tale about chance and necessity. It is an evolving story both about historically derived constraints and new possibilities and promising opportunities. Figuratively speaking, the constraints we must deal with are the cards that history—the Earth's as well as our own species' past—has given us to play with; the opportunities are how we play those vitally important cards.

Moreover, as Monod emphasizes in *Chance and Necessity*, we are not the only creatures on earth that can actively play the cards we are handed:

> Animals, and not only those that are nearest us on the evolutionary scale, unquestionably possess a brain capable of not just of retaining and recording pieces of information but also of associating and transforming them, of bringing the results of these operations back out in the form of an individual performance; yet not—and this is the essential point—in a form which permits the communication to another individual of an original, personal association or transformation. But this is what can be done with human language, which may be considered by definition to have been born on the day when creative combinations—*new* associations achieved by one person—by reason of their transmission to others no longer had to perish with [the person who invented them]. (1971: 129; also 155)

While what Monod is telling us here—at least in this English translation of his original French text—might perhaps be said more easily some other way, it seems clear enough that he is referring to what nowadays in the social sciences is often called "agency." He is saying that agency is not just characteristic of our own species history (Monod 1971: 149). Other animals, too, have agency even if, lacking our capacity for using (and misusing) language, they cannot easily communicate to others what they have learned about how to make the most—and more—of what history has given them to work with. Hence history, and not exclusively human history, is not just a tale about blind chance and absolute necessity (Corning 2019; Monod 1971: 154–55; Odling-Smee, Laland, and Feldman 2003). It is also about agency—about making choices and acting creatively.

Grant us this claim about agency, and it may be clearer why we began this book with the well-known saying "those who cannot remember the past are condemned to repeat it." As we noted then, this particular phrasing of this popular observation comes from the pen of the Spanish-American philosopher George Santayana ([1905] 2005). Not being philosophers, we simply want to list briefly five of the ways in which knowing about what has happened in the past—why you have the cards you have rather than others you might wish you had been given—can make a real difference not only in what happens in the here and now, but if all goes reasonably well, in the future, too.

1. **Ignorance**. Being ignorant of history does not only mean being at risk of repeating—presumably for the worst—what really should be over and done with. For instance, without knowing what historically marginalized people have been dealing with, it is easy for those of us who have not been similarly disadvantaged to be insensitive and even oblivious to the plight of others.
2. **Denial**. The reverse of historical ignorance is the active denial of history—perhaps because certain historical realities seem distasteful or otherwise personally objectionable. For example, countering the saying "Black Lives Matter" with the claim "All Lives Matter," which is undoubtedly true, but saying this does not acknowledge that people of color have been facing discrimination in the United States for literally centuries.
3. **Gullibility**. History can show us more than just what used to be but since has changed. History can also witness the consequences of what happened in the past. Thinking naively, for example, that something cannot possibly happen again "because that's history" may partially explain why many people a year after the COVID-19 pandemic started were fundamentally opposed to being *vaccinated* against this SARS-associated coronavirus. They survived 2020, so what's the problem? The flipside of this same kind of historical gullibility is the notion that something which worked every time in the past cannot possibly fail in the future. For instance, the Great Recession of 2008 is usually explained by the fact that too many people had taken out loans they could not actually afford.
4. **Delusion**. However difficult they may be to pin down and prove beyond a shadow of a doubt, historical facts are nonetheless facts that should not be dismissed out of hand. One example is the popular theory that Donald Trump won the presidential

election in the United States in early November 2020. Did he, or didn't he? What do the historical facts say?
5. **Destiny**. How history can be misused either unintentionally or quite deliberately is notoriously evidenced by the claim, for example, that the supposed superiority of White Europeans was not only license for them to take over the rest of the world, but that it was their destiny to do so. As Jacques Monod observed in *Chance and Necessity*: "our very human tendency to believe that behind everything real in the world stands a necessity rooted in the very beginning of things. Against this notion, this powerful feeling of destiny, we must be constantly on guard. Immanence is alien to modern science. Destiny is written concurrently with the event, not prior to it" (Monod 1971: 145).

Historical Insight

The number three has long been seen as mystical, sacred, harmonious, and perfect not only by philosophers and theologians, but in popular folktales, too: three wishes, three little pigs, three bears, three witches in Shakespeare, the Christian Holy Trinity, and the Pythagorean triangle. However, having now given you three reasons why we think history must be taken seriously, we want to offer you one more.

Considering all that we have been talking about in this book, we worry you may think we are saying "doing history" can be a science when done right. Actually, we have been trying to say the reverse. When done well, science is a kind of history. The critical difference is how much is known about what has happened "in the past" either in the laboratory or out there in the proverbial world at large. From this perspective, "doing archaeology" is a set of tools and techniques—as a means—rather than as an end in itself.

Call it history, or call it science, either way it is currently popular to defend scholarship and expert knowledge by insisting—there are even bumper stickers saying this—that "facts matter" (see Chapter 3). We certainly agree. But what is a fact? How and why do they matter?

One way to answer these questions is to ask a similarly basic one: where do facts come from? More to the point, how archaeology and the study of history contribute to our understanding not just of the past and present but also the future closely parallels how our brains make sense of the world and what is happening around us.

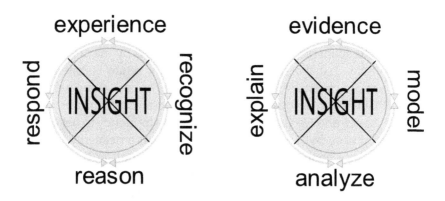

Figure 8.2. *Left:* How the human brain deals with what we experience in life; *right:* how knowing what has happened in the past can enrich our insights on what may happen in the future. © John Edward Terrell.

John B. Watson (1878–1958), B. F. Skinner (1904–1990), and other behavioral psychologists during the twentieth century might be accused nowadays of wanting us to believe that the human brain is just an organically constructed data storage device for keeping track of how positive or unrewarding our experiences in life have been. Even so, both knew there is more to what gets called "thinking" than what is included in a behaviorist's "stimulus-response" (or "operant conditioning") model of the mind (Brunkow and Dittrich 2021; Skinner 1953). Similarly, no one really needs to argue that there is much more to archaeology than just digging things out of the ground and then interpreting what they are and how old they probably are, give or take some calculated degree of uncertainty. Both psychology and archaeology add up to more than just this.

Psychology and the cognitive sciences today are still largely baffled by how our brains convert the sensual energy of its worldly experiences into constructive information that we can use to navigate our way through life (Lotto 2017; Monod 1971: 149; Terrell and Terrell 2020: 57–58). Whatever the neural mechanisms involved, however, most researchers nowadays would probably agree that the human brain—and almost every other kind of brain, too—is somehow able to (a) *recognize* patterning in what our bodily senses are telling us about what's happening in the outside world (for example, "I've seen this before!"), (b) *reason* deductively to make sense of what is being experienced ("Hey, the driver in that car ahead must be drunk as a skunk!"), and (c) *respond* accordingly (Figure 8.2, *left*).

❖ **experience** [ˌikˈspirēəns, ˌɪkˈspɪriəns] *verb*: encounter or undergo (an event or occurrence).

imagination [iˌmajəˈnāSH(ə)n, ɪˌmædʒəˈneɪʃ(ə)n] *noun*: the faculty or action of forming new ideas, images, or concepts of external objects not present to the senses; the ability of the mind to be creative or resourceful.

insight [ˈinˌsīt, ˈɪnˌsaɪt] *noun*: the capacity to gain an accurate and deep intuitive understanding of a person or thing.

reason [ˈrēzən, ˈrizən] *verb*: think, understand, and form judgments by a process of logic.

recognize [ˈrekəɡˌnīz, ˈrɛkəɡˌnaɪz] *verb*: identify (someone or something) from having encountered them before; know again.

respond [rəˈspänd, rəˈspɑnd] *verb*: act or behave in reaction to someone or something.

Unfortunately, although we have been gifted by evolution as human beings with advanced and genuinely skillful brains, what we can know about the world and about why things happen cannot be learned or discovered solely from the patterning of our own experiences (Simon 1996: 197–204). Consequently, knowing what has been happening in the past is a way for us to correct for this shortsightedness, this unavoidable cognitive bias favoring our own personal history.

But this is not all that historical insight can do for us. As we have noted in earlier chapters, the brains of many animals, and most emphatically the human brain, are capable of creatively rearranging and reinterpreting the experiences they have in dealing with the world around them. Although what is psychologically involved may be debatable, this way of dealing with life is commonly called "imagination." But having this ability is a mixed blessing. Given the human brain's creativity, how do we tell the difference between fact and fiction?

This question, similar to asking what is a fact, is one that has been debated for at least as long as there has been anyone willing to stand up publicly or privately to debate it. We have not tried to answer this question. Instead, we have written this book for three practical reasons:

1. The past plays an ever-present role in our lives through our laws and social conventions, the physical and environmental legacies of our previous acts and decisions, our genetically inherited biological characteristics, our acquired habits both good and bad, our memories, regrets and feelings of guilt, and even in our efforts to blame others for what we ourselves have done.
2. Modeling the past can give us historical insights not only on what we now know (or think we know), but also about what we do not as yet know—and therefore, what still must be learned not only about how we got to where we are today as one of the earth's dominant species, but also about the roles we have played in shaping the world we now live in.
3. Facts are experiences we use to make sense of the world and our place in it (Figure 8.2, *left*). Evidence is what we use to model and analyze how the world works—past, present, and future (Figure 8.2, *right*).

What is past is more than prologue. The past can also show us what has worked, and what has failed us. And perhaps why. However elusive the facts of history may be, history matters because without knowing what has already happened, we have no way of knowing where we may be headed during our time as a species here on Earth.

Glossary

adapt [ə'dapt] *verb*: make (something) suitable for a new use or purpose; modify.

assumption [ə'səm(p)SH(ə)n, ə'səm(p)ʃ(ə)n] *noun*: a thing that is accepted as true or as certain to happen, without proof.

black box theory: "A black box is a fiction representing a set of concrete systems into which stimuli (S) impinge and out of which reactions (R) emerge. The constitution and structure of the box are altogether irrelevant to the approach under consideration, which is purely external or phenomenological" (Bunge 1963).

categorical [ˌkadə'gôrək(ə)l] *adjective*: unambiguously explicit and direct.

category ['katəg(ə)ri] *noun*: a class or division of people or things regarded as having particular shared characteristics.

cause [kôz/ /kɔz] *noun*: a person or thing that gives rise to an action, phenomenon, or condition.

chance [CHans / tʃæns] *noun*: the probability of something happening.

choice [CHois/ /tʃɔɪs] *noun*: an act of selecting or making a decision when faced with two or more possibilities.

circumstantial ['sərkəmˌstans] *adjective*: a fact or condition connected with or relevant to an event or action; an event or fact that causes or helps to cause something to happen.

community [kuh-myoo-ni-tee] *noun*: a group of people living in the same place or having a particular characteristic in common.

consequential [ˌkänsəˈkwen(t)SHəl] *adjective*: following as a result or effect.

contingency [kənˈtinjənsē, kənˈtɪndʒənsi] *noun*: a future event or circumstance which is possible but cannot be predicted with certainty.

contingent [kənˈtinjənt] *adjective*: occurring or existing only if (certain circumstances) are the case; dependent on.

dynamic [dīˈnamik] *adjective*: characterized by constant change, activity, or progress.

dynamic relational analysis: studying changing *relational contingencies* among people, places, and events over time and space of differing character, cause, and probability.

epiphenomenon [-ˈnämənə] *noun, pl* epiphenomena: a secondary effect or byproduct that arises from but does not causally influence a process.

evolve [ēˈvälv] *verb*: develop gradually, especially from a simple to a more complex form.

experience [ˌikˈspirēəns, ˌɪkˈspɪriəns] *verb*: encounter or undergo (an event or occurrence).

explanation [ˌekspləˈnāSH(ə)n, ɛkspləˈneɪʃ(ə)n] *noun*: a statement or account that makes something clear.

hypothesis [/hīˈpäTHəsəs/] *noun*: a supposition or proposed explanation made on the basis of limited evidence as a starting point for further investigation.

imagination [iˌmajəˈnāSH(ə)n, ɪˌmædʒəˈneɪʃ(ə)n] *noun*: the faculty or action of forming new ideas, images, or concepts of external objects not present to the senses; the ability of the mind to be creative or resourceful.

insight [ˈinˌsīt, ˈɪnˌsaɪt] *noun*: the capacity to gain an accurate and deep intuitive understanding of a person or thing.

intent on/upon [in'tent] *adjective*: resolved or determined to do (something).

interpretation [in͵tərprə'tāSH(ə)n, ɪn͵tərprə'teɪʃ(ə)n] *noun*: the action of explaining the meaning of something.

model ['mädl] *verb*: devise a representation, especially a mathematical one (of a phenomenon or system).

necessity [nə'sesədē / nə'sɛsədi] *noun*: the fact of being required or indispensable.

network ['net-͵wərk] *noun*: a group or system of interconnected people or things. There are differing specific definitions of the word *network* as a noun depending on the kind of network being discussed (Kolaczyk 2009: 3–10). For instance: *graph neural networks* (Zhou et al. 2020), *computer networks* (Chowdhury et al. 2010), and *social networks* (Sekara et al. 2016).

purpose ['pərpəs] *noun*: the reason for which something is done or created or for which something exists.

random ['randəm/ /'rændəm] *adjective*: made, done, happening, or chosen without method or conscious decision.

reason ['rēzən, 'rizən] *verb:* think, understand, and form judgments by a process of logic.

recognize ['rekəg͵nīz, 'rɛkəg͵naɪz] *verb*: identify (someone or something) from having encountered them before; know again.

relational [rɪ'leɪʃ(ə)n(ə)l] *adjective*: concerning the way in which two or more people or things are connected.

respond [rə'spänd, rə'spɑnd] *verb*: act or behave in reaction to someone or something.

situational [͵sɪtʃə'weɪʃ(ə)n(ə)l] *adjective*: relating to or dependent on a set of circumstances or state of affairs.

system ['sɪstəm] *noun, pl* systems: a set of things working together as parts of a mechanism or an interconnecting network.

theory ['THirē] *noun, pl* theories: a supposition or a system of ideas intended to explain something, especially one based on general principles independent of the thing to be explained.

type [/tīp/ /taɪp/] *noun*: a category of people or things having common characteristics.

typology [/tī'pǎləjē/ /taɪ'pɑlədʒi/] *noun*: a classification according to general type, especially in archaeology, psychology, or the social sciences.

variable [verēəb(ə)l, vɛriəb(ə)] *noun*: (*mathematics*) a quantity which during a calculation is assumed to vary or be capable of varying in value.

Note

These definitions were downloaded between May 2020 and September 2021 from Lexico.com (a website created by Oxford University Press) while we were writing this book. This website was closed on 26 August 2022. Users are now redirected to Dictionary.com where similar definitions may be found.

References

Acabado, Stephen. 2021. "PH 'Prehistory': 500 years of Indigenous Erasure." Inquirer.net, 26 May. https://usa.inquirer.net/72363/ph-prehistory-500-years-of-indigenous-erasure.

Ackermann, Rebecca R., Sheela Athreya, Wendy Black, Graciela S. Cabana, Vincent Hare, Robyn Pickering, and Lauren Schroeder. 2019. "Upholding 'Good Science' in Human Origins Research: A Response to Chan et al. 2019." AfricArXiv, 6 November. https://doi.org/10.31730/osf.io/qtjfp.

Ackermann, Rebecca R., Marcella D. Baiz, James A. Cahill, Liliana Cortés-Ortiz, Ben J. Evans, B. Rosemary Grant, Peter R. Grant, Benedikt Hallgrimsson, Robyn A. Humphreys, Clifford J. Jolly, Joanna Malukiewicz, Christopher J. Percival, Terrence B. Ritzman, Christian Roos, Charles C. Roseman, Lauren Schroeder, Fred H. Smith, Kerryn A. Warren, Robert K. Wayne, and Dietmar Zinner. 2019. "Hybridization in Human Evolution: Insights from Other Organisms." *Evolutionary Anthropology* 28: 189–209. https://doi.org/10.1002/evan.21787.

Albantakis, Larissa, William Marshall, Erik Hoel, and Giulio Tononi. 2019. "What Caused What? A Quantitative Account of Actual Causation Using Dynamical Causal Networks." *Entropy* 21: 459. https://doi.org/10.3390/e21050459.

Allen, Jennifer, Baird Howland, Markus Mobius, David Rothschild, and Duncan J. Watts. 2020. "Evaluating the Fake News Problem at the Scale of the Information Ecosystem." *Science Advances* 6(14): eaay3539. https://doi.org/10.1126/sciadv.aay3539.

Allen, Jim, and James F. O'Connell. 2008. "Getting from Sunda to Sahul." In *Islands of Inquiry: Colonisation, Seafaring and the Archaeology of Maritime Landscapes*, ed. Geoffrey Clark, Foss Leach, and Sue O'Connor, 31–46. Terra Australis 29. Canberra: Australian National University Press.

Allport, Gordon W. 1954. *The Nature of Prejudice*. Reading: Addison-Wesley. Source: Digital Library of India. Added date 2017-01-21 12:12:36. Retrieved from https://archive.org/details/in.ernet.dli.2015.188638.

Alter, Stephen G. 1999. *Darwinism and the Linguistic Image: Language, Race, and Natural Theology in the Nineteenth Century*. Baltimore: Johns Hopkins University Press.

Ammerman, Albert J., and Luigi L. Cavalli-Sforza. 1971. "Measuring the Rate and Spread of Early Farming in Europe." *Man* 6: 674–88. https://doi.org/10.2307/2799190.

Anderson, Atholl. 2018. "Seafaring in Remote Oceania: Traditionalism and Beyond in Maritime Technology and Migration." In *The Oxford Handbook of Prehistoric Oceania*, ed. Ethan E. Cochrane and Terry L. Hunt, 473–92. Oxford: Oxford University Press. https://doi.org/10.1093/oxfordhb/9780199925070.013.003.

Anthony, David W. 2007. *The Horse, the Wheel, and Language: How Bronze-Age Riders from the Eurasian Steppes Shaped the Modern World*. Princeton: Princeton University Press.

Arendt, Hannah. 1951. *The Origins of Totalitarianism*. New York: Harcourt, Brace and Company.

Argote-Freyre, Frank, and Christopher M. Bellitto. 2012. "The Fall of Ancient Rome and Modern U.S. Immigration: Historical Model or Political Football?" *The Historian* 74(4): 789–811.

Athreya, Sheela, and Allison Hopkins. 2021. "Conceptual Issues in Hominin Taxonomy: Homo Heidelbergensis and an Ethnobiological Reframing of Species." *Yearbook of Physical Anthropology* 175(Suppl. 72): 4–26. https://doi.org/10.1002/ajpa.24330.

Avis, Chris, Álvaro Montenegro, and Andrew Weaver. 2007. "The Discovery of Western Oceania: A New Perspective." *Journal of Island & Coastal Archaeology* 2: 197–209. https://doi.org/10.1080/15564890701518557.

Bacon, Francis. 1620. *The New Organon, or True Directions Concerning the Interpretation of Nature*. Aphorism 84. Retrieved on 31 October 2022 from http://www.logicmuseum.com/authors/baconfrancis/novumorganum-I-68-end.htm.

Bakan, David. 1966. "The Test of Significance in Psychological Research." *Psychological Bulletin* 66: 423–37. https://doi.org/10.1037/h0020412.

Barnard, George A. 1958. "Studies in the History of Probability and Statistics: IX. Thomas Bayes's 'An Essay towards Solving a Problem in the Doctrine of Chances.'" *Biometrika* 45: 293–315. https://www.jstor.org/stable/2333180.

Barth, Fredrik. 1969. "Introduction." In *Ethnic Groups and Boundaries: The Social Organization of Culture Difference*, ed. Frederik Barth, 9–38. Boston: Little, Brown and Company.

Bateman, Richard, Ives Goddard, Richard O'Grady, Vicky Ann Funk, Rich Mooi, W. John Kress, and Peter Cannell. 1990. "Speaking of Forked Tongues: The Feasibility of Reconciling Human Phylogeny and the History of Language." *Current Anthropology* 31: 1–24. https://www.jstor.org/stable/2743338.

Batz, William A. 1974. "The Historical Anthropology of John Locke." *Journal of the History of Ideas* 35: 663–70. https://doi.org/10.2307/2709092.

Beard, Mary. 2016. *S.P.Q.R.: A History of Ancient Rome*. London: Profile Books.

Bedford, Stuart, Robert Blust, David V. Burley, Murray Cox, Patrick C. Kirch, Elizabeth Matisoo-Smith, Åshild Næss, Andrew Pawley, Christophe Sand, and Peter Sheppard. 2018. "Ancient DNA and Its Contribution to Understanding the Human History of the Pacific Islands." *Archaeology in Oceania* 53: 205–19. https://doi.org/10.1002/arco.5165.

Bedford, Stuart, Matthew Spriggs, David V. Burley, Christophe Sand, Peter Sheppard, and Glenn R. Summerhayes, eds. 2019. "Debating Lapita: Distribution, Chronology, Society and Subsistence." In *Debating Lapita: Distribution, Chronology, Society and Subsistence*, ed. Stuart Bedford and Matthew Spriggs, 5–33. Terra Australis 52. Canberra: Australian National University Press. https://www.jstor.org/stable/j.ctvtxw3gm.

Bentley, R. Alexander, Hallie R. Buckley, Matthew Spriggs, Stuart Bedford, Chris J. Ottley, Geoff M. Nowell, Colin G. Macpherson, and D. Graham Pearson. 2007. "Lapita Migrants in the Pacific's Oldest Cemetery: Isotopic Analysis at Teouma, Vanuatu." *American Antiquity* 72: 645–56. https://doi.org/10.2307/25470438.

Bernhardt, Chris. 2016. *Turing's Vision: The Birth of Computer Science*. Cambridge, MA: MIT Press.

Bilmes, Jeffrey A., and Richard Rogers. 2015. *GMTK: The Graphical Models Toolkit*. University of Washington, Seattle. Retrieved on 31 October 2022 from https://ptolemy.berkeley.edu/projects/terraswarm/pubs/503.html.

Blench, Roger. 2014. "Lapita Canoes and Their Multi-Ethnic Crews: Marginal Austronesian Languages Are Non-Austronesian. *Workshop on the Languages of Papua* 3: 20–24.

Bloomfield, Leonard. 1935. *Language*. London: George Allen & Unwin.

Borgatti, Stephen P., Martin G. Everett, and Jeffrey C. Johnson. 2018. *Analyzing Social Networks*, 2nd ed. Thousand Oaks: Sage Publications.

Borgatti, Stephen P., Ajay Mehra, Daniel J. Brass, and Giuseppe Labianca. 2009. "Network Analysis in the Social Sciences." *Science* 323: 892–95. https://doi.org/10.1126/science.1165821.

Börner, Katy, Soma Sanyal, and Alessandro Vespignani. 2007. "Network Science." *Annual Review of Information Science & Technology* 41: 537–607. https://doi.org/10.1002/aris.2007.1440410119.

Bouquet, Mary. 1996. "Family Trees and Their Affinities: The Visual Imperative of the Genealogical Diagram." *Journal of the Royal Anthropological Institute*, n.s. 2(1): 43–66. https://www.jstor.org/stable/pdf/3034632.

Bowler, Peter J. 1988. *The Non-Darwinian Revolution: Reinterpreting a Historical Myth*. Baltimore: Johns Hopkins University Press.

Box, George E. P. 1976. "Science and Statistics." *Journal of the American Statistical Association* 71: 791–99. https://doi.org/10.2307/2286841.

Brandes, Ulrik, Garry Robins, Ann McCranie, and Stanley Wasserman. 2013. "What Is Network Science?" *Network Science* 1: 1–15. https://doi.org/10.1017/nws.2013.2.

Braudel, Fernand. 1972–73. *The Mediterranean and the Mediterranean World in the Age of Philip II*. 2 vols. New York: Harper and Row Publishers.

Broekaert, Wim, Elena Köstner, and Christian Rollenger. 2020. "Introducing the 'Ties That Bind.'" *Journal of Historical Network Research* 4: i–xiii. https://doi.org/10.25517/jhnr.v4i0.83.

Broodbank, Cyprian. 2013. *The Making of the Middle Sea: A History of the Mediterranean from the Beginning to the Emergence of the Classical World*. London: Thames and Hudson.
Brubaker, Rogers. 2004. *Ethnicity without Groups*. Cambridge, MA: Harvard University Press.
Brughmans, Tom, and Matthew A. Peeples. 2018. "Network Science." In *Encyclopedia of Archaeological Sciences*, ed. Sandra L. López Varela, 1–4. Hoboken: John Wiley & Sons.
———. 2020. "Spatial Networks." In *Archaeological Spatial Analysis: A Methodological Guide*, ed. Mark Gillings, Piraye Hacıgüzeller, and Gary Lock, 273–95. London: Routledge.
Bruner, Emiliano, and Giorgio Manzi. 2006. "Saccopastore 1: The Earliest Neanderthal? A New Look at an Old Cranium." In *Neanderthals Revisited: New Approaches and Perspectives*, ed. Katerina Harvati and Terry Harrison, 23–36. Dordrecht: Springer.
Brunkow, Fernanda, and Alexandre Dittrich. 2021. "Cultural Survival in B. F. Skinner: Possibilities for Conceptual Refinement." *Behavior and Social Issues*: 1–13. https://doi.org/10.1007/s42822-020-00044-w.
Buldyrev, Sergey V., Roni Parshani, Gerald Paul, H. Eugene Stanley, and Shlomo Havlin. 2010. "Catastrophic Cascade of Failures in Interdependent Networks." *Nature* 464: 1025–28. https://doi.org/10.1038/nature08932.
Bunge, Mario. 1963. "A General Black Box Theory." *Philosophy of Science* 30: 346–58. https://www.jstor.org/stable/186066.
Burley, David V., Mark Horrocks, and Marshall I. Weisler. 2020. "Earliest Evidence for Pit Cultivation Provides Insight on the Nature of First Polynesian Settlement." *Journal of Island and Coastal Archaeology* 15: 127–47. https://doi.org/10.1080/15564894.2018.1501441.
Butterfield, Herbert. 1955. "The Rôle of the Individual in History." *History* 40: 1–17. https://www.jstor.org/stable/24403956.
Carneiro, Robert L. 1967. "On the Relationship between Size of Population and Complexity of Social Organization." *Southwestern Journal of Anthropology* 23: 234–43. https://www.jstor.org/stable/3629251.
Carr, Edward H. 1961. *What is History?* New York: Alfred A. Knopf.
Carrington, Peter J., John Scott, and Stanley Wasserman, eds. 2005. *Models and Methods in Social Network Analysis*. Cambridge: Cambridge University Press. https://doi.org/10.1017/CBO9780511811395.
Carroll, Scott P., Andrew P. Hendry, David N. Reznick, and Charles W. Fox. 2007. "Evolution on Ecological Time-Scales." *Functional Ecology* 21: 387–93. https://doi.org/10.1111/j.1365-2435.2007.01289.x.
Carter, Tara. 2015. *Iceland's Networked Society: Revealing How the Global Affairs of the Viking Age Created New Forms of Social Complexity*. Leiden: Brill. https://doi.org/10.1163/9789004293342.
Cavalli-Sforza, Luigi Luca, Paolo Menozzi, and Alberto Piazza. 1994. *The History and Geography of Human Genes*. Princeton: Princeton University Press.

Cavalli-Sforza, L. Luca, Alberto Piazza, Paolo Menozzi, and Joanna Mountain. 1990. "Comments on Bateman et al. 1990." *Current Anthropology* 31: 16–18. https://doi.org/10.1086/203800.

Cegielski, Wendy Hope. 2020. "Toward a Theory of Social Stability: Investigating Relationships Among the Valencian Bronze Age Peoples of Mediterranean Iberia." PhD diss., Arizona State University.

Chamberlin, Thomas C. (1890) 1965. "The Method of Multiple Working Hypotheses." *Science* 15: 92–96. https://www.jstor.org/stable/1716334.

Chardin, Pierre Teilhard de. 1959. *The Phenomenon of Man*. London: William Collins.

Chattoraj, Ankani, Sabyasachi Shivkumar, Yongsoo Ra, and Ralf M. Haefner. 2021. "A Confirmation Bias Due to Approximate Active Inference." *Proceedings of the Annual Meeting of the Cognitive Science Society*, 43. Retrieved from https://escholarship.org/uc/item/9c24c467.

Childe, Vere Gordon. 1925. *The Dawn of European Civilization*. London: K. Paul, Trench, Trubner & Co.; New York: Alfred A. Knopf.

———. 1937. *Man Makes Himself*. London: Watts & Company.

———. 1942. *What Happened in Prehistory*. Harmondsworth, England: Penguin.

Chowdhury, N. M. Mosharaf Kabir, and Raouf Boutaba. 2010. "Survey of Network Virtualization. Technical Report: CS-2008-25." *Computer Networks* 54: 862–76. https://doi.org/10.1016/j.comnet.2009.10.017.

Clark, Jeffrey T., and John Terrell. 1978. "Archaeology in Oceania." *Annual Review of Anthropology* 7: 293–319. https://doi.org/10.1146/annurev.an.07.100178.001453.

Clayton, Aubrey. 2020. "How Eugenics Shaped Statistics: Exposing the Damned Lies of Three Science Pioneers." *Nautilus* 92. https://nautil.us/how-eugenics-shaped-statistics-238014/.

Cochrane, Ethan E. 2018. "The Evolution of Migration: The Case of Lapita in the Southwest Pacific." *Journal of Archaeological Method and Theory* 25: 520–58. https://doi.org/10.1007/s10816-017-9345-z.

Cohen, I. Bernard. 1962. "The First English Version of Newton's *Hypotheses Non Fingo*." *Isis* 53: 379–88. https://www.jstor.org/stable/227788.

Collar, Anne, Fiona Coward, Tom Brughmans, and Barbara J. Mills. 2015. "Networks in Archaeology: Phenomena, Abstraction, Representation." *Journal of Archaeological Method and Theory* 22: 1–32. https://doi.org/10.1007/s10816-014-9235-6.

Collins, Desmond. 1976. *Human Revolution: From Ape to Artist*. Oxford, UK: Phaidon Press.

Corneli, Marco, Pierre Latouche, and Fabrice Rossi. 2018. "Multiple Change Points Detection and Clustering in Dynamic Networks." *Statistics and Computing* 28: 989–1007. https://doi.org/10.1007/s11222-017-9775-1.

Corning, Peter A. 2019. "Teleonomy and the Proximate–Ultimate Distinction Revisited." *Biological Journal of the Linnean Society* 127: 912–16. https://doi.org/10.1093/biolinnean/blz087.

Crabtree, Stefani A., and Lewis Borck. 2019. "Social Networks for Archaeological Research." In *Encyclopedia of Global Archaeology*, ed. Claire Smith, 1–12. New York: Springer. https://doi.org/10.1007/978-3-319-51726-1_2631-2.

Crabtree, Stefani A., Jennifer A. Dunne, and Spencer A. Wood. 2021. "Ecological Networks and Archaeology." *Antiquity* 95: 812–25. https://doi.org/10.15184/aqy.2021.38.

Craft, Stephanie, Seth Ashley, and Adam Maksl. 2017. "News Media Literacy and Conspiracy Theory Endorsement." *Communication and the Public* 2: 388–401. https://doi.org/10.1177/2057047317725539.

Crevecoeur, Isabelle, Marie-Hélène Dias-Meirinho, Antoine Zazzo, Daniel Antoine, and François Bon. 2021. "New Insights on Interpersonal Violence in the Late Pleistocene Based on the Nile Valley Cemetery of Jebel Sahaba." *Nature Scientific Reports* 11: 9991 https://doi.org/10.1038/s41598-021-89386-y.

"Culture." 2022. Wikipedia, 30 April. https://en.wikipedia.org/wiki/Archaeological_culture.

Daem, Dries. 2021. *Social Complexity and Complex Systems in Archaeology*. London: Routledge.

Darwin, Charles. 1859. *On the Origin of Species by Means of Natural Selection*. London: John Murray.

———. 1861. Letter to Henry Fawcett, 18 September. Darwin Correspondence Project. Retrieved from https://www.darwinproject.ac.uk/letter/DCP-LETT-3257.xml.

Dawkins, Richard. 1996. *The Blind Watchmaker: Why the Evidence of Evolution Reveals a Universe Without Design*. New York: W. W. Norton & Company.

Dawson, Helen. 2014. *Mediterranean Voyages: The Archaeology of Island Colonisation and Abandonment*. Walnut Creek: Left Coast Press. https://doi.org/10.4324/9781315424774.

———. 2019. "As Good as It Gets? 'Optimal' Marginality in the Longue Durée of the Mediterranean Islands." *Journal of Eastern Mediterranean Archaeology and Heritage* 7: 451–66. https://doi.org/10.5325/jeasmedarcherstu.7.4.0451.

———. 2021a. "At the Heart of Mare Nostrum: Islands and 'Small World Networks' in the Central Mediterranean Bronze Age." In *Bridging Social and Geographical Space Through Networks*, ed. Helen Dawson and Francesco Iacono, 9–14. Leiden: Sidestone Press.

———. 2021b. "Caught in the Current: Maritime Connectivity, Insularity, and the Spread of the Neolithic." In *Revolutions. The Neolithisation of the Mediterranean Basin: The Transition to Food Producing Economies in North Africa, Southern Europe and the Levant*, ed. Joanne Rowland, Giulio Lucarini, and Geoffrey Tassie, 85–100. Berlin: Edition Topoi. https://doi.org/10.17169/refubium-29544.

———. 2021c. "Network Science and Island Archaeology: Advancing the Debate." *Journal of Island and Coastal Archaeology* 16(2–4): 213–30. https://doi.org/10.1080/15564894.2019.1705439.

Dawson, Helen, and Irene Nikolakopoulou. 2020. "East Meets West: Aegean Identities and Interactions in the Late Bronze Age Mediterranean." eTopoi. *Journal for Ancient Studies* Special Volume 7: 155–92. https://doi.org/10.17169/refubium-28214.
Dear, Peter. 2016. "Darwin and Deep Time: Temporal Scales and the Naturalist's Imagination." *History of Science: An Annual Review of Literature, Research and Teaching* 54: 3–18. https://doi.org/10.1177/0073275315625407.
"Decolonization." 2020. Fourth International Decade for the Eradication of Colonialism. Resolution 75/123 adopted by the United Nations General on 10 December 2020. http://undocs.org/a/res/75/123.
de Nooy, Wouter. 2003. "Fields and Networks: Correspondence Analysis and Social Network Analysis in the Framework of Field Theory." *Poetics* 31: 305–27. https://doi.org/10.1016/S0304-422X(03)00035-4.
Diamond, Jared M. 1997. *Guns, Germs, and Steel: The Fates of Human Societies*. New York: W. W. Norton & Company.
Dixon, Roland B. 1928. *The Building of Cultures*. New York: Charles Scribner's Sons.
Dobrin, Lise, and Ira Bashkow. 2006. "'Pigs for Dance Songs': Reo Fortune's Empathetic Ethnography of the Arapesh Roads." *Histories of Anthropology Annual* 2: 123–54. https://doi.org/10.1353/haa.0.0015.
Douglas, Karen M., Joseph E. Uscinski, Robbie M. Sutton, Aleksandra Cichocka, Turkay Nefes, Chee Siang Ang, and Farzin Deravi. 2019. "Understanding Conspiracy Theories." *Political Psychology* 40, Suppl. 1: 3–35. https://doi.org/10.1111/pops.12568.
Eagleman, David M. 2001. "Visual Illusions, and Neurobiology." *Nature Reviews Neuroscience* 2: 920–26. https://doi.org/10.1038/35104092.
Edwards, Ward, Harold Lindman, and Leonard J. Savage. 1963. "Bayesian Statistical Inference for Psychological Research." *Psychological Review* 70: 193–242. https://doi.org/10.1037/H0044139.
Elton, Geoffrey R. 1967. *The Practice of History*. London: Fontana Books.
Feinman, Gary. 2012. "Size, Complexity, and Organizational Variation: A Comparative Approach." *Cross-Cultural Research* 45: 37–58. https://doi.org/10.1177/1069397110383658.
Ferguson, R. Brian. 2013. "Pinker's List: Exaggerating Prehistoric War Mortality." In *War, Peace, and Human Nature: The Convergence of Evolutionary and Cultural Views*, ed. Douglas P. Fry, 112–31. Oxford: Oxford University Press. https://doi.org/10.1093/acprof:oso/9780199858996.003.0007.
Fernández, Eva, Alejandro Pérez-Pérez, Cristina Gamba, Eva Prats, Pedro Cuesta, Josep Anfruns, Miquel Molist, Eduardo Arroyo-Pardo, and Daniel Turbón. 2014. "Ancient DNA Analysis of 8000 B.C. near Eastern Farmers Supports an Early Neolithic Pioneer Maritime Colonization of Mainland Europe through Cyprus and the Aegean Islands." *PLOS Genetics* 10(6). https://doi.org/10.1371/journal.pgen.1004401.

Fiedel, Stuart J., and David W. Anthony. 2003. "Deerslayers, Pathfinders, and Icemen: Origins of the European Neolithic as Seen from the Frontier." In *Colonization of Unfamiliar Landscapes. The Archaeology of Adaptation*, ed. Marcy Rockman and James Steele, 144–68. London: Routledge. https://doi.org/10.4324/9780203422908.

Fiedler, Klaus. 2011. "Voodoo Correlations Are Everywhere—Not Only in Neuroscience." *Perspectives on Psychological Science* 6: 163–71. https://doi.org/10.1177/1745691611400237.

Fisch, Menachem. 1985. "Whewell's Consilience of Inductions—an Evaluation." *Philosophy of Science* 52: 239–55. https://www.jstor.org/stable/187509.

Flannery, Kent. 1969. "Origins and Ecological Effects of Early Domestication in Iran and the near East." In *The Domestication and Exploitation of Plants and Animals*, ed. Peter J. Ucko and Geoffrey William Dimbleby, 73–100. London: Duckworth.

Foley, William A. 2000. "The Languages of New Guinea." *Annual Review of Anthropology* 29: 357–404. https://www.jstor.com/stable/223425.

Fort, Joaquim, Toni Pujol, and Marc Vander Linden. 2012. "Modeling the Neolithic Transition in the Near East and Europe." *American Antiquity* 77: 203–19. https://doi.org/10.7183/0002-7316.77.2.203.

Friedlaender, Jonathan S., Françoise R. Friedlaender, Jason A. Hodgson, Matthew Stoltz, George Koki, Gisele Horvat, Sergey Zhadanov, Theodore G. Schurr, and D. Andrew Merriwether. 2007. "Melanesian mtDNA Complexity." *PLoS ONE* 2: e248. https://doi.org/10.1371/journal.pone.0000248.

Friedlaender, Jonathan S., Françoise R. Friedlaender, Floyd A. Reed, Kenneth K. Kidd, Judith R. Kidd, Geoffrey K. Chambers, Rodney A. Lea, Jun-Hun Loo, George Koki, Jason A. Hodgson, D. Andrew Merriwether, and James L. Weber. 2008. "The Genetic Structure of Pacific Islanders." *PLoS Genetics* 4(1): e19. https://doi.org/10.1371/journal.pgen.0040019.

Friston, Karl. 2008. "Hierarchical Models in the Brain." *PLoS Computational Biology* 4(11): e1000211. https://doi.org/10.1371/journal.pcbi.1000211.

Fujimura, Joan H., Deborah A. Bolnick, Ramya Rajagopalan, Jay S. Kaufman, Richard C. Lewontin, Troy Duster, Pilar Ossorio, and Jonathan Marks. 2014. "Clines without Classes: How to Make Sense of Human Variation." *Sociological Theory* 32: 208–27. https://doi.org/10.1177/0735275114551611.

Fujimura, Joan H., and Ramya Rajagopalan. 2011. "Different Differences: The Use of 'Genetic Ancestry' versus Race in Biomedical Human Genetic Research." *Social Studies of Science* 41: 5–30. https://doi.org/10.1177/0306312710379170g.

———. 2020. "Race, Ethnicity, Ancestry, and Genomics in Hawai'i: Discourses and Practices." *Historical Studies in the Natural Sciences* 50: 596–623. https://doi.org/10.1525/hsns.2020.50.5.596.

Fuks, Daniel, and Nimrod Marom. 2021. "Sheep and Wheat Domestication in Southwest Asia: A Meta-Trajectory of Intensification and Loss." *Animal Frontiers* 11: 20–29. https://doi.org/10.1093/af/vfab029.

Furholt, Martin. 2017. "Massive Migrations? The Impact of Recent aDNA Studies on our View of Third Millennium Europe." *European Journal of Archaeology* 21: 159–91. https://doi.org/10.1017/eaa.2017.43.

———. 2021. "Ethnic Essentialism, Clash of Cultures, Biologization of Identities: How Flawed Concepts Affect the Archaeogenetics Discourse." *European Journal of Archaeology* 24: 519–55. https://doi.org/10.1017/eaa.2021.29.

Gannett, Lisa. 2003. "Making Populations: Bounding Genes in Space and in Time." *Philosophy of Science* 70: 989–1001. https://doi.org/10.1086/377383.

———. 2013. "Theodosius Dobzhansky and the Genetic Race Concept." *Studies in History and Philosophy of Biological and Biomedical Sciences* 44: 250–61. https://doi.org/10.1016/j.shpsc.2013.04.009.

Gardiner, Patrick. (1952) 1961. *The Nature of Historical Explanation*. London: Oxford University Press.

Gardner, Martin. 2001. "A Skeptical Look at Karl Popper." *Skeptical Inquirer* 25(4): 13–14, 72.

Garnier-Crussard, Antoine, Emmanuel Forestier, Thomas Gilbert, and Pierre Krolak-Salmon. 2020. "Novel Coronavirus (COVID-19) Epidemic: What Are the Risks for Older Patients?" *Journal of the American Geriatrics Society* 68: 939–40. https://doi.org/10.1111/jgs.16407.

Gerring, John. 2008. "The Mechanismic Worldview: Thinking Inside the Box." *British Journal of Political Science* 38: 161–79. https://www.jstor.org/stable/27568337.

Ghysels, Gert, Sarah Mutua, Gabriela Baya Veliz, and Marijke Huysmans. 2019. "A Modified Approach for Modelling River-Aquifer Interaction of Gaining Rivers in MODFLOW, Including Riverbed Heterogeneity and River Bank Seepage." *Hydrogeology Journal* 27: 1851–63. https://doi.org/10.1007/s10040-019-01941-0.

Gimbutas, Marija. 1997. *The Kurgan Culture and the Indo-Europeanization of Europe: Selected Articles from 1952 to 1993*. Ann Arbor: University of Michigan, Institute for the Study of Man.

Gingerich, Owen. 1973. "From Copernicus to Kepler: Heliocentrism as Model and as Reality." *Proceedings of the American Philosophical Society* 117: 513–22. https://www.jstor.org/stable/986462.

Godelier, Maurice. 2010. "Community, Society, Culture: Three Keys to Understanding Today's Conflicted Identities." *Journal of the Royal Anthropological Institute* 16: 1–11. https://www.jstor.org/stable/40541801.

Golitko, Mark. 2020. "Pacific Ethnography, Archaeology and the Pattern of Global Prehistoric Social Life." In *Theory in the Pacific, the Pacific in Theory*, ed. Tim Thomas, 102–22. London: Routledge.

Golitko, Mark, and Gary M. Feinman. 2015. "Procurement and Distribution of Pre-Hispanic Mesoamerican Obsidian 900 BC–AD 1520: A Social Network Analysis." *Journal of Archaeological Method and Theory* 22: 206–47. https://doi.org/10.1007/s10816-014-9211-1.

Golitko, Mark, Matthew Schauer, and John Edward Terrell. 2013. "Obsidian Acquisition on the Sepik Coast of Northern Papua New Guinea during the Last Two Millennia." In *Pacific Archaeology: Documenting the Past 50,000 Years*, ed. Glenn Summerhayes and Hallie Buckley, 43–57. Dunedin: University of Otago.

Golitko, Mark, and John Edward Terrell. 2021. "Three Simple Geographical Network Models for the Holocene Bismarck Sea." In *Bridging Social and Geographical Space Through Networks*, ed. Helen Dawson and Francesco Iacono, 15–30. Leiden: Sidestone Press.

Gould, D. Rae. 2013. "Cultural Practice and Authenticity: The Search for Real Indians in New England in the 'Historical' Period." In *The Death of Prehistory*, ed. Peter R. Schmidt and Stephen A. Mrozowski, 241–66. Oxford Scholarship Online. https://doi.org/10.1093/acprof:osobl/9780199684595.001.0001.

Graeber, David, and David Wengrow. 2021. *The Dawn of Everything: A New History of Humanity*. New York: Farrar, Straus and Giroux.

Gramsch, Alexander. 2015. "Culture, Change, Identity: Approaches to Interpretation of Culture Change." *Anthropologie* 53: 341–49. https://www.jstor.org/stable/26272492.

Granovetter, Mark S. 1973. "The Strength of Weak Ties." *American Journal of Sociology* 78: 1360–80. https://www.jstor.org/stable/2776392.

———. 1983. "The Strength of Weak Ties: A Network Theory Revisited." *Sociological Theory* 1: 201–33. https://www.jstor.org/stable/202051.

Grant, Madison. 1916. *The Passing of the Great Race: Or, The Racial Basis of European History*. New York: Charles Scribner's Sons.

Gray, Russell D., David Bryant, and Simon J. Greenhill. 2010. "On the Shape and Fabric of Human History." *Philosophical Transactions of the Royal Society B* 365: 3923–33. https://doi.org/10.1098/rstb.2010.0162.

Gray, Russell D., Alexei J. Drummond, and Simon J. Greenhill. 2009. "Language Phylogenies Reveal Expansion Pulses and Pauses in Pacific Settlement." *Science* 323: 479–83. https://doi.org/10.1126/science.1166858.

Green, Richard E., Johannes Krause, Adrian W. Briggs, Tomislav Maricic, Udo Stenzel, Martin Kircher, Nick Patterson, Heng Li, Weiwei Zhai, Markus Hsi-Yang Fritz, Nancy F. Hansen, Eric Y. Durand, Anna-Sapfo Malaspinas, Jeffrey D. Jensen, Tomas Marques-Bonet, Can Alkan, Kay Prüfer, Matthias Meyer, Hernán A. Burbano, Jeffrey M. Good, Rigo Schultz, Ayinuer Aximu-Petri, Anne Butthof, Barbara Höber, Barbara Höffner, Madlen Siegemund, Antje Weihmann, Chad Nusbaum, Eric S. Lander, Carsten Russ, Nathaniel Novod, Jason Affourtit, Michael Egholm, Christine Verna, Pavao Rudan, Dejana Brajkovic, Željko Kucan, Ivan Gušic, Vladimir B. Doronichev, Liubov V. Golovanova, Carles Lalueza-Fox, Marco de la Rasilla, Javier Fortea, Antonio Rosas, Ralf W. Schmitz, Philip L. F. Johnson, Evan E. Eichler, Daniel Falush, Ewan Birney, James C. Mullikin, Montgomery Slatkin, Rasmus Nielsen, Janet Kelso, Michael Lachmann, David Reich, and Svante Pääbo. 2010. "A

Draft Sequence of the Neandertal Genome." *Science* 328: 710–22. https://doi.org/10.1126/science.1188021.

Greene, Kevin. 1999. "V. Gordon Childe and the Vocabulary of Revolutionary Change." *Antiquity* 73: 97–109. https://doi.org/10.1017/S0003598X00087871.

Griffiths, Paul J. 1991. *An Apology for Apologetics: A Study in the Logic of Interreligious Dialogue*. Eugene: Wipf and Stock Publishers.

Grinnell, George. 1974. "The Rise and Fall of Darwin's First Theory of Transmutation." *Journal of the History of Biology* 7: 259–73. https://www.jstor.org/stable/4330615.

Gronenborn, Detlef. 2007. "Beyond the Models: 'Neolithisation' in Central Europe." *Proceedings of the British Academy* 144: 73–98. https://doi.org/10.5871/bacad/9780197264140.003.0005.

Groube, Les M. 1971. "Tonga, Lapita Pottery, and Polynesian Origins." *Journal of the Polynesian Society* 80: 278–316. https://www.jstor.org/stable/20704787.

Guilaine, Jean. 2013. "The Neolithic Transition in Europe: Some Comments on Gaps, Contacts, Arrhythmic Model, Genetics." In *Unconformist Archaeologist: Papers in Honour of Paolo Biagi*, ed. Elisabetta Starnini, 55–64. British Archaeological Reports, International Series. Oxford, UK: Archaeopress. https://doi.org/10.30861/9781407311463.

Haak, Wolfgang, Iosif Lazaridis, Nick Patterson, Nadin Rohland, Swapan Mallick, Bastien Llamas, Guido Brandt, Susanne Nordenfelt, Eadaoin Harney, Kristin Stewardson, Qiaomei Fu, Alissa Mittnik, Eszter Bánffy, Christos Economou, Michael Francken, Susanne Friederich, Rafael Garrido Pena, Fredrik Hallgren, Valery Khartanovich, Aleksandr Khokhlov, Michael Kunst, Pavel Kuznetsov, Harald Meller, Oleg Mochalov, Vayacheslav Moiseyev, Nicole Nicklisch, Sandra L. Pichler, Roberto Risch, Manuel A. Rojo Guerra, Christina Roth, Anna Szécsényi-Nagy, Joachim Wahl, Matthias Meyer, Johannes Krause, Dorcas Brown, David Anthony, Alan Cooper, Kurt Werner Alt, and David Reich. 2015. "Massive Migration from the Steppe Was a Source for Indo-European Languages in Europe." *Nature* 522: 207–11. https://doi.org/10.1038/nature14317.

Hall, Thomas D., P. Nick Kardulias, and Christopher Chase-Dunn. 2011. "World-Systems Analysis and Archaeology: Continuing the Dialogue." *Journal of Archaeological Research* 19: 233–79. https://doi.org/10.1007/s10814-010-9047-5.

Hamilakis, Yannis. 2018. "Archaeologies of Forced and Undocumented Migration." In *The New Nomadic Age—Archaeologies of Forced and Undocumented Migration*, ed. Yannis Hamilakis, 1–19. Sheffield, UK: Equinox eBooks Publishing.

Hamilton, William D. 1964. "The Genetical Evolution of Social Behaviour. I, II." *Journal of Theoretical Biology* 7: 1–52. https://doi.org/10.1016/0022-5193(64)90038-4. https://doi.org/10.1016/0022-5193(64)90039-6.

Harary, Frank, Robert Zane Norman, and Dorwin Cartwright. 1965. *Structural Models: An Introduction to the Theory of Directed Graphs*. New York: Wiley.

Harding, Anthony. 2013. "World Systems, Cores, and Peripheries in Prehistoric Europe." *European Journal of Archaeology* 16: 378–400. https://doi.org/10.1179/1461957113Y.0000000032.

Hariri, Reihaneh H., Erik M. Fredericks, and Kate M. Bowers. 2019. "Uncertainty in Big Data Analytics: Survey, Opportunities, and Challenges." *Journal of Big Data* 6: 44. https://doi.org/10.1186/s40537-019-0206-3.

Hart, John P., and William Engelbrecht. 2012. "Northern Iroquoian Ethnic Evolution: A Social Network Analysis." *Journal of Archaeological Method and Theory* 19: 322–49. https://doi.org/10.1007/s10816-011-9116-1.

Hart, John P., and William A. Lovis. 2013. "Reevaluating What We Know about the Histories of Maize in Northeastern North America: A Review of Current Evidence." *Journal of Archaeological Research* 21: 175–216. https://doi.org/10.1007/s10814-012-9062-9.

Hashemi, Lobat, Balgobin Nandram, and Robert Goldberg. 1998. "Bayesian Analysis for a Single 2 x 2 Table." *Statistics in Medicine* 16: 1311–28. https://doi.org/10.1002/(sici)1097-0258(19970630)16:12<1311::aid-sim568>3.0.co;2-3.

Hobbes, Thomas. 1651. *Leviathan. Leviathan or the Matter, Forme, & Power of a Common-Wealth Ecclesiastical and Civill*. London: Andrew Crooke. Retrieved from https://www.gutenberg.org/files/3207/3207-h/3207-h.htm.

Hodder, Ian, and Angus Mol. 2016. "Network Analysis and Entanglement." *Journal of Archaeological Method and Theory* 23: 1066–94. https://doi.org/10.1007/s10816-015-9259-6.

Hoenigswald, Henry M. 1987. "Language Family Trees, Topological and Metrical." In *Biological Metaphor and Cladistic Classification: An Interdisciplinary Perspective*, eds. Henry M. Hoenigswald and Linda F. Wiener, 257–67. Philadelphia: University of Pennsylvania Press.

Hofmann, Daniela, Emily Hanscam, Martin Furholt, Martin Bača, Samantha S. Reiter, Alessandro Vanzetti, Kostas Kotsakis, Håkan Petersson, Elisabeth Niklasson, Herdis Hølleland, and Catherine J. Frieman. 2021. "Forum: Populism, Identity Politics, and the Archaeology of Europe." *European Journal of Archaeology* 24: 519–55. https://doi.org/10.1017/eaa.2021.29.

Hofmanová, Zuzana, Susanne Kreutzer, Garrett Hellenthal, Christian Sell, Yoan Diekmann, David Díez-del-Molino, Lucy van Dorp, Saioa López, Athanasios Kousathanas, Vivian Link, Karola Kirsanow, Lara M. Cassidy, Rui Martiniano, Melanie Strobel, Amelie Scheu, Kostas Kotsakis, Paul Halstead, Sevi Triantaphyllou, Nina Kyparissi-Apostolika, Dushka Urem-Kotsou, Christina Ziota, Fotini Adaktylou, Shyamalika Gopalan, Dean M. Bobo, Laura Winkelbach, Jens Blöcher, Martina Unterländer, Christoph Leuenberger, Çiler Çilingiroğlu, Barbara Horejs, Fokke Gerritsen, Stephen J. Shennan, Daniel G. Bradley, Mathias Currat, Krishna R. Veeramah, Daniel Wegmann, Mark G. Thomas, Christina Papageorgopoulou, and Joachim Burger. 2016. "Early Farmers from across Europe Directly Descended from Neolithic Aegeans." *Proceedings of the National Academy of Sciences* 113: 6886–91. https://doi.org/10.1073/pnas.1523951113.

Holland-Lulewicz, Jacob. 2021. "From Categories to Connections in the Archaeology of Eastern North America." *Journal of Archaeological Research*: 1–43. https://doi.org/10.1007/s10814-020-09154-w.

Holland-Lulewicz, Jacob, and Amanda D. Roberts Thompson. 2021. "Incomplete Histories and Hidden Lives: The Case for Social Network Analysis in Historical Archaeology." *International Journal of Historical Archaeology*. https://doi.org/10.1007/s10761-021-00638-z.

Horden, Peregrine, and Nicholas Purcell. 2000. *The Corrupting Sea: A Study of Mediterranean History*. Oxford, UK: Blackwell.

Hubbard, Raymond. 2004. "Alphabet Soup: Blurring the Distinctions between P's and A's in Psychological Research." *Theory & Psychology* 14: 295–327. https://doi.org/10.1177/0959354304043638.

Hunley, Keith, Michael Dunn, Eva Lindström, Ger Reesink, Angela Terrill, Meghan E. Healy, George Koki, Françoise R. Friedlaender, and Jonathan S. Friedlaender. 2008. "Genetic and Linguistic Coevolution in Northern Island Melanesia." *PLoS Genetics* 4(10): e1000239. https://doi.org/10.1371/journal.pgen.1000239.

Hurston, Zora Neale. 1942. *Dust Tracks on a Road*. Philadelphia: J. B. Lippincott Company.

Iacono, Francesco, Elisabetta Borgna, Maurizio Cattani, Claudio Cavazzuti, Helen Dawson, Yannis Galanakis, Maja Gori, Cristiano Iaia, Nicola Ialongo, Thibault Lachenal, Alberto Lorrio, Rafael Micó, Barry Molloy, Argyro Nafplioti, Kewin Peche-Quilichini, Cristina Rihuete Herrada, and Roberto Risch. 2021. "Establishing the Middle Sea: The Late Bronze Age of Mediterranean Europe (1700–900 BC)." *Journal of Archaeological Research*: 1–75. https://doi.org/10.1007/s10814-021-09165.

Ingold, Tim. 2015. *The Life of Lines*. London: Routledge.

———. 2017. "On Human Correspondence." *Journal of the Royal Anthropological Institute* 23: 9–27. https://doi.org/10.1111/1467-9655.12541.

Irwin, Geoffrey. 1992. *The Prehistoric Exploration and Colonisation of the Pacific*. Cambridge: Cambridge University Press.

———. 2008. "Pacific Seascapes, Canoe Performance, and a Review of Lapita Voyaging with Regard to Theories of Migration." *Asian Perspectives* 47: 12–27. https://doi.org/10.1353/asi.2008.0002.

Irwin, Geoffrey, and Richard G. J. Flay. 2015. "Pacific Colonisation and Canoe Performance: Experiments in the Science of Sailing." *Journal of the Polynesian Society* 124: 419–43. https://www.jstor.org/stable/44012033.

Jacob, François. 1982. *The Possible and The Actual*. New York: Pantheon.

Johnson, Allen W., and Timothy K. Earle. 2000. *The Evolution of Human Societies: From Foraging Group to Agrarian State*. Stanford: Stanford University Press.

Jolly, A. M., S. Q. Muth, J. L. Wylie, and J. J. Potterat. 2001. "Sexual Networks and Sexually Transmitted Infections: A Tale of Two Cities." *Journal of Urban Health* 78: 433–45. https://doi.org/10.1093/jurban/78.3.433.

Kahneman, Daniel, and Amos Tversky. 1973. "On the Psychology of Prediction." *Psychological Review* 80: 237–51. https://doi.org/10.1037/h0034747.

Kant, Immanuel. 1784. "What Is Enlightenment?" Retrieved on 1 November 2016 from http://www.columbia.edu/acis/ets/CCREAD/etscc/kant.html#:~:text=Enlightenmentpercent20ispercent20man'spercent20emergencepercent20from,ownpercent20mindpercent20withoutpercent20another'spercent20guidance (English); https://www.gutenberg.org/ebooks/30821 (German).

Kirch, Patrick V. 2000. *On the Road of the Winds: An Archaeological History of the Pacific Islands before European Contact.* Berkeley: University of California Press.

Knoke, David, and Song Yang. 2008. *Social Network Analysis.* Thousand Oaks: Sage Publications.

Koikkalainen, Saara, and David Kyle. 2016. "Imagining Mobility: The Prospective Cognition Question in Migration Research." *Journal of Ethnic and Migration Studies* 42: 759–76. https://doi.org/10.1080/1369183X.2015.1111133.

Kolaczyk, Eric D. 2009. *Statistical Analysis of Network Data.* New York: Springer.

Kosiba, Steve. 2019. "New Digs: Networks, Assemblages, and the Dissolution of Binary Categories in Anthropological Archaeology." *American Anthropologist* 121: 447–63. https://doi.org/10.1111/aman.13261.

Kristiansen, Kristian. 2014. "Towards a New Paradigm? The Third Science Revolution and Its Possible Consequences in Archaeology." *Current Swedish Archaeology* 22: 11–34. https://doi.org/10.37718/CSA.2014.01.

Kristiansen, Kristian, and Thomas B. Larsson. 2005. *The Rise of Bronze Age Society: Travels, Transmissions and Transformations.* Cambridge: Cambridge University Press.

Kuhn, Thomas S. 1970. *The Structure of Scientific Revolutions*, 2nd ed. Chicago: University of Chicago Press.

Lahr, M. Mirazón, F. Rivera, R. K. Power, A. Mounier, B. Copsey, F. Crivellaro, J. E. Edung, J. M. Maillo Fernandez, C. Kiarie, J. Lawrence, A. Leakey, E. Mbua, H. Miller, A. Muigai, D. M. Mukhongo, A. Van Baelen, R. Wood, J.-L. Schwenninger, R. Grün, H. Achyuthan, A. Wilshaw, and R. A. Foley. 2016. "Inter-Group Violence among Early Holocene Hunter-Gatherers of West Turkana, Kenya." *Nature* 529: 394–98. https://doi.org/10.1038/nature16477.

Lambdin, Charles. 2012. "Significance Tests as Sorcery: Science Is Empirical—Significance Tests Are Not." *Theory & Psychology* 22: 67–90. https://doi.org/10.1177/0959354311429854.

Landau, Misia. 1984. "Human Evolution as Narrative." *American Scientist* 72: 262–68. https://www.jstor.org/stable/27852647.

Latham, Robert Gordon.1850. *The Natural History of the Varieties of Man.* London: J. Van Voorst.

Legendre, Pierre, Marie-Josée Fortin, and Daniel Borcard. 2015. "Should the Mantel Test Be Used in Spatial Analysis?" *Methods in Ecology and Evolution* 6: 1239–47. https://doi.org/10.1111/2041-210X.12425.

Le Guin, Ursula K. 1979. *The Language of the Night: Essays on Fantasy and Science Fiction*. Edited by Susan Wood. New York: G. P. Putnam's Sons.
Leppard, Thomas, P. 2022. "Process and Dynamics of Mediterranean Neolithization (7000–5500 BC)." *Journal of Archaeological Research* 30: 231–83. https://doi.org/10.1007/s10814-021-09161-5.
Lesser, Alexander. 1961. "Social Fields and the Evolution of Society." *Southwestern Journal of Anthropology* 17: 40–48. https://www.jstor.org/stable/3628867.
Levins, Richard. 1966. "The Strategy of Model Building in Population Biology." *American Scientist* 54: 421–31. https://www.jstor.org/stable/27836590.
———. 1968. *Evolution in Changing Environments*. Princeton: Princeton University Press.
———. 2006. "Strategies of Abstraction." *Biology and Philosophy* 21: 741–55. https://doi.org/10.1007/s10539-006-9052-8.
Linseele, Veerle, 2021. "Early Livestock in Egypt: Archaeozoological Evidence." In *Revolutions. The Neolithisation of the Mediterranean Basin: The Transition to Food Producing Economies in North Africa, Southern Europe and the Levant*, ed. Joanne Rowland, Giulio Lucarini, and Geoffrey Tassie, 59–68. Berlin: Edition Topoi.
Lipson, Mark, Pontus Skoglund, Matthew Spriggs, Frederique Valentin, Stuart Bedford, Richard Shing, Hallie Buckley, Iarawai Phillip, Graeme K. Ward, Swapan Mallick, Nadin Rohland, Nasreen Broomandkhoshbacht, Olivia Cheronet, Matthew Ferry, Thomas K. Harper, Megan Michel, Jonas Oppenheimer, Kendra Sirak, Kristin Stewardson, Kathryn Auckland, Adrian V. S. Hill, Kathryn Maitland, Stephen J. Oppenheimer, Tom Parks, Kathryn Robson, Thomas N. Williams, Douglas J. Kennett, Alexander J. Mentzer, Ron Pinhasi, and David Reich. 2018. "Population Turnover in Remote Oceania Shortly after Initial Settlement." *Current Biology* 28: 1157–65. https://doi.org/10.1016/j.cub.2018.02.051.
Lopez, Anthony C. 2017. "The Evolutionary Psychology of War: Offense and Defense in the Adapted Mind." *Evolutionary Psychology* 15: 1474704917742720. https://doi.org/10.1177/1474704917742720. PMID: 29237297.
Lorenz, Chris. 2011. "History and Theory." In *The Oxford History of Historical Writing, Volume 5: Historical Writing Since 1945*, ed. Axel Schneider and Daniel Woolf, 13–35. Oxford: Oxford University Press.
Lotto, Beau. 2017. *Deviate: The Creative Power of Transforming Your Perception*. London: Weidenfeld & Nicolson.
Lucarini, Giulio, and Anita Radini, 2021. "A Disregarded Nobility: The Role and Exploitation of Wild Plants in North Africa during the Holocene, Analyzed through an Integrated Functional Analysis on Non-Knapped Stone Tools." In *Revolutions. The Neolithisation of the Mediterranean Basin: The Transition to Food Producing Economies in North Africa, Southern Europe and the Levant*, ed. Joanne Rowland, Giulio Lucarini, and Geoffrey Tassie, 69–83. Berlin: Edition Topoi.

Lucas, Gavin. 2018. *Writing the Past: Knowledge and Literary Production in Archaeology*. London: Routledge.

Lupyan, Gary, and Benjamin Bergen. 2016. "How Language Programs the Mind." *Topics in Cognitive Science* 8: 408–24. https://doi.org/10.1111/tops.12155.

Lyman, R. Lee. 2021. "On the Importance of Systematics to Archaeological Research: The Covariation of Typological Diversity and Morphological Disparity." *Journal of Paleolithic Archaeology* 4(3). https://doi.org/10.1007/s41982-021-00077-6.

MacArthur, Robert H. 1972. *Geographical Ecology: Patterns in the Distribution of Species*. Princeton: Princeton University Press.

MacKendrick, Paul. 1960. *The Mute Stones Speak: The Story of Italian Archaeology*. New York: St. Martin's Press.

Marks, Jonathan. 2021. *Why Are There Still Creationists? Human Evolution and the Ancestors*. New York: John Wiley & Sons.

Marler, Joan. 1996. "The Life and Work of Marija Gimbutas." *Journal of Feminist Studies in Religion* 12: 37–51. https://www.jstor.org/stable/25002285.

Martin, John Levi. 2003. "What Is Field Theory?" *American Journal of Sociology* 109: 1–49. https://doi.org/10.1086/375201.

Marx, Karl. 1904. *A Critique of Political Economy*. Translated by N. I. Stone from the 2nd German ed. Chicago: Charles H. Kerr & Company. Retrieved on 5 July 2021 from https://www.gutenberg.org/ebooks/46423.

Mellars, Paul, and Chris Stringer. 1989. "Introduction." In *The Human Revolution: Behavioural and Biological Perspectives on the Origins of Modern Humans*, ed. Paul Mellars and Chris Stringer, 1–14. Edinburgh: Edinburgh University Press.

Meyer-Delius, Daniel, Christian Plagemann, Georg Von Wichert, Wendelin Feiten, Gisbert Lawitzky, and Wolfram Burgard. 2008. "A Probabilistic Relational Model for Characterizing Situations in Dynamic Multi-Agent Systems." In *Data Analysis: Machine Learning and Applications*, ed. Christine Preisach, Hans Burkhardt, Lars Schmidt-Thieme, and Reinhold Decker, 269–76. Berlin: Springer.

Michel, Matthias, and Megan A. K. Peters. 2021. "Confirmation Bias without Rhyme or Reason." *Synthese* 199: 2757–72. https://doi.org/10.1007/s11229-020-02910-x.

Mills, Barbara. 2017. "Social Network Analysis in Archaeology." *Annual Review of Anthropology* 46: 379–97. https://doi.org/10.1146/annurev-anthro-102116-041423.

Mills, Barbara J., Jeffrey J. Clark, Matthew A. Peeples, W. R. Haas, Jr., John M. Roberts, Jr., J. Brett Hill, Deborah L. Huntley, Lewis Borck, Ronald L. Breiger, Aaron Clauset, and M. Steven Shackley. 2013. "Transformation of Social Networks in the Late Pre-Hispanic US Southwest." *Proceedings of the National Academy of Sciences U.S.A.* 110: 5785–90. https://doi.org/10.1073/pnas.1219966110.

Mlekuž, Dimitrij, Mihael Budja, Robert Payton, and Clive Bonsall. 2008. "'Mind the Gap': Caves, Radiocarbon Sequences, and the Mesolithic-Neolithic Transi-

tion in Europe—Lessons from the Mala Triglavca Rockshelter Site." *Geoarchaeology* 23: 398–416. https://doi.org/10.1002/gea.20220.
Monod, Jacques. 1971. *Chance and Necessity: An Essay on the Natural Philosophy of Modern Biology*. Translated by Austryn Wainhouse. New York: Alfred A. Knopf.
Montenegro, Álvaro, Richard T. Callaghan, and Scott M. Fitzpatrick. 2016. "Using Seafaring Simulations and Shortest-Hop Trajectories to Model the Prehistoric Colonization of Remote Oceania." *Proceedings of the National Academy of Sciences* 113: 12685–90. https://doi.org/10.1073/pnas.1612426113.
Morris, Ian. 2003. "Mediterraneanization." *Mediterranean Historical Review* 18: 30–55. https://doi.org/10.1080/0951896032000230471.
Mumford, Stephen, and Rani Lill Anjum. 2013. *Causation: A Very Short Introduction*. Oxford: Oxford University Press.
Murphy, Kevin Patrick. 2002. "Dynamic Bayesian Networks: Representation, Inference and Learning." PhD diss., University of California, Berkeley.
Newman, Mark E. J. 2001. "The Structure of Scientific Collaboration Networks." *Proceedings of the National Academy of Sciences U.S.A.* 98: 404–49. https://doi.org/10.1073/pnas.98.2.404.
———. 2010. *Networks: An Introduction*. London: Oxford University Press.
Newton, Douglas. 1989. "Mother Cassowary's Bones: Daggers of the East Sepik Province, Papua New Guinea." *Metropolitan Museum Journal* 24: 305–25. https://doi.org/10.2307/1512887.
Nooteboom, Bart. 1986. "Plausibility in Economics." *Economics and Philosophy* 2: 197–224. https://doi.org/10.1017/S1478061500002632.
Novotny, Vojtech, and Pavel Drozd. 2000. "The Size Distribution of Conspecific Populations: The Peoples of New Guinea." *Proceedings of the Royal Society of London. Series B: Biological Sciences* 267: 947–52. https://doi.org/10.1098/rspb.2000.1095.
Nuzzo, Regina. 2014. "Scientific Method: Statistical Errors." *Nature* 506: 150–52. https://doi.org/10.1038/506150a.
Oatley, Thomas, W. Kindred Winecoff, Andrew Pennock, and Sarah Bauerle Danzman. 2013. "The Political Economy of Global Finance: A Network Model." *Perspectives on Politics* 11: 133–53. https://doi.org/10.1017/S1537592712003593.
Odling-Smee, F. John, Kevin N. Laland, and Marcus W. Feldman. 2003. *Niche Construction: The Neglected Process in Evolution*. Princeton: Princeton University Press.
Orzack, Steven Hecht, and Elliot Sober. 1993. "A Critical Assessment of Levins's 'The Strategy of Model Building in Population Biology' (1966)." *Quarterly Review of Biology* 68: 533–46. https://www.jstor.org/stable/3037250.
Otárola-Castillo, Erik, and Melissa G. Torquato. 2018. "Bayesian Statistics in Archaeology." *Annual Review of Anthropology* 47: 435–53. https://doi.org/10.1146/annurev-anthro-102317-045834.
Pálsson, Gísli. 2021. "Cutting the Network, Knotting the Line: A Linaeological Approach to Network Analysis." *Journal of Archaeological Method and Theory* 28: 178–96. https://doi.org/10.1007/s10816-020-09450-1.

Pawley, Andrew. 2007. "The Origins of Early Lapita Culture: The Testimony of Historical Linguistics." In *Pacific Explorations: Lapita and Western Pacific Settlement*, ed. Andrew Pawley, Stuart Bedford, Christophe Sand, and Sean P. Connaughton, 17–49. Terra Australis 26. Canberra: Australian National University Press. https://www.jstor.org/stable/j.ctt24h9sg.4.

Pawley, Andrew, and Medina Pawley. 1994. "Early Austronesian Terms for Canoe Parts and Seafaring." In *Austronesian Terminologies: Continuity and Change*, ed. Andrew Pawley and Malcolm Ross, 329–61. Canberra: Australian National University Press.

Peeples, Matthew A. 2019. "Finding a Place for Networks in Archaeology." *Journal of Archaeological Research* 27: 451–99. https://doi.org/10.1007/s10814-019-09127-8.

Pilaar Birch, Suzanne E. 2018. "From the Aegean to the Adriatic: Exploring the Earliest Island Fauna." *Journal of Island and Coastal Archaeology* 13: 256–68. https://doi.org/10.1080/15564894.2017.1310774.

Pinker, Steven. 2002. *The Blank Slate: The Modern Denial of Human Nature*. New York: Penguin Books.

———. 2011. *The Better Angels of Our Nature: Why Violence Has Declined*. New York: Viking.

Platt, John R. 1964. "Strong Inference." *Science* 146: 347–53. https://www.jstor.org/stable/1714268.

Poincaré, Henri. 1905. *Science and Hypothesis*. London: Walter Scott Publishing Co. Retrieved on 21 August 2011 from https://www.gutenberg.org/ebooks/37157.

Popper, Karl R. 1962. *Conjectures and Refutations: The Growth of Scientific Knowledge*. New York: Basic Books, Publishers.

Posth, Cosimo, Kathrin Nägele, Heidi Colleran, Frédérique Valentin, Stuart Bedford, Kaitip W. Kami, Richard Shing, Hallie Buckley, Rebecca Kinaston, Mary Walworth, Geoffrey R. Clark, Christian Reepmeyer, James Flexner, Tamara Maric, Johannes Moser, Julia Gresky, Lawrence Kiko, Kathryn J. Robson, Kathryn Auckland, Stephen J. Oppenheimer, Adrian V. S. Hill, Alexander J. Mentzer, Jana Zech, Fiona Petchey, Patrick Roberts, Choongwon Jeong, Russell D. Gray, Johannes Krause, and Adam Powell. 2018. "Language Continuity Despite Population Replacement in Remote Oceania." *Nature Ecology and Evolution* 2: 731–40. https://doi.org/10.1038/s41559-018-0498-2.

Price, T. Douglas, and Gary M. Feinman. 2010. "Social Inequality and the Evolution of Human Social Organization." In *Pathways to Power. Fundamental Issues in Archaeology*, ed. T. Douglas Price and Gary M. Feinman, 1–14. New York: Springer. https://doi.org/10.1007/978-1-4419-6300-0_1.

Prichard, James C. 1813. *Researches into the Physical History of Man*. Reprinted edition, 1973. Chicago: University of Chicago Press.

Pritchard, Jonathan K., Matthew Stephens, and Peter Donnelly. 2000. "Inference of Population Structure Using Multilocus Genotype Data." *Genetics* 155: 945–59. https://doi.org/10.1093/genetics/155.2.945.

Pugach, Irina, Ana T. Duggan, D. Andrew Merriwether, Françoise R. Friedlaender, Jonathan S. Friedlaender, and Mark Stoneking. 2018. "The Gateway from Near into Remote Oceania: New Insights from Genome-Wide Data." *Molecular Biology and Evolution* 35: 871–76. https://doi.org/10.1093/molbev/msx333.

Râmakrishna. 1907. *The Gospel of Râmakrishna*. New York: The Vedanta Society. Retrieved on 18 July 2020 from https://books.google.com/books?id=JFEMAAAAYAAJ&pg=PR3#v=onepage&q&f=false.

Ramenofsky, Ann F., Alicia K. Wilbur, and Anne C. Stone. 2003. "Native American Disease History: Past, Present and Future Directions." *World Archaeology* 35: 241–57. https://www.jstor.org/stable/3560225.

Reece, Robert L. 2019. "Color Crit: Critical Race Theory and the History and Future of Colorism in the United States." *Journal of Black Studies* 50: 3–25. https://doi.org/10.1177/0021934718803735.

Reich, David. 2018. *Who We Are and How We Got Here: Ancient DNA and the New Science of the Human Past*. New York: Pantheon.

Renfrew, Colin. 1972. *The Emergence of Civilization: The Cyclades and the Aegean in the Third Millennium B.C.* Oxford, UK: Oxbow Books.

———. 1977. "Alternative Models for Exchange and Spatial Distribution." In *Exchange Systems in Prehistory*, ed. Timothy K. Earle and Jonathon E. Ericson, 71–90. New York: Academic Press. https://doi.org/10.1016/B978-0-12-227650-7.50010-9.

———. 1987. *Archaeology & Language: The Puzzle of Indo-European Origins*. Cambridge: Cambridge University Press.

"Repatriation." 2021. "'Give Us Our People Back': Muscogee Push University of Alabama to Return Moundville Remains." AL.com, 18 November. Retrieved from https://www.al.com/news/2021/11/give-us-our-people-back-muscogee-push-university-of-alabama-to-return-moundville-remains.html.

Rito, Teresa, Daniel Vieira, Marina Silva, Eduardo Conde-Sousa, Luísa Pereira, Paul Mellars, Martin B. Richards, and Pedro Soares. 2019. "A Dispersal of *Homo Sapiens* from Southern to Eastern Africa Immediately Preceded the Out-of-Africa Migration." *Scientific Reports* 9: 4728. https://doi.org/10.1038/s41598-019-41176-3.

Robb, John. 2010. "Beyond Agency." *World Archaeology* 42: 493–520. https://doi.org/10.1080/00438243.2010.520856.

———. 2013. "Material Culture, Landscapes of Action, and Emergent Causation: A New Model for the Origins of the European Neolithic." *Current Anthropology* 54: 657–83. https://doi.org/10.1086/673859.

Robb, John, and Preston Miracle. 2007. "Beyond 'Migration' versus 'Acculturation': New Models for the Spread of Agriculture." In *Going Over: The Mesolithic-Neolithic Transition in North-West Europe*, ed. Alasdair Whittle and Vicki Cummings, 99–115. Proceedings of the British Academy 144. Oxford: Oxford University Press, British Academy. https://doi.org/10.5871/bacad/9780197264140.003.0006.

Roberts, Patrick, Julien Louys, Jana Zech, Ceri Shipton, Shimona Kealy, Sofia Samper Carro, Stuart Hawkins, Clara Boulanger, Sara Marzo, Bianca Fiedler, Nicole Boivin, Mahirta, Ken Aplin, and Sue O'Connor. 2020. "Isotopic Evidence for Initial Coastal Colonization and Subsequent Diversification in the Human Occupation of Wallacea." *Nature Communications* 11(1): 1–11. https://doi.org/10.1038/s41467-020-15969-4.

Roe, Ann. 1953. *The Making of a Scientist*. New York: Dodd, Mead and Company.

Roscoe, Paul. 1989. "The Pig and the Long Yam: The Expansion of a Sepik Cultural Complex." *Ethnology* 28: 219–31. https://doi.org/10.2307/3773512.

Rovelli, Carlo. 2017. *Reality Is Not What It Seems: The Journey to Quantum Gravity*. New York: Penguin Random House.

———. 2018. *The Order of Time*. New York: Riverhead Books.

Ruse, Michael. 2013. *The Gaïa Hypothesis: Science on a Pagan Planet*. Chicago: University of Chicago Press.

Sanger, Matthew. 2021. "Joining the Circle: Native American Philosophy Applied to the Study of Late Archaic Shell Rings of the Southeast United States." *Journal of Archaeological Method and Theory* 28: 737–65. https://doi.org/10.1007/s10816-021-09532-8.

Santayana, George. (1905) 2005. *The Life of Reason: The Phases of Human Progress*, Vol. 1. Retrieved on 21 July 2021 from https://www.gutenberg.org/ebooks/15000.

Schortman, Edward M. 2014. "Networks of Power in Archaeology." *Annual Review of Anthropology* 43: 167–82. https://www.annualreviews.org/doi/abs/10.1146/annurev-anthro-102313-025901.

Schurgin, Mark W. 2018. "Visual Memory, the Long and the Short of It: A Review of Visual Working Memory and Long-Term Memory." *Attention, Perception, & Psychophysics* 80: 1035–56. https://doi.org/10.3758/s13414-018-1522-y.

Scott, John. 2000. *Social Network Analysis: A Handbook*, 2nd ed. London: Sage.

Sekara, Vedran, Arkadiusz Stopczynski, and Sune Lehmann. 2016. "Fundamental Structures of Dynamic Social Networks." *Proceedings of the National Academy of Sciences* 113: 9977–82. https://doi.org/10.1073/pnas.1602803113.

Service, Elman R. 1975. *The Origins of the State and Civilization: The Process of Cultural Evolution*. New York: W. W. Norton & Company.

Shaw, Ben, Judith H. Field, Glenn R. Summerhayes, Simon Coxe, Adelle C. F. Coster, Anne Ford, Jemina Haro, Henry Arifeae, Emily Hull, Geraldine Jacobsen, Richard Fullagar, Elspeth Hayes, and Lisa Kealhofer. 2020. "Emergence of a Neolithic in Highland New Guinea by 5000 to 4000 Years Ago." *Science Advances* 6(13): eaay4573. https://doi.org/10.1126/sciadv.aay4573.

Shennan, Stephen, Sean S. Downey, Adrian Timpson, Kevan Edinborough, Sue Colledge, Tim Kerig, Katie Manning, and Mark G. Thomas. 2013. "Regional Population Collapse Followed Initial Agriculture Booms in Mid-Holocene Europe." *Nature Communications* 4: 2486. https://doi.org/10.1038/ncomms3486.

Sherratt, Andrew. 1981. "Plough and Pastoralism: Aspects of the Secondary Products Revolution." In *Pattern of the Past: Studies in Honour of David Clarke*, ed. Ian Hodder, Glynn Isaac, and Norman Hammond, 261–305. Cambridge: Cambridge University Press.

———. 1993a. "What Would a Bronze Age World System Look Like? Relations between Temperate Europe and the Mediterranean in Later Prehistory." *Journal of European Archaeology* 1: 1–58. https://doi.org/10.1179/096576693800719293.

———. 1993b. "Who Are You Calling Peripheral? Dependence and Independence in European Prehistory." In *Trade and Exchange in Prehistoric Europe*, ed. Chris Scarre and Frances Healy, 245–55. Oxford, UK: Oxbow Books.

———. 1994. "Core, Periphery, and Margin." In *Development and Decline in the Mediterranean Bronze Age*, ed. Clay Mathers and Simon Stoddart, 335–45. Sheffield: J. R. Collis.

Sherratt, Andrew, and Susan Sherratt. 1998. "Small Worlds: Interaction and Identity in the Ancient Mediterranean." In *The Aegean and the Orient in the Second Millennium: Proceedings of the 50th Anniversary Symposium*, Cincinnati, 18–20 April 1997, ed. Eric. H. Cline and Diane Harris-Cline, 329–43. Liège: Université de Liège, Histoire de l'art et archéologie de la Grèce antique; Austin: University of Texas at Austin.

Simon, Herbert A. 1978. "Rationality as Process and as Product of Thought." *American Economic Review* 68: 1–16. https://www.jstor.org/stable/1816653.

———. 1996. *The Sciences of the Artificial*, 3rd ed. Cambridge, MA: MIT Press.

Skinner, B. F. 1953. *Science and Human Behavior*. New York: Macmillan.

Skoglund, Pontus, Cosimo Posth, Kendra Sirak, Matthew Spriggs, Frederique Valentin, Stuart Bedford, Geoffrey R. Clark, Christian Reepmeyer, Fiona Petchey, Daniel Fernandes, Qiaomei Fu1, Eadaoin Harney, Mark Lipson, Swapan Mallick, Mario Novak, Nadin Rohland, Kristin Stewardson, Syafiq Abdullah, Murray P. Cox, Françoise R. Friedlaender, Jonathan S. Friedlaender, Toomas Kivisild, George Koki, Pradiptajati Kusuma, D. Andrew Merriwether, Francois-X. Ricaut, Joseph T. S. Wee, Nick Patterson, Johannes Krause, Ron Pinhasi, and David Reichl. 2016. "Genomic Insights into the Peopling of the Southwest Pacific." *Nature* 538: 510–13. https://doi.org/10.1038/nature19844.

Smith, Edward Bishop, Raina A. Brands, Matthew E. Brashears, and Adam M. Kleinbaum. 2020. "Social Networks and Cognition." *Annual Review of Sociology* 46: 159–74. https://doi.org/10.1146/annurev-soc-121919-054736.

Soares, Pedro, Teresa Rito, Jean Trejaut, Maru Mormina, Catherine Hill, Emma Tinkler-Hundal, Michelle Braid, Douglas J. Clarke, Jun-Hun Loo, Noel Thomson, Tim Denham, Mark Donohue, Vincent Macaulay, Marie Lin, Stephen Oppenheimer, and Martin B. Richards. 2011. "Ancient Voyaging and Polynesian Origins." *American Journal of Human Genetics* 88: 239–47. https://doi.org/10.1016/j.ajhg.2011.01.009.

Sober, Elliot. 1980. "Evolution, Population Thinking, and Essentialism." *Philosophy of Science* 47: 350–83. https://www.jstor.org/stable/186950.

Spencer, Herbert, 1857. "Progress: Its Law and Causes." *The Westminster Review* 67 (American Edition, April): 244–67. New York: Leonard Scott & Co. Downloaded from https://hdl.handle.net/2027/mdp.39015031985347.

Spriggs, Matthew. 2011. "Archaeology and the Austronesian Expansion: Where Are We Now?" *Antiquity* 85: 510–28. https://doi.org/10.1017/S0003598X00067910.

Spriggs, Matthew, and David Reich. 2020. "An Ancient DNA Pacific Journey: A Case Study of Collaboration between Archaeologists and Geneticists." *World Archaeology* 51: 620–39. https://doi.org/10.1080/00438243.2019.1733069.

Spriggs, Matthew, Frederique Valentin, Stuart Bedford, Ron Pinhasi, Pontus Skoglund, David Reich, and Mark Lipson. 2019. "Revisiting Ancient DNA Insights into the Human History of the Pacific Islands." *Archaeology in Oceania* 54: 53–56. https://doi.org/10.1002/arco.5180.

Stanton, William. 1960. *The Leopard's Spots: Scientific Attitudes toward Race in America 1815–59*. Chicago: University of Chicago Press.

Stephenson, Todd Andrew. 2000. *An Introduction to Bayesian Network Theory and Usage*. IDIAP Research Report-RR 00–03. Martigny: IDIAP. https://infoscience.epfl.ch/record/82584/files/rr00-03.pdf?ln=en.

Stocking, George W., Jr. 1987. *Victorian Anthropology*. New York: Free Press.

———. 1988. "Bones, Bodies, Behavior." In *Bones, Bodies, Behavior: Essays on Biological Anthropology*, ed. George W. Stocking, Jr., 3–17. Madison: University of Wisconsin Press.

Strassberg, Sarah Saxton, and Creanza Nicole. 2021. "Cultural Evolution and Prehistoric Demography." *Philosophical Transactions of the Royal Society* B 376. https://doi.org/10.1098/rstb.2019.0713.

Stojanowski, Christopher M., Andrew C. Seidel, Laura C. Fulginiti, Kent M. Johnson, and Jane E. Buikstra. 2016. "Contesting the Massacre at Nataruk." *Nature* 539: E8–E10. https://doi.org/10.1038/nature19778.

Summerhayes, Glenn. 2009. "Obsidian Network Patterns in Melanesia—Sources, Characterisation and Distribution." *Bulletin of the Indo-Pacific Prehistory Association* 29: 109–24. https://doi.org/10.7152/BIPPA.V29I0.9484.

———. 2019. "Austronesian Expansions and the Role of Mainland New Guinea: A New Perspective." *Asian Perspectives* 58: 250–60. https://doi.org/10.1353/asi.2019.0015.

Templeton, Alan. 1998. "Human Races: A Genetic and Evolutionary Perspective." *American Anthropologist* 100: 632–50. https://doi.org/10.1525/aa.1998.100.3.632.

———. 2019. *Human Population Genetics and Genomics*. London: Elsevier.

Terrell, John Edward. 1986. "Causal Pathways and Causal Processes: Studying the Evolutionary Prehistory of Human Diversity in Language, Customs, and Biology." *Journal of Anthropological Archaeology* 5: 187–98. https://doi.org/10.1016/0278-4165(86)90013-9.

———. 1990. "Storytelling and Prehistory." *Archaeological Method and Theory* 2: 1–29. https://www.jstor.org/stable/20170203.

———. 2001a. "Ethnolinguistic Groups, Language Boundaries, and Culture History: A Sociolinguistic Model." In *Archaeology, Language, and History: Essays on Culture and Ethnicity*, ed. John Edward Terrell, 199–221. Westport, CT: Bergin & Garvey.
———. 2001b. "The Uncommon Sense of Race, Language, and Culture." In *Archaeology, Language, and History: Essays on Culture and Ethnicity*, ed. John Edward Terrell, 11–30. Westport, CT: Bergin & Garvey.
———. 2002. "Tropical Agroforestry, Coastal Lagoons, and Holocene Prehistory in Greater near Oceania." In *Vegeculture in Eastern Asia and Oceania*, ed. Shuji Yoshida and Peter J. Matthews, 195–216. Japan Center for Area Studies Symposium Series 16. Osaka: National Museum of Ethnology.
———. 2004. "The 'Sleeping Giant' Hypothesis and New Guinea's Place in the Prehistory of Greater near Oceania." *World Archaeology* 36: 601–9. https://www.jstor.org/stable/4128294.
———. 2006. "Human Biogeography: Evidence of Our Place in Nature." *Journal of Biogeography* 33: 2088–98. https://doi.org/10.1111/j.1365-2699.2006.01581.x.
———. 2010. "Social Network Analysis of the Genetic Structure of Pacific Islanders." *Annals of Human Genetics* 74: 211–32. https://doi.org/10.1111/j.1469-1809.2010.00575.x.
———. 2013a. "Polynesians and the Seductive Power of Common Sense." *Cultural Geographies* 20: 135–52. https://doi.org/10.1177/1474474011432663.
———. 2013b. "Social Network Analysis and the Practice of History." In *Network Analysis in Archaeology*, ed. Carl Knappett, 17–41. Oxford: Oxford University Press. https://doi.org/10.1093/acprof:oso/9780199697090.003.0002.
———. 2015. *A Talent for Friendship: Rediscovery of a Remarkable Trait*. New York: Oxford University Press.
Terrell, John Edward, and John P. Hart. 2008. "Domesticated Landscapes." In *Handbook of Landscape Archaeology*, ed. Bruno David and Julian Thomas, 328–32. Walnut Creek: Left Coast Press.
Terrell, John Edward, John P. Hart, Sibel Barut, Nicoletta Cellinese, Antonio Curet, Tim Denham, Chapurukha M. Kusimba, Kyle Latinis, Rahul Oka, Joel Palka, Mary E. D. Pohl, Kevin O. Pope, Patrick Ryan Williams, Helen Haines, and John E. Staller. 2003. "Domesticated Landscapes: The Subsistence Ecology of Plant and Animal Domestication." *Journal of Archaeological Method and Theory* 10: 323–68. https://www.jstor.org/stable/20177484.
Terrell, John Edward, Terry L. Hunt, and Chris Gosden. 1997. "Human Diversity and the Myth of the Primitive Isolate." *Current Anthropology* 38: 155–95. https://doi.org/10.1086/204604.
Terrell, John Edward, and Judith Modell. 1994. "Anthropology and Adoption." *American Anthropologist* 96: 155–61. https://www.jstor.org/stable/682656.
Terrell, John Edward, and Esther M. Schechter. 2007. "Deciphering the Lapita Code: The Aitape Ceramic Sequence and Late Survival of the 'Lapita Face.'" *Cambridge Archaeological Journal* 17: 59–85. https://doi.org/10.1017/S0959774307000066.

Terrell, John Edward, and Gabriel Stowe Terrell. 2020. *Understanding the Human Mind: Why You Shouldn't Trust What Your Brain Is Telling You*. London: Routledge.
Terrell, John Edward, and Robert L. Welsch. 1997. "Lapita and the Temporal Geography of Prehistory." *Antiquity* 71: 548–72. https://doi.org/10.1017/S0003598 X0008532X.
Torrence, Robin, and Pamela Swadling. 2008. "Social Networks and the Spread of Lapita." *Antiquity* 82: 600–16. https://doi.org/10.1017/S0003598X00097258.
Toynbee, Arnold J. (1934) 1961. *A Study of History*. Oxford: Oxford University Press.
Travers, Jeffrey, and Stanley Milgram. 1969. "An Experimental Study of the Small World Problem." *Sociometry* 32: 425–43. https://doi.org/10.2307/2786545.
Trigger, Bruce G. 1980. *Gordon Childe: Revolutions in Archaeology*. London: Thames & Hudson.
———. 1989. *A History of Archaeological Thought*. Cambridge: Cambridge University Press.
Trinkaus, Erik, and Pat Shipman. 1993. *The Neandertals: Changing the Image of Mankind*. London: Alfred A. Knopf.
Tse, Peter Ulric. 2013. *The Neural Basis of Free Will: Criterial Causation*. Cambridge, MA: MIT Press.
Tucker, Aviezer. 2010. "Where Do We Go from Here? Jubilee Report on *History and Theory*." *History and Theory* 49: 64–84. https://doi.org/10.1111/j.1468-23 03.2010.00560.x.
Valeggia, Claudia R., and Eduardo Fernandez-Duque. 2021. "Moving Biological Anthropology Research beyond p<0.05." *American Journal of Biological Anthropology* 177: 193–95. https://doi.org/10.1002/ajpa.24444.
Valentin, Frédérique, Stuart Bedford, Hallie R. Buckley, and Matthew Spriggs. 2010. "Lapita Burial Practices: Evidence for Complex Body and Bone Treatment at the Teouma Cemetery, Vanuatu, Southwest Pacific." *Journal of Island and Coastal Archaeology* 5: 212–35. https://doi.org/10.1080/1556489 1003648092.
Valentin, Frédérique, Florent Détroit, Matthew J. T. Spriggs, and Stuart Bedford. 2016. "Early Lapita Skeletons from Vanuatu Show Polynesian Craniofacial Shape: Implications for Remote Oceanic Settlement and Lapita Origins." *Proceedings of the National Academy of Sciences* 113: 292–97. https://doi.org/10.1073/pnas.1516186113.
van de Loosdrecht, Marieke S., Marcello A. Mannino, Sahra Talamo, Vanessa Villalba-Mouco, Cosimo Posth, Franziska Aron, Guido Brandt, Marta Burri, Cäcilia Freund, Rita Radzeviciute, Raphaela Stahl, Antje Wissgott, Lysann Klausnitzer, Sarah Nagel, Matthias Meyer, Antonio Tagliacozzo, Marcello Piperno, Sebastiano Tusa, Carmine Collina, Vittoria Schimmenti, Rosaria Di Salvo, Kay Prüfer, Jean-Jacques Hublin, Stephan Schiffels, Choongwon Jeong, Wolfgang Haak, and Johannes Krause. 2020. "Genomic and Dietary

Transitions during the Mesolithic and Early Neolithic in Sicily." *bioRxiv.* https://doi.org/10.1101/2020.03.11.986158.

Vauchez, André. 1997. *Sainthood in the Later Middle Ages.* New York: Cambridge University Press.

Veth, Peter, Kane Ditchfield, Mark Bateman, Sven Ouzman, Marine Benoit, Ana Paula Motta, Darrell Lewis, Sam Harper, and Balanggarra Aboriginal Corporation. 2019. "Minjiwarra: Archaeological Evidence of Human Occupation of Australia's Northern Kimberley by 50,000 BP." *Australian Archaeology* 85: 115–25. https://doi.org/10.1080/03122417.2019.1650479.

Veth, Peter, Ingrid Ward, and Kane Ditchfield. 2017. "Reconceptualising Last Glacial Maximum Discontinuities: A Case Study from the Maritime Deserts of North-Western Australia." *Journal of Anthropological Archaeology* 46: 82–91. https://doi.org/10.1016/j.jaa.2016.07.016.

Wade, Nicholas. 2014. *A Troublesome Inheritance: Genes, Race and Human History.* New York: Penguin Press.

Wallace, Anthony F. C. 1956. "Revitalization Movements." *American Anthropologist* 58: 264–81. https://doi.org/10.1525/aa.1956.58.2.02a00040.

Wasserman, Stanley, and Katherine Faust. 1994. *Social Network Analysis: Methods and Applications.* Cambridge: Cambridge University Press.

Watson, James B. 1990. "Other People Do Other Things: Lamarckian Identities in Kainantu Subdistrict, Papua New Guinea." In *Cultural Identity and Ethnicity in the Pacific*, ed. Jocelyn Linnekin and Lin Poyer, 17–41. Honolulu: University of Hawaii Press.

Watts, Duncan J., and Steven H. Strogatz. 1988. "Collective Dynamics of 'Small-World' Networks." *Nature* 393: 440–42. https://doi.org/10.1038/30918.

Weisberg, Michael. 2006. "Richard Levins' Philosophy of Science." *Biology and Philosophy* 21: 603–5. https://doi.org/10.1007/s10539-006-9048-4.

Welsch, Robert L., and John Edward Terrell. 1998. "Material Culture, Social Fields, and Social Boundaries." In *The Archaeology of Social Boundaries*, ed. Miriam Stark, 50–77. Washington, DC: Smithsonian Institution Press.

Welsch, Robert L., John Terrell, and John A. Nadolski. 1992. "Language and Culture on the North Coast of New Guinea." *American Anthropologist* 94: 568–600. https://www.jstor.org/stable/680563.

Whewell, William. 1840. *The Philosophy of the Inductive Sciences, Founded upon Their History*, 2 vols. London: John W. Parker.

Williams, George C. (1966) 2018. *Adaptation and Natural Selection: A Critique of Some Current Evolutionary Thought.* Princeton: Princeton University Press.

Willie, Edson. 2019. "A Melanesian View of Archaeology in Vanuatu." In *Archaeologies of Island Melanesia: Current Approaches to Landscapes, Exchange, and Practice*, ed. Mathieu Leclerc and James Flexner, 211–14. Terra Australis 51. Canberra: Australian National University Press.

Wilson, Edward O. 1975. *Sociobiology: The New Synthesis.* Cambridge, MA: Harvard University Press.

———. 2012. *The Social Conquest of the Earth.* New York: Liveright (a division of W. W. Norton).

Wittfogel, Karl A. 1957. *Oriental Despotism: A Comparative Study of Total Power.* New Haven: Yale University Press.

Wright, Sewall. 1943. "Isolation by Distance." *Genetics* 28: 114–38. https://doi.org/10.1093/genetics/28.2.114.

Wu, Xueling, and Fang Hu. 2020. "Analysis of Ecological Carrying Capacity Using a Fuzzy Comprehensive Evaluation Method." *Ecological Indicators* 113: 106243. https://doi.org/10.1016/j.ecolind.2020.106243.

Wurzer, Gabriel, Kerstin Kowarik, and Hans Reschreiter, eds. 2015. *Agent-Based Modeling and Simulation in Archaeology.* Cham: Springer International Publishing.

Wynn, Thomas, and Frederick Coolidge. 2011. "The Implications of the Working Memory Model for the Evolution of Modern Cognition." *International Journal of Evolutionary Biology* 2011. https://doi.org/10.4061/2011/741357.

Yore, Larry D., Brian M. Hand, and Marilyn K. Florence. 2004. "Scientists' Views of Science, Models of Writing, and Science Writing Practices." *Journal of Research in Science Teaching* 41: 338–69. https://doi.org/10.1002/tea.20008.

Zhou, Jie, Ganqu Cui, Shengding Hu, Zhengyan Zhang, Cheng Yang, Zhiyuan Liu, Lifeng Wang, Changcheng Li, and Maosong Sun. 2020. "Graph Neural Networks: A Review of Methods and Applications." *AI Open* 1: 57–81. https://doi.org/10.1016/j.aiopen.2021.01.001.

Zilhão, João. 2001. "Radiocarbon Evidence for Maritime Pioneer Colonization at the Origins of Farming in West Mediterranean Europe." *Proceedings of the National Academy of Sciences* 98: 14180–85. https://doi.org/10.1073/pnas.241522898.

Index

Acabado, Stephen, 183
adapt
  definition of, 195
  relational contingencies and, 29
adaptation, as concept, 7
  environmental, 69
adaptive, 7
admixture
  as concept, 7
  in human diversity models, 95
aDNA. *See* ancient DNA
Albantakis, Larissa, 112
Allen, Jennifer, 70
Ammerman, A., and L. Cavalli-Sforza, 136–37
analysis. *See* data analysis; dynamic relational analysis; relational analysis; social network analysis
Ancestry theory, 88, 91, 99, 106–7
ancient DNA (aDNA), 122
ancient Pacific voyaging, historical research on, 40–54, 57n1
  analysis of, 49–51
  assumptions in, 42–43
  background information on, 43–44
  current theories on, 43–45
  data collection in, 50
  discussion and evaluation of, 45, 48, 51, 54
  evidence for, 49–51, 54
  explanations for, 44–45, 48
  after global Ice Age, 43
  during mid-Holocene era, 49
  modeling explanations in, 45, 48
  network models for, 46–47
  to New Guinea, 43, 49

  obsidian frequencies at archaeological sites, 52–54, 58n2
  summaries of, 54–57
  working hypothesis for, 48–49
  working models for, 45–48
Arendt, Hannah, 68
Aristotle, 163
assumptions
  definition of, 62, 195
  in dynamic relational analysis, 20–24
  in historical research on ancient Pacific voyaging, 42–43
  prior, 63
  in social network analysis, 20–24
  theories and, 63
Augustus, Romulus, 2

Bacon, Francis, 10, 130
Bakan, George, 157
Barth, Fredrik, 73
baseline plausibility analysis
  DNA analysis, 118–22
  purpose of, 122–24
  quantitative, 115–17
  subjective, 117–18, 121
  suppositional claims, 116
Bayes Theorem, 110–15, 128n1
  causal and conditional statements in, 111
  contingent probabilities in, 111, 114, 116
  COVID-19 pandemic and, 113–15
  dynamic Bayesian networks, 112–13
  dynamic relational analysis and, 112–13
  history and, 111–13

network modeling and, 112
probability determination with, 114
subjective baseline analysis and, 121
Beard, Mary, 59
Bedford, Stuart, 119
Bernhardt, Chris, 33
Big Data, 131–34, 144
biological complexity, study of
  homeostasis and, 38
  mathematical analysis of, 37
  model clusters in, 37
  self-regulation, 38
black box theory, 123
  definition of, 195
"The Blind Men and the Elephant" parable, 133, 147n2
Borck, Lewis, 1
Borgatti, Stephen, 16
Börner, Katy, 1
Bowler, Peter, 87
Box, George, 83
Brainerd-Robinson coefficient, 169
Broad Spectrum Revolution, 143
Brubaker, Rogers, 73
Butterfield, Herbert, 71

Carneiro, Robert, 72
Carr, Edward Hallet, 35, 60
categorical, 5, 195
categorical modeling, 94–95
categorical thinking
  concepts in, 7
  dynamic relational analysis and, 19
  efficiency of, 6
  evolution and, 5
  information gathering and, 131
  relational thinking compared to, 5–7
  social network analysis and, 19
  terms associated with, 7
categorical ties, in social network analysis, 22–23
category, 5, 195
causal conditional statements, 111
cause
  definition of, 195
  in dynamic relational analysis, 25
  social networks as, 17–18
Cavalli-Sforza, L., 93

Chamberlin, T. C., 84
chance
  definition of, 188, 195
  history and, 188–89
  in three-factor contingency analysis, 125–27
Chance and Necessity (Monod), 188–89, 191
characterizations, as models, 85–86
Childe, Vere Gordon, 73, 137, 142–43
choice
  definition of, 188, 195
  history and, 188–89
  in three-factor contingency analysis, 125
circumstantial, 7
  definition of, 195
circumstantial contingencies
  in control theories, 72
  in ecological theories, 69
  in functional theories, 68
  in human diversity models, 99–101, 106, 108
  Neolithic Revolution and, 141
  Papua New Guinea analysis, 163
  in participant theories, 70
  in structural theories, 66
circumstantial relational contingencies, 27–28
Clarke, Graham, 142
climate change, as ecological theory, 69
clusters, 84
Cohen, I. Bernard, 150–51
communication, history as act of, 179
community, 7
  definition of, 98, 195
  human diversity models and, 98
complete social networks, 16. *See also* whole social networks
computer networks, 4, 197
conditional statements, 111
connections, in social network analysis, 13
consequential, 7
  definition of, 196
  relationships, 11–12
consequential contingencies
  in control theories, 72
  in ecological theories, 69

in functional theories, 68
in human diversity models, 99, 101, 106, 108
Neolithic Revolution and, 141
Papua New Guinea analysis, 163
in participant theories, 70
as relational, 27–28
in structural theories, 66
consilience of induction, 132
The Consilience of Induction (Whewell), 132
conspiracy theories, 80
participant theories and, 70
contingency. *See also* circumstantial contingencies; consequential contingencies; situational contingencies
as concept, 7
definition of, 196
DNA analysis and, 120
in dynamic relational analysis, 25
intentional, 124
in Papua New Guinea study, 175
relational, 21, 25–29
contingent, 7. *See also* circumstantial
definition of, 196
dynamic relational analysis and, 25
contingent probabilities
in Bayes Theorem, 111, 114, 116
in DNA analysis, 121–22
in history, 184
control theories, of history, 64–65, 71–74
Copernicus, Nicolaus, 63, 132, 149
Crabtree, Stefani, 1
Creation Story theory, 88–90, 99, 106–7

Darwin, Charles, 71, 129–30, 180–81
on human diversity models, 91, 93
On the Origin of Species, 10–11, 83, 87, 93, 107
data analysis. *See also* Big Data
of archaeological sites, 160
density and, 158
dynamic relational analysis and, 158–59, 161–76
model-building in, 152
network modeling, 7
of situational data, 145
social network analysis and, 158–59

statistical analysis, 154–58
typological analysis, 151–54
data collection
on ancient Pacific voyaging, 50
information gathering as, 145–46
Dawson, Helen, 138–39
DBNs. *See* dynamic Bayesian networks
Dear, Peter, 93
decolonization, 183
delusions, about history, 190–91
density, 7
data analysis and, 158
De revolutionibus orbium coelestium (Copernicus), 63, 132, 149
design, 85–86
Diamond, Jared M., 67
DNA analysis, 118–22
ancient DNA information in, 122
contingency and, 120
contingent probability in, 121–22
geographic distribution of, 119–22
migration factors for, 119–20
domestication, as ecological theory, 69
Dust Tracks on a Road (Hurston), 178
dyads
in dynamic relational analysis, 22
social network analysis as, 21–22
dynamic, 19, 196
dynamic Bayesian networks (DBNs), 112–13
dynamic relational analysis (DYRA), 4–5
Bayes Theorem and, 112–13
categorical thinking and, 19
cause in, 25
complexity of modeling, 24–25
consequential relationships and, 11–12
contingency in, 25
contingent elements in, 25
data analysis and, 158–59, 161–76
definition of, 5, 11, 13, 19
goal of, 21
historical research with, 21
homophily and, 23
model construction and, 23–24
modeling strategies, 25
network models, 28–30
for Papua New Guinea material culture and society, 161–76

of population growth, 26–27
questions and, 36–37
relational contingencies in, 21, 25–29
relational probability and, 23
social network analysis compared to, 13
structural dyads in, 22
variables in, 25
working assumptions of, 20–24

ecological theories, of history, 64–65, 67, 69, 71
Edwards, Ward, 118, 148
Einstein, Albert, 11, 62
Elton, G. R., 59
entities, in social network analysis, 15
environmental adaptation theory, 69
epiphenomenon, 165
definition of, 196
evidence
components of, 60
of marine interaction in Bronze Age Mediterranean, 76–77
for Papua New Guinea material culture and society, 167–69
evolution, categorical thinking and, 5
evolve
definition of, 196
relational contingencies and, 29
exemplars, 85–86
experience, 193, 196
explanation
definition of, 130, 196
in historical research on ancient Pacific voyaging, 44–45, 48
of history, 61, 184–88
in information gathering, 130–31

facts, history and, 61, 194
family, 7
Faust, Katherine, 7–8, 14, 17. *See also* social network analysis
Fawcett, Henry, 129
feedback cycles, 30
Feinman, Gary, 159, 186
Fisher, Ronald, 155
Flay, Richard, 121
foresight, historical, 188–91

functional theories, of history, 64–65, 67–68

Gardiner, Patrick, 34
Gimbutas, Marija, 129, 144–45
Gingerich, Owen, 149–50
Godelier, Maurice, 98
"Goldilocks Rule," for good questions, 36
Golitko, Mark 159
Gould, D. Rae, 178
Granovetter, Mark, 23, 96–97
graph neural networks, 4, 197
graph theory, social network analysis and, 14, 20
Groube, Les, 126

Hart, John P., 69, 135–36
heliocentric model, 150
Hill, David, 182
history
as act of communication, 179
Bayes Theorem and, 111–13
chance and, 188–89
choice and, 188–89
conceptual approach, 1–3
contingent probability in, 184
core-periphery approach, 75–76, 79
decolonization, 183
definition of, 60
delusions about, 190–91
diversity and, 185–86
explanations of, 61, 184–88
facts and, 61, 194
foresight and, 188–91
human agency and, 64–65
ignorance of, 190
inequality and, 186
insight into, 191–94
justification of, 182–83
living past and, 180
of marine interaction in Bronze Age Mediterranean, 74–79
models for, 62–64, 85, 87, 194
necessity and, 188–89
origins and, 185–86
patterns in, 3
purpose of, 180–82
racism in, 183

randomness and, 188
of repatriation, 182
scope of, 81
small world networks approach, 75–79
theories, 62–74
urbanism and, 186
of violence and warfare, 187–88
writing of, 60, 62
The History and Geography of Human Genes (Cavalli-Sforza), 93
Hobbes, Thomas, 187
homophily
  dynamic relational analysis and, 23
  social network analysis and, 23
human agency
  history and, 64–65
  in relational contingencies, 30
  in three-factor contingency analysis, 124, 128
human diversity models, 87–103
  admixture in, 95
  Ancestry theory, 88, 91, 99, 106–7
  biblical theories, 89–90
  categorical modeling in, 94–95
  circumstantial contingencies in, 99–101, 106, 108
  communities and, 98
  consequential contingencies in, 99, 101, 106, 108
  Creation Story theory, 88–90, 99, 106–7
  Darwin on, 91, 93
  evaluation of, 105
  hypotheses for, 99–101
  interaction structures in, 103
  kinship systems, 91, 94
  mathematical models, 96
  network mapping in, 100, 102–5, 107
  population models, 95
  problem statements, 87–88
  racial modeling in, 94–95
  situational contingencies in, 99–100, 106, 108
  social cooperation models, 95
  social network models, 95, 97
  social networks theory, 89, 94, 106
  societies in, 91, 94
  theories for, 88–91, 93–94, 99, 106–7
  trellis model, 96
  working models for, 94–98
Hurston, Zora Neale, 178
hypothesis/hypotheses, 6–7. *See also* Bayes Theorem; explanation; supposition
  black box theory and, 123
  conceptual approach to, 109–10
  definition of, 196
  heliocentric model, 150
  for human diversity models, 99–101
  Kurgan hypothesis, 144–45
  for marine interaction in Bronze Age Mediterranean, 76
  null hypothesis significance testing, 154–57
  for Papua New Guinea material culture and society, 166–67
  for research, 39

imagination, 193, 196
individual, as concept, 7
Industrial Revolution, 143
information gathering
  Big Data, 131–34, 144
  "The Blind Men and the Elephant" parable, 133, 147n2
  categorical thinking and, 131
  circumstantial data and, 145
  consequential data and, 145
  consilience of induction, 132
  contextual approach to, 129–30
  data gathering as, 145–46
  explanation in, 130–31
  model-building and, 131
  for Neolithic Revolution, 134–45
  relational thinking and, 131
  situational data and, 145
Ingold, Tim, 26
insight
  definition of, 193, 196
  historical, 191–94
  into history, 191–94
intentional, 7
intentional contingencies, 124
intentionality, in relational contingencies, 30

intent on/upon
  definition of, 197
  relational contingencies and, 29
interpretation
  definition of, 130, 197
  network science and, 12
Irwin, Geoffrey, 45, 121

Jaccard index, 171
Jacob, François, 8, 37

Kahneman, Daniel, 117, 120
Kant, Immanuel, 153
Karr, Jean-Baptiste Alphonse, 180
Kepler, Johannes, 63
kinship systems, 91, 94
Kuhn, Thomas, 70
Kurgan hypothesis, 144–45

Lahr, Marta Mirazón, 187
Lambdin, Charles, 148, 155
Landau, Misia, 179
The Language of the Night (Le Guin), 1
Latham, Robert Gordon, 95
Le Guin, Ursula K., 1
Leppard, Thomas, 72
Lesser, Alexander, 42
Levins, Richard, 24–25, 37–38, 84–85, 150, 182
Lindman, Harold, 118
logic of research, 38–39
Lovis, William A., 69
Lucas, Gavin, 130–31, 148

MacArthur, Robert H., 36
MacKendrick, Paul, 55
The Making of a Scientist (Roe), 33
marine interaction, in Bronze Age Mediterranean
  analysis of, 76–77
  core-periphery approaches, 75–76, 79
  evaluation of, 77–78
  evidence for, 76–77
  matrix of contacts, 77
  small world networks approach, 75–79
  theories of, 74–75
  working hypothesis for, 76
  working models for, 75–76
  World Systems Analysis, 75–76
migration control theory, 72
Mills, Barbara, 15–16
models, modeling and. *See also* human diversity models; network models; representation; *specific models*
  in ancient Pacific voyaging research, 45, 48
  categorical, 94–95
  characterizations as, 85–86
  clusters and, 84
  complexity of, 24–25
  construction of, 23–24
  in data analysis, 152
  definitions of, 7, 85, 87, 197
  design of, 85–86
  in dynamic relational analysis, 23–25, 28–30
  exemplars, 85–86
  heliocentric, 150
  for historical research on ancient Pacific voyaging, 45–48
  for history, 62–64, 85, 87, 194
  history of, 7–8, 84
  of human diversity, 87–103, 105
  information gathering and, 131
  for marine interaction in Bronze Age Mediterranean, 75–76
  mathematical, 96
  for Neolithic Revolution in Europe, 137–39
  for Papua New Guinea material culture and society, 165–66, 168–70
  plausible, 8
  population, 95
  purpose and scope of, 85
  racial, 94–95
  research, 6–7, 39, 45–48
  social cooperation, 95
  social network, 95, 97
  strategies for, 23–24
  structural, 31
  trellis, 96
  types of, 85
Monod, Jacques, 188–89, 191

The Mute Stones Speak (MacKendrick), 55

The Natural History of the Varieties of Man (Latham), 95
natural state theory, 163–64
The Nature of Historical Explanation (Gardiner), 34
necessity
    definition of, 188, 197
    history and, 188–89
    in three-factor contingency analysis, 125
Neolithic Revolution in Europe
    analysis of, 139–40
    archaeological sites, 138
    circumstantial contingencies and, 141
    consequential contingencies and, 141
    cultural diffusion and, 137
    evidence and, 139–40, 143–45
    hunting and gathering behaviors, 135–36
    information gathering for, 134–45
    Kurgan hypothesis, 144–45
    problem statements, 136
    situational contingencies and, 141
    theories on, 136–37
    working model for, 137–39
network mapping, 100, 102–5, 107
network models
    for ancient Pacific voyaging, 46–47
    Bayes Theorem and, 112
    data analysis and, 7
    dynamic relational analysis and, 28–30
    in relational contingencies, 29
networks. *See also* social network analysis
    computer, 4, 197
    definition of, 4, 197
    friendship, 22–23
    graph neural, 4, 197
    mapping of, 100, 102–5, 107
    modeling for, 7
    social, 4, 197
    in social network analysis, 14–15
    systems in, 18
network science, interpretation and, 12
network structure, as concept, 7

The New Organon (Bacon), 10
Newton, Isaac, 150
NHST. *See* null hypothesis significance testing
nodes, in social networks, 17
null hypothesis significance testing (NHST), 154–57
Nuzzo, Regina, 110

Odoacer (Roman military officer), 2
On the Origin of Species (Darwin), 10–11, 83, 87, 107
Osiander, Andreas, 149–50
Otárola-Castillo, Erik, 109, 111, 115

Papua New Guinea, material culture and society in, DYRA of, 161–76
    apportionment of variation in, 166
    Brainerd-Robinson coefficient in, 169
    circumstantial contingencies, 163
    consequential contingencies, 163
    contingencies in, 175
    epiphenomenon and, 165
    evaluation of, 172–73, 174
    evidence for, 167–69
    Jaccard index in, 171
    language classifications, 167–68
    linguistic distance and, 163
    natural state theory for, 163–64
    Partial Mantel Test, 173
    problem statements, 161–62
    situational contingencies, 163
    social network distance and, 163, 171
    social network models, 168–70
    social use theory for, 163–65
    technological types, 167
    working hypotheses, 166–67
    working models for, 165–66
Partial Mantel Test, 173
participant theories, of history, 64–65, 70–71
patterns
    in history, 3
    in social networks, 17
Pearson, Karl, 155
Pinker, Steven, 187
Platt, John R., 85

plausible models, 8
Poincaré, Henri, 24
Popper, Karl, 117
population
   as concept, 7
   models, 95
population growth, dynamic relational analysis of, 26–27
The Possible and the Actual (Jacob), 8
The Practice of History (Elton), 59
Price, T. Douglas, 186
Prichard, James Cowles, 95
prior assumptions, 63
probabilities
   in Bayes Theorem, 111, 114
   contingent, 111, 114, 116, 121–22
   relational, 22–23
problem statements
   in human diversity models, 87–88
   Neolithic Revolution in Europe, 136
   in Papua New Guinea analysis, 161–62
   questions and, 39–43
   in research, 39–43
Ptolemy, Claudius, 63, 132, 149
purpose
   definition of, 197
   relational contingencies and, 29
   in three-factor contingency analysis, 124
purposeful, 7

quantum gravity, theory of, 62
questions, 35–37
   background information for, 40, 42
   dynamic relational analysis and, 36–37
   "Goldilocks Rule" for, 36
   problem statements and, 39–43

racism, 183
Ramenofsky, Ann F., 68
random/randomness
   definition of, 188, 197
   history and, 188
reason, 193, 197
recognize/recognition, 193, 197
Reich, David, 119
relational, 7. *See also* connection

   definition of, 6, 197
relational analysis. *See also* dynamic relational analysis
   definition of, 196
   networks and networking, 4
   scope of, 12–13
   social relationships, 4
relational contingencies
   adapt as type of, 29
   casual statements, 28
   circumstantial, 27–28
   consequential, 27–28
   in dynamic relational analysis, 21, 25–29
   evolve as type of, 29
   feedback cycles, 30
   human agency in, 30
   intentionality in, 30
   intent on/upon as type of, 29
   network models in, 29
   prior situations and, 28
   purpose as type of, 29
   purposeful behavior and, 30
   situational, 28
   temporal pathways and, 30
relational probabilities
   dynamic relational analysis and, 23
   in social network analysis, 22–23
relational thinking
   categorical thinking compared to, 5–7
   concepts in, 7
   information gathering and, 131
   terms connected to, 7
relationships. *See also* social networks
   as concept, 7
   social, 4
repatriation, 182
representations, models as, 85–86
research. *See also* ancient Pacific voyaging
   analysis of, 39
   on ancient Pacific voyaging, 40–54, 57n1, 58n2
   current theories and, 39, 43–45
   discussion and evaluation of, 39
   evidence and, 39
   logic of, 38–39
   models, 6–7, 39, 45–48
   problem statements, 39–43

project planning, 39–40
working hypothesis for, 39
Researches into the Physical History of Man (Prichard), 95
respond, 193, 197
revitalization, in participant theory, 70
revolutions, in archaeology, 142–43
Robb, John, 109
Roe, Anne, 33
Roman Empire, 2
Rovelli, Carlo, 11–12

Sahaba, Jebel, 187
Santayana, George, 2, 190
Sanyal, Soma, 1
Savage, Leonard J., 118
Schortman, Edward M., 17–18
scientific revolution, as participant theory, 70
Scott, John, 21
Secondary Products Revolution, 143
Shakespeare, William, 182
Sherratt, Andrew, 76
situational, 7. *See also* circumstantial
  data as, 145
  definition of, 197
situational contingencies
  in control theories, 72
  in ecological theories, 69
  in functional theories, 68
  in human diversity models, 99–100, 106, 108
  Neolithic Revolution and, 141
  Papua New Guinea analysis, 163
  in participant theories, 70
  as relational, 28
  in structural theories, 66
Skinner, B. F., 192
small world networks approach, to history, 75–79
  in the Mediterranean, 78
SNA. *See* social network analysis
Sober, Elliot, 163
social control theory, 72
Social Network Analysis (Faust and Wasserman), 17
social network analysis (SNA), 4–5, 11
  actors in, 14, 21–22
  agenda of, 13
  categorical thinking and, 19
  categorical ties in, 22–23
  connections and, 13
  data analysis and, 158–59
  data selection in, 21
  definition of, 12–13, 18
  as dyad, 21–22
  dynamic relational analysis compared to, 13
  edges and, 13–14
  entities in, 15
  graph theory and, 14, 20
  homophily and, 23
  links and, 13
  network relationships in, 14–15
  network structures in, 14–15
  processes and, 19
  relational probabilities in, 22–23
  scope of, 13
  as social science, 21
  structural causation in, 17
  as structural models, 31
  suppositions in, 18
  systems and, 19
  ties and, 13–14
  whole networks in, 20–22
  working assumptions of, 20–24
  as working model, 20
social network models, for Papua New Guinea analysis, 168–70
social networks, 4, 197
  actors in, 17
  causal relationships in, 16
  as causes, 17–18
  complete, 16
  in constant state of flux, 15
  entire, 16
  historical context for, 13
  models for, 95, 97
  nodes in, 17
  Papua New Guinea analysis and, 163, 171
  patterning in, 17
  social networks theory, 89, 94, 106
  structural analysis of, 17
  as structures, 16–17
  as systems, 18–19

vertices in, 17
whole, 16, 20–22
social networks theory, 89, 94, 106
social relationships, 4
social use theory, 163–65
Sociobiology (Wilson, Edward O.), 71
Spencer, Herbert, 185–86
Spriggs, Matthew, 119, 123
statistical analysis, 154–58
  correlations, 156
  null hypothesis significance testing, 154–57
Stocking, George, 89
Stojanowski, Christopher, 187
Stone, Anne C., 68
structural theories, 64–67
  circumstantial contingencies in, 66
  consequential contingencies in, 66
  cultural determinism and, 66
  geographic determinism and, 66
  racial determinism and, 66
  situational contingencies in, 66
  social network analysis and, 67
subjective baseline analysis, Bayes Theorem and, 121
supply control theory, 72
suppositions
  definition of, 62–63
  in social network analysis, 18
systems. *See also* networks
  definition of, 197
  in networks, 18
  social network analysis and, 19
  social networks as, 18–19

temporal pathways, relational contingencies and, 30
Terrell, John Edward, 63, 69, 116, 192
theory, theories and. *See also* Bayes Theorem; suppositions
  Ancestry theory, 88, 91, 99, 106–7
  assumptions and, 63
  biblical theories, 89–90
  black box theory, 123
  conspiracy, 80
  control, 64–65, 71–74
  Creation Story theory, 88–90, 99, 106–7
  definition of, 62–63, 198
  ecological, 64–65, 67, 69, 71
  functional, 64–65, 67–68
  historical, 62–74
  for human diversity models, 88–91, 93–94, 99, 106–7
  for marine interaction in Bronze Age Mediterranean, 74–75
  natural state theory, 163–64
  on Neolithic Revolution, 136–37
  participant, 64–65, 70–71
  research, 39, 43–45
  social networks theory, 89, 94, 106
  social use theory, 163–65
  structural, 64–67
thinking. *See* categorical thinking; relational thinking
three-factor contingency analysis
  chance in, 125–27
  choice in, 125
  historical explanation in, 125–26
  human agency in, 124, 128
  intentional contingencies, 124
  necessity in, 125
  purposefulness in, 124
ties, social network analysis and, 13–14
Torquato, Melissa, 109, 111, 115
Trump, Donald, 34, 190–91
Turing, Alan, 34–35
Turing's Vision (Bernhardt), 33
Tversky, Amos, 117, 120
type, 7. *See also* category
  definition of, 198
type noun, 152
typological analysis
  of culture, 152
  data analysis and, 151–54
  type noun, 152
  typology noun, 152–53
typology, 198
typology noun, 152

urbanism, 186

variables
  definition of, 198
  in dynamic relational analysis, 25
Vauchez, André, 68

vertices, in social networks, 17
Vespignani, Alessandro, 1
violence and warfare, 187–88

Wallace, Anthony, 70
Wallerstein, Immanuel, 75
warfare. *See* violence and warfare
Wasserman, Stanley, 7–8, 14, 17. *See also* social network analysis
Watson, John B., 192
Weisberg, Michael, 37
What is History (Carr), 60

Whewell, William, 132
whole social networks, 16
    in social network analysis, 20–22
Willie, Edson, 178
Wilson, Edward O., 71
Wilson, Peter Lamborn, 2
Wittfogel, Karl, 72
World Systems Analysis (WSA), 75–76
World-System Theory (WST), 75
Writing the Past (Lucas), 130, 148
WSA. *See* World Systems Analysis
WST. *See* World-System Theory

CPSIA information can be obtained
at www.ICGtesting.com
Printed in the USA
JSHW062226140323
38487JS00006B/35